HOW TO SEARCH THE SCRIPTURES

HOW TO
SEARCH THE SCRIPTURES

by
Lloyd M. Perry
and
Robert D. Culver

Foreword by
Harry L. Evans
President, Trinity College
and Trinity Evangelical Divinity School

BAKER BOOK HOUSE
Grand Rapids, Michigan

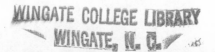

Library of Congress Catalog Card Number: 67-18190

Standard Book Number: 8010-6871-1

First printing, September 1967
Second printing, January 1971

PHOTOLITHOPRINTED BY CUSHING - MALLOY, INC.
ANN ARBOR, MICHIGAN, UNITED STATES OF AMERICA
1971

*Dedicated to all who desire
to become better acquainted with
the Bible. May God guide you by
His Holy Spirit as you use this
book to search the Scriptures*

Study to show thyself approved unto God, a workman that needeth not to be ashamed, rightly dividing the Word of Truth. — II Timothy 2:15

FOREWORD

I am happy to commend the work of the two distinguished members of our Divinity School faculty who have collaborated in producing this inspiring and helpful volume.

The most notable features of the Perry-Howard book published in 1956 by Revell on *How to Study Your Bible* have been retained in the present volume, especially those unique how-to-do-it chapters that demonstrate and illustrate Dr. Perry's practical methods of inductive Bible study.

To this original volume have been added chapters that enhance the value of the work immeasurably. The initial chapter on the organization, evaluation and translation of the Scriptures cannot but whet the appetite for Bible study. The clear, concise and evangelical presentation of the doctrine of Holy Scripture is a classic for both brevity and thoroughness. The brief chapter on the covenantal and dispensational systems of Biblical interpretation will be helpful, and the unique section that deals with a homiletical approach to the Scriptures should prove invaluable not only to preachers and theological students but to Sunday school teachers and others who sense their need of help in preparing to share the riches of the Word with others.

The authors have succeeded eminently in motivating their readers to do what our Lord commanded, namely, to "Search the scriptures, because . . . these are they which bear witness of me" (John 5:39).

— Harry L. Evans, President,
Trinity College and Trinity
Evangelical Divinity School

Acknowledgments

The authors disclaim any originality in organizing the material that forms the background for the study methods herein proposed. We have drawn on such volumes as Merrill C. Tenney's *The New Testament: A Survey;* Edward J. Young's *An Introduction to the Old Testament;* Henry H. Halley's *Bible Handbook;* W. H. Griffith-Thomas' *Methods of Bible Study; The New Analytical Bible; The Scofield Reference Bible; Commentary* edited by F. Davidson, A. M. Stibbs, and E. F. Kevan; John J. Ross's *Thinking through the New Testament,* and several others. In all cases we have cited authorities whose works are fairly accessible to the general reader.

We are indebted to a great number of Bible students who in divinity school classes, Sunday school classes, and youth groups have worked through these study methods. The examples that appear in this book are their actual work. They are not the work of experts but the results of the type of study which laymen in every walk of life can match in their own study.

Our sincere hope is that Christians will be inspired to "search the Scriptures daily," and that the practical suggestions and examples that follow will help the conscientious student to translate desire into actuality, and to realize in his own experience the thrill of personal communication from God through Bible study.

L. M. P.
R. D. C.

INTRODUCTION

"I want to study the Bible, but I don't know how. Where can I get a book that will show me how to do it?"

If this is a question you have asked, then this book is for you, for it is designed to show just how an ordinary Christian can pursue a program of Bible study on his own and profit thereby.

Strangely enough, there are not many books of this type. There are almost numberless books about the Bible and thousands of expositions of the Bible or some part thereof; but there are very few that offer practical methods of approach to the Bible so that a beginner can learn and apply the methods for himself. And yet nothing is more important and more profitable than individual Bible study.

This volume seeks to establish basic inductive methodology for personal Bible study. It is inductive because it comes to the text of Scripture objectively to find out what the Bible has to say. It seeks to read the meaning of the text and not to read meanings into it. Eleven specific methods of study provide a "how-to-do-it" procedure for studying Bible books, chapters, paragraphs, minute parts, doctrines, biographies, prayers, miracles, parables, poetry, and Bible writers. In each case an example of the method is included which has been prepared by a young person or adult from a divinity school class, Sunday school class or youth group. These methods of study can be applied to units of Scripture irrespective of their inherent nature.

A burning conviction has guided the authors and permeated the material presented — a conviction that

> All scripture is given my inspiration of God and is profitable for doctrine, for reproof, for correction, for instruction in righteousness: That the man of God may be perfect, thoroughly furnished unto all good works (II Tim. 3:16, 17).

For one who has such a conviction, real lasting profit can be gained from searching the Scriptures. The finding of the Book of the Law by Hilkiah in the house of the Lord (II Chron. 34:14-21) and the perusal of its contents resulted in one of the five reformations or revivals recorded in the book of II Chronicles. The discovery of the Word of God always brings innumerable blessings. Sir Walter Scott, in "The Monastery," wrote:

> Within that awful volume lies
> The mystery of mysteries.
> Happiest they of human race
> To whom God has granted grace
> To read, to fear, to hope, to pray,
> To lift the latch and force the way;
> And better had they ne'er been born
> Who read to doubt or read to scorn.

In order to gain the greatest profit from Bible study, the individual must *search the Scriptures* (John 5:39). This involves investigation and exploration after the manner of the scientist. This systematic search should be carried out with thoroughness. The clear-cut command to Joshua was that the Book of the Law should not depart out of his mouth and that he should meditate therein both day and night. Such meditation should involve attention and intention with application as the objective. It was G. Campbell Morgan who stated that the Bible yields its treasures to honest toil more readily than any other serious literature, but that it never yields to indolence.

The frustration of the Ethiopian in Acts 8 in his inability to understand the Scriptures except someone should guide him, has been the experience of many since his day. The central message of the Bible is clear: it is the proclamation that Jesus Christ is Lord and that there is salvation through faith in Him as Savior. But there are many passages in the Bible that are not easy to understand. The Bible is not an ordinary book; actually it is a "library" of sixty-six books.

For one who is not familiar with this "library," the best place to begin reading is at the beginning of the New Testament. The story of Christ as set forth in the four Gospels is the key to the understanding of the Bible. Following them it would be well to proceed to such letters as that of James and Paul's letters to the Philippians and to Timothy. As one matures in Bible knowledge, he will go on to Romans, Galatians, and the Corinthian epistles. After such an introduction to the New Testament, the reader will find it helpful to turn to some of the Old Testament books, reading them concurrently with his New Testament reading.

Since the Bible has a quality that other literature does not possess, it must be read with this in mind. The Bible is a revelation of spiritual truth the understanding of which depends upon spiritual sensitivity. This requires the indwelling and illumination of the Holy Spirit, who takes the things of Christ and makes them real to us. Regeneration, or the new birth, is therefore a prerequisite to the understanding of the Scriptures.

In a classic passage in I Corinthians, Paul announces this truth. "For after that in the wisdom of God the world by wisdom knew not God, it pleased God by the foolishness of preaching to save them that believe" (I Cor. 1:21). In God's wise plan He barred men from knowing Him by their innate wisdom, and chose to reveal Himself only to faith.

The searching of our hearts is good preparation for the searching of the Scriptures. Both James and Peter, in their epistles, picture the truth of God's Word as a seed to be planted in our lives. But the soil of our hearts must be prepared for the reception of the "incorruptible seed." James urges us to put away "filthiness and rank growth of wickedness" (James 1:21), and Peter admonishes us to "put away all malice and all guile and insincerity and envy and all slander" (I Peter 2:1).

Heart preparation should also be accompanied by a choice

of the right time and place for Bible study. Try to be alone and uninterrupted. Do not rush into God's presence and out again without taking time to free your mind of distractions and to become accustomed to the nearness of God. Find or make the time that you need for this important heart preparation.

In seeking to understand the Scriptures, seek to discover the primary meaning of the writer as he wrote, not the meaning you would like to read into his words.

We should proceed on the principle that "when the plain sense makes good sense, we should seek no other sense." A passage should be taken literally unless the context shows that it is to be understood otherwise. The greatest care must be taken not to twist Scripture to fit previously formed patterns of thought or doctrine.

"A text without a context is a pretext." For this reason each part of Scripture, whether a single word or an entire book, must be seen in its contextual relationships. Each word must be evaluated with respect to its usage in the sentence. A sentence must be interpreted in the light of the surrounding paragraph. A paragraph, in turn, must be related to the surrounding chapter or larger segment. Each segment must be viewed in its relation to the entire book. And added light will be thrown on a whole book when it is seen in its place in the entire Bible.

The truth of God is a many-sided truth, and in studying the Bible it is important to consider everything that is taught on any particular subject. Your study may reveal some apparent contradictions, but as you advance these will be resolved and you will achieve a well-rounded synthesis that avoids extremes and one-sided views.

Special attention should be given to any word or phrase or idea that recurs frequently in Scripture. Notice, for example, the repeated use by Mark of the word "straightway," or Paul's oft-repeated "in Christ" in Ephesians, or the Psalmist's "Selah." Taking note of such repetition will enable you to perceive the emphasis placed on certain aspects of Scripture, thus learning to stress the truths the Bible stresses, to feel and reflect the Bible's own emphasis, and to that degree be more "Biblical."

Bible study is never an end in itself. We study the Bible not merely to know the Bible but to know God, to know ourselves, and to know God's will for us. Our aim should be so to see God in His Word that our lives will be changed to conform to the pattern set forth in the Lord Jesus Christ (II Cor. 3:18). Creed and conduct must never be divorced. We must, as James said, be "doers of the word and not hearers only" (James 1:22).

There are dangers in Bible study. It is possible to become spiritually proud. Paul tells us that "knowledge puffs up" (I Cor. 8:1). We may also become merely academic and come short of receiving the Word with meekness (James 1:21) and applying it to our own lives (James 1:23, 24). The end result of all Bible study should be its *application to life.*

TABLE OF CONTENTS

Chapter I

AN INTRODUCTION TO THE SCRIPTURES

A. THEIR ORGANIZATION

All the Bible centers in Christ, but because He came at the time He did in history, our Bible divides into an Old Testament and a New Testament.

All that was written prior to His coming, and preparatory to His coming, forms the Old Testament, and all that was written after His coming forms the New Testament. It is as simple as that.

But some subdivisions of the Old and New Testaments may help us to better understand this compilation of books. The thirty-nine books of the Old and the twenty-seven books of the New need not be an unintelligible and forbidding list of names. They can be grouped in various ways according to their content. Indeed they have already been arranged in a manner that lends itself to this, for the books do not appear in the chronological order of their writing in either the Old or New Testament, but rather in a manner that follows a unique plan.

Let us study several suggested outlines, some traditional, some novel, in order to acquaint ourselves with the order and progress in the Bible.

A TRADITIONAL ENGLISH BIBLE DIVISION

OLD TESTAMENT	NEW TESTAMENT
I. *Pentateuch.* Five Books	I. *Biographical.* Four Books
1. Genesis	1. Matthew

2. Exodus
3. Leviticus
4. Numbers
5. Deuteronomy

II. *Historical Books.* Twelve
    1. Joshua
    2. Judges
    3. Ruth
    4. I Samuel
    5. II Samuel
    6. I Kings
    7. II Kings
    8. I Chronicles
    9. II Chronicles
    10. Ezra
    11. Nehemiah
    12. Esther

III. *Poetical Books.* Five
    1. Job
    2. Psalms
    3. Proverbs
    4. Ecclesiastes
    5. Song of Solomon

IV. *Major Prophetical Books*
    Five
    1. Isaiah
    2. Jeremiah
    3. Lamentations
    4. Ezekiel
    5. Daniel

2. Mark
3. Luke
4. John

II. *Historical.* One
    Acts of the Apostles

III. *The Pauline Epistles.*
    Fourteen (including
    Hebrews)
    1. Romans
    2. I Corinthians
    3. II Corinthians
    4. Galatians
    5. Ephesians
    6. Philippians
    7. Colossians
    8. I Thessalonians
    9. II Thessalonians
    10. I Timothy
    11. II Timothy
    12. Titus
    13. Philemon
    14. Hebrews (authorship
        uncertain)

IV. *General Epistles.* Seven
    1. James
    2. I Peter
    3. II Peter
    4. I John
    5. II John
    6. III John
    7. Jude

V. *Minor Prophetical Books.* V. *Prophetical.* One
Twelve   Revelation
   1. Hosea
   2. Joel
   3. Amos
   4. Obadiah
   5. Jonah
   6. Micah
   7. Nahum
   8. Habakkuk
   9. Zephaniah
10. Haggai
11. Zechariah
12. Malachi

A COMPOSITE OUTLINE
of
OLD AND NEW TESTAMENTS

OLD TESTAMENT[1]
(Based on the traditional Hebrew division)

LAW OF MOSES	THE PROPHETS	THE HAGIOGRAPHA
Genesis	The Former Prophets:	The Poetical Books:
Exodus	Joshua	Psalms
Leviticus	Judges	Proverbs
Numbers	I and II Samuel	Job
Deuteronomy	I and II Kings	
	The Latter Prophets:	The Megilloth (little rolls):
	Isaiah	Song of Solomon
	Jeremiah	Ruth
	Ezekiel	Lamentations
		Ecclesiastes
		Esther

The Twelve:	Historical Books:
Hosea	Daniel
Joel	Ezra
Amos	Nehemiah
Obadiah	I and II
Jonah	Chronicles
Micah	
Nahum	
Habakkuk	
Zephaniah	
Haggai	
Zechariah	
Malachi	

NEW TESTAMENT[2]

THE RECORDS OF THE LIFE OF CHRIST
  Matthew
  Mark
  Luke
  John

THE RECORDS OF THE EARLY CHURCH
  The Record: Acts
  Literature of Protest: James and Galatians
  The Pauline Program: I and II Thessalonians, I and II Corinthians, Romans
  The Pauline Imprisonment: Philemon, Ephesians, Colossians, Philippians

THE PROBLEMS OF THE EARLY CHURCH

The Pastoral Epistles:	I Timothy
	Titus
	II Timothy
The Suffering Church:	I Peter
The Break from Judaism	Hebrews

The Period of Heresies:　II Peter; Jude; I, II, III John
The Expectant Church:　Revelation

THE BIBLE BOOKS IN SEVEN GROUPS[3]

OLD TESTAMENT	NEW TESTAMENT
1. 17 Historical	4. 4 Gospels
2. 5 Poetical	5. Acts
3. 17 Prophetic	6. 21 Epistles
	7. Revelation

HISTORICAL: The Rise and Fall of the Hebrew Nation.
POETICAL: Literature of the Nation's Golden Age.
PROPHETIC: Literature of the Nation's Dark Days.
GOSPELS: The Man Whom the Nation Produced.
ACTS: His Reign Among All Nations Begins.
EPISTLES: His Teachings and Principles.
REVELATION: Forecast of His Universal Dominion.

REVELATION TO CULMINATION[4]

REVELATION: Genesis to Deuteronomy
PREPARATION: Joshua to Esther
ASPIRATION: Job to Song of Solomon
EXPECTATION: Isaiah to Malachi
MANIFESTATION: Matthew to John
REALIZATION: Acts to Epistles
CULMINATION: Revelation

REVELATION AND REALIZATION[5]

OLD TESTAMENT

1. Revelation — Christ to His Church (Gospels)
2. Realization — Christ in His Church (Rest of the N. T.)
   a. In Outward Expression: (History) Acts
   b. In Inward Experience: (Doctrine) Epistles

   c. In Onward Expectation: (Prophecy) Revelation

A PANORAMIC VIEW OF THE BIBLE[6]

The books of the Bible fall into groups. Speaking broadly there are five great divisions in the Scriptures, and these may be conveniently fixed in the memory by five key words, Christ being the one theme (Luke 24:25-27):

PREPARATION MANIFESTATION PROPAGATION
The Old Testament   The Gospels   The Acts

      EXPLANATION   CONSUMMATION
      The Epistles   The Apocalypse

B. THEIR EVALUATION

The Christian who feels no urgency to study his Bible needs his appetite whetted. He could do nothing better than to thumb through the Bible, pausing along the way to meditate on the many statements it makes concerning itself. He should thereby come to a new appreciation of the Word of God and a hunger to know its contents.

Consider, first of all, eleven illustrations by which the Bible is pictured.

   1. The Bible is a *priceless possession*. Psalm 19:7-10; 119:72.
   2. The Bible is a *light*. Psalm 119:105, 130; Proverbs 6:23.
   3. The Bible is *rain* which produces life and fruit. Isaiah 55:10, 11.
   4. The Bible is *food*. Jeremiah 15:16; I Peter 2:1, 2; I Corinthians 3:1, 2; Hebrews 5:12-14.

5. The Bible is a *fire* which burns away the chaff and which ignites us to action. Jeremiah 23:29; 20:9.

6. The Bible is a *hammer* which disintegrates our pretenses and reveals our true nature. Jeremiah 23:29.

7. The Bible is a *seed* which when it falls on good soil grows and bears fruit in a new divine life. Matthew 13:1-23; Mark 4:1-20; Luke 8:4-15; I Peter 1:23.

8. The Bible is a *mirror* in which we find ourselves revealed (James 1:22-25) and in which the Lord Jesus Christ can be seen. II Corinthians 3:18.

9. The Bible is *water* whereby we are washed and cleansed. Ephesians 5:26.

10. The Bible is a *sword* to be wielded in our defense against the enemy. Ephesians 6:17.

11. The Bible is a *critic* which pierces our innermost being, discerning our thoughts and motives. Hebrews 4:12.

❉ ❉ ❉

Consider, besides, these significant statements of the Bible regarding itself:

"These words, which I command thee this day, shall be in thine heart: And thou shalt teach them diligently unto thy children, and shalt talk of them when thou sittest in thine house, and when thou walkest by the way, and when thou liest down, and when thou risest up" (Deut. 6:6, 7). "The Lord thy God . . . humbled thee, and suffered thee to hunger, and fed thee with manna, which thou knewest not, neither did thy fathers know; that he might make thee know that man doth not live by bread only, but by every word that proceedeth out of the mouth of the Lord doth man live" (Deut. 8:2, 3). "Therefore shall ye lay up these my words in your heart and in your soul, and bind them for a sign upon your hand, that they may be as frontlets between your eyes" (Deut. 11:18).

* * *

"This book of the law shalt not depart out of thy mouth; but thou shalt meditate therein day and night, that thou mayest observe to do according to all that is written therein: for then thou shalt make thy way prosperous, and then thou shalt have good success" (Josh. 1:8). "Ezra had prepared his heart to seek the law of the Lord, and to do it, and to teach in Israel statutes and judgments" (Ezra 7:10).

* * *

"Blessed is the man . . . (whose) delight is in the law of the Lord; and in his law doth he meditate day and night. And he shall be like a tree planted by the rivers of water, that bringeth forth his fruit in his season; his leaf also shall not wither; and whatsoever he doeth shall prosper" (Ps. 1:1-3). "The law of the Lord is perfect, converting the soul: the testimony of the Lord is sure, making wise the simple. The statutes of the Lord are right, rejoicing the heart: The commandment of the Lord is pure, enlightening the eyes. The fear of the Lord is clean, enduring forever: the judgments of the Lord are true and righteous altogether. . . . Moreover by them is thy servant warned: and in keeping of them there is great reward" (Ps. 19:7-9, 11).

* * *

"Wherewithal shall a young man cleanse his way? by taking heed thereto according to thy word. With my whole heart have I sought thee: O let me not wander from thy commandments. Thy word have I hid in mine heart, that I might not sin against thee" (Ps. 119:9-11).[7] "Open thou mine eyes, that I may behold wondrous things out of thy law" (Ps. 119:18). "It is good for me that I have been afflicted: that I might learn thy statutes" (Ps. 119:71). "O how love I thy law! It is my meditation all the day" (Ps. 119:97). "Great peace have they which love thy law: and nothing shall offend them" (Ps. 119:165).

* * *

"The grass withereth, the flower fadeth: but the Word of our God shall stand for ever" (Isa. 40:8). "Thus saith the Lord, the heaven is my throne, and the earth is my footstool: . . . but to this man will I look, even to him that is poor and of a contrite spirit, and trembleth at my word" (Isa. 66:1, 2).

* * *

"[Jesus] answered and said, It is written, man shall not live by bread alone, but by every word that proceedeth out of the mouth of God. . . . Jesus said unto him, It is written again, Thou shalt not tempt the Lord thy God. . . . Then saith Jesus unto him, get thee hence, Satan; for it is written. . . . Then the devil leaveth him" (Matt. 4:4-11). "Jesus answered and said unto them, Ye do err, not knowing the scriptures, nor the power of God" (Matt. 22:29). "And beginning at Moses and all the prophets, he expounded unto them in all the scriptures the things concerning himself. . . . And they said to one another, Did not our heart burn within us, while he talked with us by the way, and while he opened to us the scriptures? . . . Then opened he their understanding, that they might understand the scriptures" (Luke 24:27, 32, 45).

* * *

"For whatsoever things were written aforetime were written for our learning, that we through patience and comfort of the scriptures might have hope" (Rom. 15:4). "Let the word of Christ dwell in you richly in all wisdom" (Col. 3:16). "When ye received the word of God, which ye heard of us, ye received it not as the word of men, but as it is in truth, the word of God, which effectually worketh also in you that believe" (I Thess. 2:13). "Give attendance to reading, to exhortation, to doctrine. . . . Meditate upon these things; give thyself wholly to them; that thy profiting may appear to all" (I Tim. 4:13, 15).

*   *   *

"All scripture is given by inspiration of God, and is profitable for doctrine, for reproof, for correction, for instruction in righteousness: That the man of God may be perfect, thoroughly furnished unto all good works" (II Tim. 3:16, 17). "Preach the word; be instant in season, out of season; reprove, rebuke, exhort with all longsuffering and doctrine" (II Tim. 4:2). "The word preached did not profit them, not being mixed with faith in them that heard it" (Heb. 4:2).

*   *   *

"But be ye doers of the word, and not hearers only, deceiving your own selves" (James 1:22). "Blessed are they that do his commandments, that they may have right to the tree of life. . . . For I testify unto every man that heareth the words of the prophecy of this book, If any man shall add unto these things, God shall add unto him the plagues that are written in this book: And if any man shall take away from the words of the book of this prophecy, God shall take away his part out of the book of life, and out of the holy city, and from the things which are written in this book" (Rev. 22:14, 18, 19).

*   *   *

The student of the Bible will find inspiration in recalling statements which have been made by great leaders in the past. These men have been leaders in the secular world, yet have held a deep respect for the Book which we desire to study.

John Quincy Adams (1767-1848), sixth president of the United States, famous for promulgating the Monroe Doctrine:

"So great is my veneration for the Bible that the earlier my children begin to read it the more confident will be my

hope that they will prove useful citizens of their country.
. . ."

Sir Francis Bacon (1561-1626), father of the inductive
method which underlies modern science, and famous for
his "Essays":

"There never was found, in any age of the world, either
religion or law that did so highly exalt the public good as
the Bible."

Sir William Blackstone (1723-1780), the foremost expositor
of English law in his generation:

(In his famous "Commentaries on the Laws of England")
"The Bible has always been regarded as part of the Common Law of England."

Thomas Carlyle (1795-1881), great British man of letters
who inveighed against *laissez-faire* theories of government and influenced the ages to come:

"The Bible is the truest utterance that ever came by alphabetic letters from the soul of man, through which, as
through a window divinely opened, all men can look into
the stillness of eternity, and discern in glimpses their far-distant, long-forgotten home. It is the one book wherein, for
thousands of years, the spirit of man has found light and
nourishment. It is the finest bit of literature ever written
by the pen of man."

Samuel Taylor Coleridge (1772-1834), English poet and
philosopher:

"In the Bible there is more that finds me than I have
experienced in other books put together: the words of the
Bible find me at greater depth of my being, and what-

ever finds me brings with it an irresistible evidence of its having proceeded from the Holy Spirit."

Charles A. Dana (1819-1897), editor of the *New York Sun*, noted for his writings on the Civil War:

"The grand old Book still stands; and this old earth, the more its leaves are turned over and pondered, the more it will sustain and illustrate the pages of the Sacred Word."

Charles Dickens (1812-1870), English author who wrote to improve conditions among the underprivileged of London:

"The New Testament is the very best book that ever was or ever will be known in the world."

Timothy Dwight (1752-1817), first president of Yale University:

"The Bible is a window in this prison-world, through which we may look into eternity."

W. E. Gladstone (1809-1898), British Prime Minister who achieved notable social reforms:

"I have spent seventy years of my life studying that Book to satisfy my heart; it is the Word of God. The Bible is stamped with a Specialty of Origin, and an immeasurable distance separates it from all competitors. I bank my life on the statement that I believe this Book to be the solid rock of Holy Scriptures."

Johann Wolfgang von Goethe (1749-1832), the greatest of German poets and dramatists:

"It is a belief in the Bible, the fruits of deep meditation, which has served me as the guide of my moral and literary life. The further the ages advance in cultivation, the more can the Bible be used."

General Ullyses S. Grant (1822-1885), American soldier and eighteenth president of the United States:

"Hold fast to the Bible as the sheet-anchor of your liberties; write its precepts in your hearts, and practice them in your lives."

Horace Greeley (1811-1872), founder and editor of the *New York Tribune*, famous for his advice, "Go west, young man, go west":

"It is impossible to enslave mentally or socially a Bible-reading people. The principles of the Bible are the groundwork of human freedom."

Patrick Henry (1736-1799), first governor of Virginia, of "Give me liberty or give me death" fame:

"The Bible is worth all other books which have ever been printed."

Thomas Huxley (1825-1895), famous English biologist who invented the term "agnostic" and helped to popularize Darwin's evolutionary views:

"The Bible has been the Magna Charta of the poor and oppressed. The human race is not in a position to dispense with it."

Andrew Jackson (1767-1845), seventh president of the United States:

"That book, sir, is the rock on which our republic rests."

Immanuel Kant (1724-1804), celebrated German philosopher:

"The existence of the Bible, as a book for the people, is

the greatest benefit which the human race has ever experienced. Every attempt to belittle it is a crime against humanity."

Dr. Howard A. Kelly (1858-1943), one of the greatest surgeons of the twentieth century, who pioneered the use of radium in treating cancer, gynecologist at Johns Hopkins Hospital:

"I testify that the Bible is the Word of God, because it is food for the spirit just as definitely as bread and meat are food for the body. The Bible appeals strongly to me as a physician because it is such excellent medicine; it has never failed to cure a single patient if only he took his prescription honestly."

General Robert E. Lee (1807-1870), American soldier and one of the world's great military commanders:

"In all my perplexities and distresses, the Bible has never failed to give me light and strength."

Abraham Lincoln (1809-1865), sixteenth president of the United States, famous for his fight against human slavery:

"I believe the Bible is the best gift God has ever given to man. All the good from the Saviour of the world is communicated to us through this book; but for this book we could not know right from wrong. All the things desirable to man are contained in it."

Sir David Livingstone (1813-1873), Scottish missionary and explorer in Africa:

"All that I am I owe to Jesus Christ revealed to me in His Divine Book."

Lord Thomas Babington Macaulay (1800-1859), one of England's greatest historians:

"The English Bible — a book, which, if everything else in our language should perish, would alone suffice to show the whole extent of its beauty and power."

Napoleon Bonaparte (1769-1821), Emperor of France, famous for his military conquests:

"The Bible is no mere book, but a living Creature, with a power that conquers all that oppose it."

Sir Isaac Newton (1642-1727), English scientist and philosopher who, among other notable contributors, discovered the law of gravity:

"There are more sure marks of authenticity in the Bible than in any profane history."

William Lyon Phelps (1865-1943), "Uncle Billy" Phelps to the thousands of men who studied literature under him at Yale University:

"I believe a knowledge of the Bible without a college course is more valuable than a college course without the Bible. The Bible has been a greater influence on the course of English literature than all other forces put together."

John Ruskin (1819-1900), England's great writer, artist, and art critic:

"Whatever merit there is in anything that I have written is simply due to the fact that when I was a child my mother daily read me a part of the Bible and daily made me learn a part of it by heart."

Sir Walter Scott (1771-1832), great Scotch poet and novelist, author of "Ivanhoe," "The Talisman," etc.:

"The most learned, acute and diligent student can not, in the longest life, obtain an entire knowledge of this one volume. The more deeply he works the mine, the richer and more abundant he finds the ore; new light continually beams from this source of heavenly knowledge, to direct the conduct and illustrate the work of God and the ways of men; and he will at last leave the world confessing that the more he studied the Scriptures, the fuller conviction he had of his own ignorance, and of their inestimable value."

Lord Alfred Tennyson (1809-1892), one of England's greatest poets:

"Bible reading is an education in itself."

General George Washington (1732-1799), first president of the United States:

"It is impossible to rightly govern the world without God and the Bible."

Daniel Webster (1782-1852), America's greatest orator, celebrated jurist and statesman:

"If we abide by the principles taught in the Bible, our country will go on prospering and to prosper; but if we and our posterity neglect its instructions and authority, no man can tell how sudden a catastrophe may overwhelm us and bury all our glory in profound obscurity."

Woodrow Wilson (1856-1924), twenty-eighth president of the United States, president of Princeton University:

"Our civilization cannot survive materially unless it is redeemed spiritually. The Bible is the word of life. I beg that you will read it and find this out for yourself. You will find the things you have wondered about and been troubled about all your life as men have been always; and the more you read it, it will become plain to you what things are worthwhile and what are not, what things make men happy. . . . When you have read the Bible you will know that it is the Word of God, because you will have found in it the key to your own heart, your own happiness, and your own duty."

❋   ❋   ❋

C. Their Translation

From the earliest times men saw the necessity of translating the Bible so that everyone could read it in his own language. One of the languages into which the Bible has been translated, obviously, is English. And it will be enlightening to trace briefly the history of English translations.

The very first of these dates back to A.D. 650, Caedmon, who became a great Anglo-Saxon poet, wrote many of the Bible's central passages in the form of Saxon poems. At about the time of Caedmon's death, in A.D. 700, two bishops, Eadhelm and Egbert, made Saxon translations of the Psalms and of the Gospels. Their work was crude, however, and was far surpassed when the Venerable Bede, thirty-five years later, produced his Saxon translation of the Gospel of John.

John Wycliffe in 1384 completed the first English translation of the entire Bible. Translated from the Latin Vulgate, and stilted and mechanical as was its style, it was nonetheless a great landmark in the history of the English Bible. But Wycliffe's work could not be widely circulated because the printing press had not yet been invented. Only a few hundred copies, in all likelihood, were produced, each laboriously and meticulously copied by hand. There are one hundred and seventy copies still in existence.

The development, in 1454, by John Gutenberg, of movable type printing prepared the way for the first wide-scale circulation of the Scriptures. And the invention came none too soon. With the rise of the Renaissance and the Reformation, there came a century second only to our own twentieth century in the number of translations which it produced. There were those of Miles Coverdale and John Rogers, the "Great Bible," the Genevan New Testament which first recognized the division of the text into verses, and the standard Roman Catholic Douay-Rheims version.

But the greatest of the sixteenth century Bibles was that of William Tyndale. Going back to the original Greek of the New Testament, Tyndale produced a fresh new translation in a free idiomatic English of great beauty. Evidence of its greatness lies in the fact that when the King James Version was produced almost a century later, one-third of it retained Tyndale's wording, and the remaining two-thirds retained his general literary structure. Some scholars go as far as to say that 90 per cent of Tyndale is reproduced in the King James Version.

In 1604 a conference of bishops and clergy was held to resolve some differences in the church. Out of this conference came the suggestion for a new up-to-date translation of the Bible. The idea met generally with disdain, but King James, who presided over the meetings and who had wide literary interest, championed the cause and ordered fifty-four scholars from Oxford, Cambridge, and Westminster to set about the task.

In 1611 they presented their finished work, the Authorized, or King James Version, which ever since has been the example of unparalleled beauty in English literary expression.

It seems strange to us today, looking back, to discover that initially the King James Version met with suspicion and hostility. The charge of tampering with Holy Scripture and of degrading it by reducing it to the vernacular of the day was hurled against the translators. But this has generally been the lot of men who, watching the changes in language, have sought to produce new translations of the Scripture in the language spoken in their own times.

It is expedient that there be new translations from time to time. Just as the New Testament was written in ordinary, rather than literary Greek, it would seem that God intends each country and each generation to read the Bible in its own every-day language.

And so it came about that the King James Version underwent revisions. Some of these were minor, simply bringing the spelling and vocabulary up to date, like the revisions of 1613, 1629, 1638, 1762, and 1769.

But toward the end of the nineteenth century Bible scholars were insisting on more than minor revisions. Too many very ancient Greek manuscripts had been recently uncovered, throwing new light on the original text of the New Testament. In 1885 there appeared the English Revised Version and in 1901 the American Standard Version, both showing improvement over the King James Version. But much as these versions were preferred by scholars and careful students, neither has replaced the King James Version in the affection of the people or in its tremendous influence both on the literary style and on the moral character of the English-speaking world. No greater tribute could be paid to the King James Version of the Bible than to recognize that for more than three hundred years it has held sway as the crowning literary achievement of the world.

Nonetheless, the twentieth century has seen a feverish production of new translations. Discoveries of new information are constantly improving our reconstructions of the original text, and there is the feeling that God did not intend us to read His Word in "Bible English."

Great variety exists among these translations. Some are painfully literal, word-for-word translations. Others go to the opposite extreme of freely paraphrasing in twentieth century idiom. Some have the avowed purpose of introducing novelty. Others seek to retain the traditional wording as far as possible, making changes only where it is necessary to bring the wording up to date or to make it more understandable.

For the person who wants to study the Bible there is great value in reading more than one translation, remembering that words in one language are seldom the exact equivalent of words in another language, and that translations are always approximations of the original. In the light of this the student will learn a great deal by comparing different versions for the additional light they will throw on the Bible's meaning.

The following list includes some of the modern translations and offers guidance in their selection and use.

Young, Robert: *Literal Translation of the Holy Bible*; 1887; reprinted, 1953.

The Twentieth Century New Testament; 1901.

Moffatt, James: *The Historical New Testament*; 1901.

Weymouth, Richard F.: *The New Testament in Modern Speech*; 1903.
A reverent, reliable translation that maintains its popularity undiminished. The footnotes of recent printings, however, are not acceptable to conservative Christians.

American Baptist Publication Society: *The Holy Bible — An Improved Edition*; 1913.

Moffatt, James: *The Bible — A New Translation*; 1922.
Dr. Moffatt is much too free with the text to make his

translation acceptable to conservative Christians, though a reading of his version may bring many new insights. His language is modern colloquial British English.

Goodspeed, Edgar J.: *The New Testament, an American Translation*; 1923.

A University of Chicago scholar, Dr. Goodspeed is liberal in his theological bent, but writes in a brisk American idiom.

Goodspeed, E. J., and Smith, J. M. P.: *The Bible, an American Translation;* 1931.

Williams, Charles B.: *The New Testament*; 1937.

This version is noted for its careful translation of the tenses of the Greek verbs, and is highly recommended for supplementary study.

The Holy Bible; Revised Standard Version; New Testament, 1946; *Old Testament,* 1952.

Produced by 32 scholars under the authorization of the National Council of Churches of Christ. Many conservative scholars have protested against the frequent reconstruction of the Old Testament Hebrew text without manuscript or other objective evidences, but in the main, especially in the New Testament, it is a thoroughly reliable and readable modern English version which follows very closely the style of the King James Version. Its paragraphing and versification of poetry are helpful and its style reverent and clear. Its supplementary use is highly recommended.

Phillips, J. B.: *Letters to Young Churches;* 1948.

A modern paraphrasing of the New Testament Epistles which very successfully reproduces the Scriptures' powerful directness.

Hooke, S. H., editor: *The Basic Bible;* 1950.

A rather misguided effort to limit the Bible to a vocabulary of 1000 words.

Phillips, J. B.: *The Gospels;* 1953.

The free flowing English of Phillips' paraphrasing reflects his training as a newspaper reporter as well as an interpreter of the Scriptures to young people.

Verkuyl, Gerrit: *The Berkeley Version of the Bible;* 1959.

A dignified modern version well worth reading, with helpful footnotes that throw light on the text.

MODERN ROMAN CATHOLIC TRANSLATIONS

Confraternity of Christian Doctrine: *The New Testament of Our Lord and Saviour Jesus Christ;* 1941. If occasion arises to deal with a Roman Catholic, it may be well to use an authorized Catholic translation. This version is quite dependable, although the footnotes often argue against the obvious truths it proclaims.

Knox, Ronald A.: *The New Testament of Our Lord and Saviour Jesus Christ;* 1951.

Here is another acceptable version for dealing with a Roman Catholic who will accept only a translation bearing the imprimatur of his church.

Notes

1. Edward J. Young, *An Introduction to the Old Testament* (Grand Rapids: Wm. B. Eerdmans Publishing Co., 1950), p. 47.
2. Merrill C. Tenney, *New Testament Survey* (Grand Rapids: Wm. B. Eerdmans Publishing Co., 1961), pp. xi-xvi.
3. Halley's *Bible Handbook*, p. 30 (23rd Edition).
4. W. H. Griffith Thomas, *Methods of Bible Study.*
5. *Ibid.*
6. *The Scofield Reference Bible,* Introduction.
7. The entire 119th Psalm focuses on the Word of God under various designations such as "statutes," "judgments," testimonies," etc. Read it through in its entirety noting the Psalmist's attitude toward the Word of God and his reliance upon it.

Chapter II

THE CHRISTIAN DOCTRINE OF HOLY SCRIPTURE

What confidence Christians ought to have in the book men call the Bible[1] and which, in view of its several parts, is also called the Scriptures, is indicated by many incidents related in that book. For example, Jesus reports Abraham as saying, in Paradise, that even a resurrected saint's message would have no higher persuasive power than the Old Testament Scriptures (Luke 16:29-31). In an especially vehement rhetorical flight, Paul, the author of the Epistle to the Galatians, declares that even an angel from heaven could have no authority to correct or modify the message of his book (Gal. 1:3). The same author, in the book of Romans, several times raises important problems of belief for which invariably the solution is introduced by such formulae as "What saith the scripture?" (4:3. cf. 9:17; 10: 10; 11:2). In each case the Old Testament passage cited is treated as the final word on the matter.

Among all Christians, of whatever special denominational persuasion, this pattern of dependence on the word of Scripture as the final word in doctrinal matters has been the rule. The Reformers[2] of the sixteenth and seventeenth centuries declared the Scriptures alone to be the only source of knowledge for faith and doctrine. And though in practice Roman Catholic tradition has set the Bible aside in many matters (for example, the dogmas of the sacrifice of the mass and of purgatory), and the pope in his "teaching office" has contradicted the Scriptures (for example, the dogmas of the immaculate conception and the assumption of the virgin Mary), even the Roman Church asserts in official standards[3] that the Bible is the final religious authority and without any error whatsoever.

Now it is proper to ask, Why is this true? We will be on the right track if we ask another question first: Why do Christians generally believe *any* important religious teaching to be true? Is it not because it is taught directly in some clear declaration of the Bible? Why do all Christians assert the truth of such an apparently improbable affirmation as the Trinity of the Godhead? That there is only one God who eternally exists in three persons? Is it because the Apostles' Creed says so? By no means. It is because certain texts assert that there is but one God, certain others that the Father is God, others that the Son is God, and certain others that the Spirit is God. Further passages associate the three together in such a manner as clearly to indicate that they three are one object of worship yet must not be confused as if they were one person. No Christian teacher has ever explained this teaching in a manner fully satisfying to the intellect; yet every Christian finds the Trinity to be a Mystery his mind can accept because God Himself has revealed it. To the Christian, having accepted what God has spoken, the Spirit of God imparts further insights that illuminate all of his life. As a result he cannot conceive of life at all without the Triune God — a Lord Christ who prayed the Father and sent the Comforter. In this Triune God he consciously lives and moves and has his being.

This process of arriving at a settled religious conviction shared by all other Christian believers does not, of course, uniformly occur in every believer. But it happened to the first believers. Though frequently attacked, to the present hour no Christian denomination has ever officially discarded the doctrine.

The Biblical basis of the doctrine of the Trinity is arrived at both deductively and inductively. If one wishes,

he may say it is one or the other. Essentially the process is
to bring several Biblical statements related to the same
subject together, as in the case of the Trinity, then to summarize their teaching as do the ancient ecumenical creeds
(Apostles', Nicean, Athanasian, Chalcedonian). This is neither pure induction nor deduction, neither analysis nor
synthesis. Rather, men of God in the various conclaves
placed together the Biblical affirmations on the Godhead
— Father, Son, and Holy Ghost — made a modest attempt at
explanation[4] (one *substance*, three *persons*) and insisted
on acceptance of a Mystery.

This Mystery is the strength of Christianity, not its weak-
ness. It is not a "problem"; it is a citadel, a dynamic, the
very soul of the church.

Furthermore, Christians affirm the divine authority of the
Bible for the same kind of reasons. There are dozens of
passages affirming that men spoke and wrote messages giv-
en to them by God, later collected in what we now call
the Bible. There are other passages affirming the divine
authority of the Scriptures in matters of faith, others affirming their *sole* authority in such matters. Statements of
Jesus in the Bible that "the scriptures cannot be broken,"
that "one jot or one tittle shall in no wise pass from the
Law [Old Testament] until all be fulfilled" (Matt. 5:18),
have led Christians to believe them to be without error.

It may be asserted safely, then, that "Holy Scripture" or
"Inspiration of the Bible" (to name a large subject by an
important part of it) is not a name merely for a book or
the opinion of it held by certain Christians, but a doctrine of Christianity. It is a doctrine constructed in the
same way that all evangelical Christian doctrines have
been constructed.

But, a special problem arises in this connection. The
doctrine of the Trinity, in view of the absence of the incar-
nate Son of God from the scenes of earth and the invisibility
of the Father and the Son, is not capable of empirical veri-

fication or non-verification. You believe it or you do not, on grounds faith deems sufficient. The same is true of all the doctrines of Christianity. For example, the statement that "Christ died" is not likely to be seriously questioned as a fact. Generally speaking, it needs no verification; all men die. Mohammed died, too. The death of Christ is not a Christian doctrine. But the statement "Christ died for our sins, according to the Scriptures" is a fact with interpretation; i.e., a *doctrine* of Christianity, specifically spelled out in Prophetic (Isa. 53) and Apostolic Scriptures (Rom. 3, 4, 5). This is incapable of empirical verification. You believe it or you do not, on grounds faith deems sufficient, as in the case of the Trinity.

Now this empirical, experimental "walk-by-sight" epoch that began with the age of discovery five hundred years ago seeks to verify the inspiration of the Bible the way it does the atomic theory of matter and the corpuscular or wave theory of light. The Bible is, after all, a bound volume of paper and ink within a cover. It can be seen. So, men think that since it is palpable to the senses it can be tested and analyzed like all other sense data. Thus the Bible is examined not according to its claims but according to what are often called its "phenomena." A list of kings in Genesis does not quite match one in Chronicles.[5] A passage in Genesis says Jacob leaned on a bed's head while one in Hebrews says he leaned on a staff.[6] The reports of the superscription on Jesus' cross[7] are not verbally the same. The reports of the sayings and events of Jesus' life vary somewhat from Gospel to Gospel. Now, say the empiricists (that is, the "scientific-approach-to-religion" people), we must not decide what the Bible is in the way we decide what the Godhead is. We must rather *observe the phenomena* of the Bible, then form a *tentative hypothesis* (as in science) to explain them.[8] Next we must seek to *verify the hypothesis* by tests. If it stands up under testing we will call our hypothesis a *theory*. This is not final either, for science does not claim to achieve certainty, only probability or a pragmatic basis of operation.

This method does not really work well for Christian faith, for the heart rests only in certainties. If God's asseverations may not be received with certainty, then men will not be Christians in any historic sense of that word.

As a matter of fact, in areas where the Bible is capable of being put to empirical tests of truthfulness in factual reporting, it comes off very well. But that is another story. Yet the results of such testing do not, even at very best, produce divine doctrines for us. The most the "test tube" of archaeology, our most productive modern method of historical verification, can prove is that the Bible is a good history book. If it is a good history book, of course, men will find it easier to believe it to be a good book of doctrine, too. True, the Bible reports many miracles, including the resurrection of Jesus from the dead. But conviction of the truth here will come to the heart only as the message is brought home to the heart by the inward witness of the Holy Spirit. This is what the Bible means when it says, "Faith cometh by hearing and hearing by the word of God," and "God chose by the foolishness of preaching to save them that believe," and again, Jesus' words to Peter, "Flesh and blood hath not revealed this unto thee, but my Father which is in heaven."

This is not circular reasoning,[9] proving the Bible by the Bible. It is rather to begin the process of reasoning with acceptance of a testimony — the testimony of God concerning His Word and His Son. It can be verified throughout life and on into eternity. This is the way all of life is. The babe begins a marvelous relationship by suckling his mother's breast, because Mother offers and the babe receives. Faith in Mother, however, receives stronger reasons later, but from the side of faith, not of rejection. To talk of circular reasoning in such a situation is like trying to measure the height of a building with a thermometer.

I. Our first consideration must be the God of the Bible.
What kind of being is He?

A recent splendid work on Systematic Theology departs
from the usual arrangement of doctrines wherein the logical
first position of the Doctrine of Scripture as the source of
theology is abandoned for one wherein Scripture is treated
after the doctrine of God and the Works of God. The author
explains, "We live in a day when many devout believers in
God through Christ have been alienated from the orthodox
view of the Bible to such an extent they can scarcely give
it serious consideration." Then he adds, "I have a feeling
that after a review of the doctrine of God, many of our
friends will be more open to the orthodox view of the Bible
than they would otherwise be."[10]

The Bible begins with the fact of God — "In the beginning God." No effort is directed to prove or define Him.
As the story of the ages rolls along, the reader meets a personal Spirit who communicates with man, His noblest creature. This divine Spirit is seen to be without limit in time,
or space, or power. He is the Author of all that is. He is
the Father of time, the Sustainer of all existence, and the
Lord of History. A famous theologian sums it up in the
sentence, "God is that infinite and eternal Spirit in whom
all things have their source, support, and end."[11] It is
affirmed in the Bible that this Person, as said above, is
Lord of History. He planned it and controls it. Nothing,
from the fall of an empire or a stellar galaxy to the fall of a
sparrow[12] or a raindrop, is outside His control. The free
acts of men, even the evil acts of wicked men,[13] are included mysteriously in this grasp. The doctrine of the last
previous four sentences is called Providence and is hardly
questioned in any respect by Christian theologians and
Bible interpreters. This God could send the Israelites to
Egypt at just the time in that nation's history when they
would be kindly received. He could later bring them to

Canaan at just the epoch when they might grow to a great nation. He could direct Ahashuerus to be sleepless at just the time when he might seek diversion in just the passage from his documents that would turn his interest to the Jews and thereby effect their deliverance. All these things God could and *did* do. Any ordinary book of theology or doctrine will furnish long lists of passages from the Bible supporting and amplifying the above statements. Christians when first faced directly with this plain fact of Bible teaching sometimes quail before it. It seems to be such a stern reality — if it be reality. But when they kneel in prayer they always assume it, especially when they pray for God to change the perverse, ungodly wills of their unbelieving relatives and loved ones. The more the Christian reflects on these things, the more certain he will be that, unless God can and does control all things: the growth of the hair in Hitler's mustache, the production of hormones in an angry murderer's adrenal glands, as well as the rising of the sun and the falling of raindrops — unless God be omnipotent, He is no God at all! He is certainly no help through prayer and devotion.

To accept this doctrine of God and His Providence as true — as most of the persons interested enough in the Christian doctrine of Scripture to deny it or affirm it do — is to render a doctrine of authoritative, inerrant Scripture possible and worthy of consideration. Such a God could have His revealed will inerrantly written in a book by human hands working freely.

II. Our second consideration follows naturally from the first: The Scriptures inform us that the all-powerful and all-knowing Creator-God *prepared the human writers of Scripture* specifically for their task.

It will help us to see the importance of this if we observe certain interesting features of the Bible. We note, in the first place, that the Bible is a collection of many different kinds of literature — law, narrative, lyric poetry, didactic poetry, personal epistles, open letters, sermons, state papers, prophetic visions, apocalypse, etc. — and this is only a beginning of classification. We note also that it is written to different generations of men in widely different epochs. Some were ancient bedouins; others were a nation of slaves on the move through deserts; still others settled agriculturalists; at the latest epoch — a rather "cultivated" juncture of history — a cosmopolitan, urbane generation scattered through the cities of the Roman Empire. This last was the case with every book of the New Testament. Note how the names of cities figure even in the names of several of them (Corinth, Ephesus, Philippi, Colosse). Finally, it is clear that the writings of the Bible in their various parts represent fully the personality of the particular writers involved. This is not a mere inference drawn from the "phenomena of Scripture," that is, the observed data such as Paul's vehemence, Isaiah's elegance, or Amos' rusticity. Rather it is a rather clear assumption of each author who permits his commission to be stated in his writings. Take, for example, what John says in Revelation 1:19, "Write [says Jesus] "the things which are [chaps 2, 3], and the things which shall be hereafter [*after these things*, Greek, chaps. 4-22]." So John did just that. We find him taking some dictation from the risen Lord or the revealing angel occasionally. He is even once told to omit description of what he was seeing. But always he writes "in his own words," as we say, except when rarely he is supplied specific words to write. In such cases the portion is introduced by "and he said," or some similar expression. Compare the similar situation with regard to the book of Leviticus (1:1).

It is important, therefore, to discover that several Bible writers specifically claim preparation to write their portions, first, for their own generation, and after that for us who read the sacred Book today. As Paul says of one of the most famous writers, "David, after he had served his own

generation by the will of God, fell on sleep, and was laid
unto his fathers (Acts 13:36). This same Paul writes of
his own preparation that God "separated" him "from" his
"mother's womb," called him "to reveal" Christ and "preach
him among the heathen." If God wanted the Gentiles and
the Hellenized Jews of the world evangelized, if He wanted
an oriental religion translated and transfused into a European social and national setting, then He had to get ready
a man of scholarly instincts, incisive logic, vigorous, self-
disciplined personality, and a good education in two cul-
tures — Oriental and European — for the task. A Jew reared
in the university city of Tarsus[14] (where else would he
have picked up knowledge of the writings of Aratus and
Cleanthes — Acts 17:27, 28) by a Pharisee[15] ("strictest sect
of the Jews"[16]) family with Roman citizenship,[17] later edu-
cated in the best Rabinnical learning "at the feet of Gama-
liel," one of the most famous teachers in the history of
Judaism — such a man, we may certainly say, had been, by
special providence and *special grace*, prepared both by
heredity and environment for the task of writing nearly
half of the books of the New Testament. No Christian has
any problem in understanding how such a man as this,
brought to complete submission to the Holy Spirit and filled
by the same Spirit, could write a book like Romans, completely expressing God's thoughts and words in sentences
that were nevertheless fully his own. Nothing seems more
fitting and natural. It is a remarkable testimony to the
narrowness of the mind of man that professed Christian
theologians should have ever had any "problem" with the
so-called human element in a divine book. Anyone who
looks long at the doctrine of the image of God in man
should not think this any more remarkable in a book than
the miracle of the divine and human natures of Christ.
Both are in complete harmony with the "fitness" of things.

Similar claims of special providential preparation are

made by the author of Jeremiah (1:4 ff.). Evidences of it are in many books.

Before leaving this thought, observe that these assertions will not seem either strange or remarkable to men convinced of the Christian view of God.

III. A further distinct feature of the Christian doctrine of Scripture that further illuminates the key position of the human authors is that God *fully certified each of these men to his own generation as a man with authority to speak* [or write] *for God.*[19] In fact, this is one of the most certain features of the doctrine of Scripture as the Bible itself presents that doctrine. This will explain why certain ancient Jewish books on religious subjects were received as Holy Scripture; i.e., are canonical, and others either perished from man's knowledge or became what scholars are wont to call "pseudepigraphal" (of spurious authorship) or "apocryphal" (hidden, suppressed books).

Space does not allow full development of this aspect of the subject, though little is needed to establish the point. Since Moses is the author of the earliest portion of the Bible, let the story begin with him:

(1) When the great legislator, general, judge, revelator and benefactor had led the Israelites to the border of Canaan and he knew he was about to die without a successor in his manifold offices, he delivered a strong proscription; i.e., a negative command in detail. The Israelites were to have nothing whatsoever to do with the false and essentially vicious methods of gaining alleged divine revelation practiced by the inhabitants of Canaan. His exact words, containing a remarkable list of heathen religious practices, are to be found in Deuteronomy 18:9-14. Many of these are practiced in various parts of the world (including astrology, consulting dead ancestors, etc.) to the present hour.

(2) At the same time Moses announced the establish-

ment of a new office (if we may distinguish an *office* from a *function* which was at least as old as Abraham, Gen. 20: 7), the office of prophet. He declared that the prophets would speak for God as certainly as he, Moses, had spoken for God throughout the forty years of their association with him, and expressly commanded the Israelites to obey the prophets' words as they had heeded his own. These matters are plainly set forth in Deuteronomy 18:5-19.

(3) At this juncture something extremely important for the doctrine of Holy Scripture — the basis for infallible recognization of the authentic prophet and his oracle, or detection of the inauthentic, took place. Moses announced five marks — we call them certifying signs — of the authentic messenger of God. They were (a) that the prophet would in every case be a Hebrew — of the family of Israelites, or as they came to be called in much later times, "the Jews." Twice it is specified, "The Lord thy God will raise up unto thee a Prophet from the midst of thee, *of thy brethren,* like unto me; unto him ye shall hearken" (Deut. 18:15; cf. v. 18). Paul only confirms this old principle when he says of the Jews that their great advantage is "that unto them were committed the oracles of God" (Rom. 3:2). This is not because the Hebrews have ever manifested any marked degree of "aptitude for religion," as Jewish writers seem inclined to claim. Whoever was so spiritually stiffnecked as the people who set aside their Scriptures, went "a whoring" after pagan idols, stoned the prophets and crucified the Savior? It is rather, it seems likely, that since the people being readied for the advent of the world's Redeemer were Jewish, they were not to be disadvantaged in this preparation by the spiritual ministry of foreigners. The advantages of an indigenous ministry are, then, as old as Moses and certainly not of recent discovery. It should therefore be no surprising thing that every book of the Bible either claims a Jewish author or is hardly otherwise to be explained.

The second certifying sign was (b) that the prophet would invariably speak in the name of Jehovah, the God of Israel. This fact, implied in Deuteronomy 18:15 and 18, is stated positively in verse 22 and negatively in verse 20 with the grim provision that the false "prophet . . . that shall speak in the name of other gods, even that prophet shall die." Deuteronomy 13 furnishes a detailed explanation as to how this sacrilege was to be verified and punished. So there are no Baal or Moloch oracles in the Bible. All are in the name of the God of Abraham, Isaac, and Jacob.

A third, and very important mark of the true messenger of the Lord was (c) his ability accurately to predict the future, that is, the near future, in some verifiable manner. The exact words are, "And if you say in thine heart, How shall we know the word which the Lord hath not spoken? When a prophet speaketh in the name of the Lord, if the thing follow not, nor come to pass, that is the thing which the Lord hath not spoken, but the prophet hath spoken it presumptuously: thou shalt not be afraid of him" (Deut. 18:21, 22). Abraham and Sarah had faith strengthened by the fulfillment of predictive prophecy (Gen. 12:1-3; 15: 14-16; 18:10-14; 21:1, 2) in the birth of their son Isaac in their old age. Moses himself was not at first the staunch, obedient believer that he came to be. Again it was a fulfilled prophecy, in part, that helped him (Exod. 3:11, 12. cf. 19:1 ff.; 4:14; cf. 27, 28).

The fourth sign was to be (d) ability to perform miracles. This is related to the gift of prophecy just treated, though it is presented by Moses in Deuteronomy 13:1 ff., somewhat earlier.

The fifth and last, in some respects the most important, is rather difficult to formulate. Moses' words about it, in part, are: "If there arise among you a prophet or a dreamer of dreams, and giveth thee a sign or a wonder [signs and wonders are miraculous works], And the sign or the wonder come to pass, whereof he spake unto thee, saying, Let us go after other gods, which thou hast not known, and let us serve them; thou shalt not hearken unto the words of that prophet, or that dreamer of dreams: for the Lord your God proveth you, to know whether ye love the Lord your God with all your heart and with all your soul" (Deut. 13:1-3. The whole chapter continues the same thought).

Some authors have considered this to show that the good moral character of the prophet was the fifth mark. But such is not the case; it is rather (e) the *content of his message*. The final, decisive mark to be found in the prophet's message was agreement with Moses' message — the monotheistic Jehovah faith and the covenant of Sinai which had taken God forty years to deliver and establish in the hearts of a few, at least, of the Israelites. No new revelation of eternal truth from the heart of an eternal, unchanging God can ever annul or set aside an older revelation. The Bible will show growth and variety of detail; the men whose history and thinking it reports will be at different levels of spiritual apprehension, under different sorts of divine administration (instance the end of the sacrifices by the sacrifice of Christ); but, that Bible will be a dynamic unity of doctrine, faith, and message from beginning to end. Millions of intelligent Christians have found it so. They simply do not discover that inner disharmony and contradiction of message that the too-helpful, unbelieving critics say is there. Scholarly writers have demonstrated that unity[20] against many gainsayers.

Not every book of the Bible states that its immediate author met all these tests. But since the earliest portion of the Old Testament, the Pentateuch, details them and all the rest of the Old Testament points back to the Pentateuch as basic religious authority[21] (including the Lord Jesus, who certainly is more to be trusted than certain critics), we may safely assert that the provisions were carefully respected. The reader who desires more information on this aspect of the subject is referred to evangelical works on the subject, in addition to the present authors' work mentioned above. See Robert D. Culver, "Were the Old Testament Prophecies Really Prophetic?" in *Can I Trust My Bible,* Moody Press, 1962, and *The Sufferings and the Glory,* Christian Service Press, Moline, Illinois, 1958.

Let us call attention to the case of one preaching prophet, Elijah. Like a bolt from the blue, he appears on the pages of Scripture at I Kings 17:1, saying to Ahab, "As the LORD God of Israel liveth, before whom I stand, there shall not be dew nor rain these years but according to my word." This (a) Hebrew prophet whose very name means "My God is Jehovah," (b) speaking in Jehovah's name (c) predicts a drought to be ended only at his signal. Three years later in a (d) mighty act of miraculous power, God confirmed his messenger's claims with a miracle of fire and sent rain at the prophet's word, thus claiming the people's hearts for himself and (e) the Mosaic faith again. Read the thrilling end of the story (I Kings 18:36-46).

In times of absence of prophets, people mourned their absence and knew of it by the absence of the "signs" (Ps. 74:9). When the last great Prophet, the very Son of God, came, he was certified in the same way (Acts 2:22; Matt. 11:1-6); the apostles and other writers of New Testament Scripture likewise (II Cor. 12:12). The men of the first Christian century knew that the epoch of revelation was over when the apostles died and the signs ceased (Heb. 2:1-5), just as the people living in the four "silent centuries between the Testaments" knew revelation had been interrupted, as Jewish writings coming from that period testify (I Macc. 4:46).

These five marks of true divine communication by divinely accredited messengers enabled the ancient people of God infallibly to detect imposters and to recognize the genuine. How we today, living at a great distance from the time the Bible was written and received, come to assurance that these things transpired as just described, or that God indeed has enscripturated divine revelation in this Book, is another matter, to be treated later herein.

One further observation must be made. There were several methods whereby an accredited messenger of God (an apostle or prophet) could confer his God-given authority upon a written oracle; i.e., make it "canonical," as later church writers came to say. He might write the book himself and issue it as Scripture. This is certainly the case with a Psalm of David, an Epistle of Peter, Paul, or John, or the prophecy of Jeremiah, Habakkuk, or Malachi. This does not, of course, preclude his use of a secretary to whom he might dictate his words. Or, he might sponsor the composition of another whose work he regarded as correct in every regard. Such is almost certainly the case in Paul's relation to the writings of Luke (Gospel and Acts) and of Peter in relation to the Gospel of Mark. A third method grows out of the unique spiritual authority of the Apostles in the early church. These men had Christ's special authority (Matt. 10:14-20; John 17:18-20; 20:19-23). One of them, Peter, had a very remarkable dispensation in this regard (Matt. 16:19, 20). Now all the books of the New Testament were written and received by churches in an age when Apostles were living and presiding in their special functions as unique channels of Christ's authority. If we did not know the name of the author of a single book received by the church as Scripture under the leadership of these men, the case would be scarcely different from what it is now with only one book, Hebrews, clearly anonymous as to authorship. The same principle applies to the anonymous books of the Old Testament in relation to the prophets of that epoch. All the historical books of the Old Testament except Ezra and Nehemiah, many Psalms, and most of the Proverbs are anonymous. Yet they are Scripture. Prophets led the people of God in including them in the body of Sacred Writings.

These matters are essential to the doctrine of Holy Scrip-

ture but cannot be treated more at length here. The writer
directs the readers to evangelical books and articles on the
subject of "Canon" and "Canonicity."

IV. We have now arrived at the central feature of our
subject — *Revelation*. Stated propositionally: *God revealed
the matter of Holy Scriptures to His appointed messengers.*
    No subject is more a matter of dispute among theolo-
gians[22] today than this one. It is safe to assert, however,
and it is asserted here without any disrespect for the learning of certain gentlemen who think otherwise, that there is
no disagreement over the essential meaning of divine revelation as applied to Scripture among men who have abandoned their own wisdom for God's wisdom, as Haldane said
of the doctrine of justification in his famous commentary on
Romans so long ago.
    To attempt an extended study of the various Greek and
Hebrew words for "reveal" or "revelation" is only somewhat
helpful. It is far from decisive. What is decisive is a consideration of the clear teaching of the Bible on the subject of
the impartation from God to chosen men the matters of
sacred record in the Bible.
    The Bible itself provides a doctrinal summary on this
matter: "God, having of old time spoken unto the fathers
in the prophets in divers portions and in divers manners,
hath at the end of these days spoken unto us in a Son"
(Heb. 1:1, 2 ASV margin). The Old Testament ("of old
time") epoch was one in which God spoke through prophets. It took place in "divers portions," that is, through a
rather large number of men who lived from the time of
Moses (or perhaps the author may even be thinking of
Adam or Enoch) to the time of Malachi, the last prophet
of the Old Testament Scriptural epoch. Some portions were
large, such as the book of Isaiah, coming from about 700
B.C. Some were small, such as the 23rd Psalm (David's),
coming from about the year 1000 B.C. A conservative es-

timate of the length of the period during which written Old Testament Scripture was being unfolded by God to prophets and through them to the people of God is 1000 years — from Moses, about 1400 B.C., to Malachi, about 400 B.C.

It was also in "divers manners." The way God revealed Himself, His truth, and facts of His sovereign will, was hardly the same in any two cases. We find it hard to interpret the information we are given. When David wrote "The heavens declare the glory of God, and the firmament showeth his handiwork," he was only reporting what God's works of creation, preservation, and providence tell all men, only, by the Holy Spirit, purified and corrected from any taint of sinful interpretation. (Cf. Ps. 139:6; 51:5, 6; II Sam. 23:1-3, especially v. 3). This is God's Spirit speaking by His natural creation through man's rational and spiritual faculties. God speaks through nature to us all, but we had best go to Scripture to get the details straightened out.

Apparently an inner voice or conviction of the Holy Spirit — never explained to us — accounts for the revelation of some of the most precious announcements of Messiah and the coming salvation. Such is the apparent reference of the statement that "the Spirit of Christ which was in them did signify when it testified beforehand the sufferings of Christ, and the glory that should follow" (I Peter 1:11, an interpretation of Isa. 53).

Psalm 51 (note the superscription) is spiritual truth brought to the author's attention and formed into settled spiritual conviction as the Spirit spoke through an exceedingly painful spiritual experience.

And there are many others: dreams and their interpretation (Dan. 2), visions of both subjective and objective sort (Dan. 7; Ezek. 1-7). In the case of Moses, there was used a writing produced by "the finger of God" — a phrase that certainly does not answer all questions about what kind of writing tools God may use (Exod. 31:18; 32: 16). With Moses, and only with Moses, God spoke "mouth to mouth" (Num. 12:8) or "face to face" (Exod. 33:11). God also spoke through history, interpreted by Spirit-guided men. The books that compose the historical section beginning with Joshua and ending with Esther is a record of events that happened, interpreted according to the Spirit of God at work in the hearts of God's chosen prophetic writers. History, as such, is not revelation, but history, interpreted by God, *is* divine revelation.

God also spoke through institutions such as the ritual system and its ministers. In fact, all of the Old Testament, in one way or another, spoke and speaks of Christ, as the New Testament expressly declares. But the methods are various. No one knows how many there may have been. The book of Hebrews hints at the typical message of the Old Testament without spelling it out.

To return to the second part of our basic text in dealing with the idea of revelation, Hebrews 1:2 states that "God . . . hath at the end of these days spoken unto us by a Son." God spoke of Himself through the announcement, birth, life, death, resurrection, and ascension of a Son from Heaven. The author of Hebrews is emphasizing not the deity of Christ (which he elsewhere affirms) but a contrast in revelatory methods. The Old Testament revelation came in bits and pieces through prophets over a thousand years in a multitude of ways. But the New Testament revelation came in a brief time in and through one remarkable man, a Son of God from heaven.

A certain recent theory of revelation holds that revelation is wholly of the nature of personal acquaintance with God, wholly devoid of factual ("propositional") content.[23] This theory did not arise out of Biblical convictions drawn from passages teaching it in the Bible, but out of certain philosophical opinions. These opinions are mainly those of "existentialism" — "Existence is prior to essence." This is often labeled "anti-rational" and it is, but in their view of nature and the Bible the advocates of this view frequently are very "rationalistic" — denying many of the miracles, even the resurrection of the body of Jesus. It would take us far afield to discuss the view here. Suffice it to say, that in spite of the strange Biblical exegesis of these interpreters, the Bible reports to us that God revealed many "facts" and "propositions" to men of old — the "pattern" for a tabernacle, the duration of the Babylonian exile, the city of our Savior's birth, the nature of our Lord's resurrection body, the existence of angels, the promise of our Lord's second coming, etc. This theory receives notice far beyond what its pure novelty and irrational dogmatism deserve. And, happily, like most fads in theology, it seems to be passing out of fashion.

Some of the questions that arise in connection with our assertions on the subject of revelation; for example, how we can say that a book like III John (a bit of personal correspondence) is God speaking through Christ, find their answer in what was said earlier under "Certification of writers" and later under the next topic.

V. Our next consideration is that *God inspired the Bible*. This is only a way of saying that in some unspecified manner the record of revelation which we call the Bible is a divinely written book, hence truthful and of divine authority. No, we do not affirm that it was written in heaven or dictated by word of mouth by God to men on earth. In fact, men always get into trouble when they seek to define this truth too precisely. This is for the same reason that they get into trouble when they seek to define too precisely the doctrine of the Trinity or the Person of Christ. Usually, in stating one aspect of the truth, such venturesome spirits exclude what seems to be its opposite, in an effort to be thoroughly consistent. This is simply to say that the Trinity is a supernatural reality; the person of Christ a miracle. Both of these truths, like the truth that there is a book men wrote — truly the most thoroughly human book in all the world that is also in the very most real and proper sense the Word of God — are mysteries, divine mysteries.

Furthermore, it is sinful to call the mysteries of God *problems*. The Trinity and the Person of Christ are not problems; they are the very heart of Christian truth, the glory of our faith. We believe them not because our minds discovered them, or having been told them our minds fully understand them, but because God Almighty did let us know about them. So it is with the Bible. It partakes of the same character. This is to say that in addition to being a deposit of revelation, it is itself as a whole a datum of divine revelation. Thus its poets rapturously sing and its prophets and apostles boldly proclaim.

In an effort, insofar as possible, to let the Bible speak for itself on this subject, we will first introduce three of the strongest texts, all from the New Testament, on this subject, in each case presenting an exegesis, followed by a summary of its teaching. The first now follows.

"And that from a child thou hast known the holy scriptures. . . . All scripture is given by inspiration of God, and is profitable for doctrine, for reproof, for correction, for instruction in righteousness: that the man of God may be perfect, throughly furnished unto all good works" (II Tim. 3:15-17).

The first item of interest is the proper name for the doctrine and the book. It is "holy scriptures," or, in shorter form, "scripture." As we shall see, "inspiration," while of long use and filled with pious meaning, is not a very good word, since it is very inexact and misleading, never used elsewhere in the Bible, in any way, of the Bible.

The next is the disconcerting fact that "is given by" in verse 16 is an interpolated interpretation — intended to help translate, but joined with "inspiration," really being a rather inept carry-over from the Latin Vulgate. The situation is thus: The first clause of verse 16 in Greek is *pasa* (all) *graphe* (scripture) *theopneustos* (God-breathed). The clause requires the supply of "is" between "scripture" and "God-breathed" for translation into English. Hence we should read, "All scripture (is) God-breathed." Now a study of the form "God-breathed" will show that it does not mean "God-breathed-into" but "God-breathed-out" — not "*in*spired" but "*out*spired." An illustration will help. The father shows his child how to inflate a toy balloon. After placing the opening to his lips he inhales deeply, then, pressing the opening firmly against protruding lips, he "*in*spires" the balloon, or as we are more apt to say, "*in*flates" it. This is exactly what *theopneustos* in II Timothy 3:16 does *not* mean! Change the figure to one less pleasing but much more to our point. Watch the rugged, slicker-clad cowboy (on TV commercial, of course) gallop his horse past a huddled clump of wet herefords, then quickly dismount and stride swiftly beneath the canvas shelter. There a companion hands him a king-size specimen of brand X cigarettes. He lights it; he inhales deeply (with great satisfaction). Then he *ex*hales (breathes out) and *creates* thereby a cloud of white smoke, so to speak. Now, just so is the Bible a God-breathed-out (i.e., God-created) book. This gives it the power and utility described in the rest of the quotation.

The Scripture author here is using a figure of speech known to interpreters as "anthropomorphism" — God under a human manner of speaking. But this particular anthropomorphism is a fairly common figure of speech in the Bible and one used with such plainness in several other passages that there need be no doubt of its meaning. When God creates the universe it is represented as being by His spoken (breath over vocal cords) word (Gen. 1:3, 6, 9, 14, 20, 24, 26; cf. Heb. 11:1 ff.). Psalm 33, in a poetic commentary on this fact, decisively states, "By the word of the LORD were the heavens made; and all the host of them *by the breath of his lips*" (v. 6). It is hard to think of stronger evidence than this that in a context relating to origin of something, the divine breath stands for God's creative activity. Verse 9 goes on to say, "For he spake, and it was done; he commanded, and it stood fast."[25]

We may, then, with assurance, affirm that when we read in the Authorized Version of II Timothy 3:16 that "All scripture is given by inspiration of God," we should understand it to mean that all Scripture is divinely created. The Bible is a God-created book, hence profitable in the manner the passage so forcefully states.

We move on to a second great passage — II Peter 1: 15-21. Space forbids treating all the passage. The great Apostle is interested in showing that the Christian Scriptures are not "cunningly devised fables" (v. 16) and that the Scriptures are more firm assurance and brighter light even than great personal spiritual experiences such as he, with James and John, had on the "holy mount" (vv. 16-18). He concludes, "We have also a more sure word of prophecy; whereunto ye do well that ye take heed, as unto a light that shineth in a dark place . . . knowing this, first, that no prophecy of the scripture is of any private interpretation. For the prophecy came not in old time by the will of man: but holy men of God spake as they were moved by the Holy Ghost" (II Peter 1:19-21).

The best understanding of the word "prophecy" (vv. 19, 21) is simply Scripture, received as a whole. If one insist on the narrower sense, it is of a single portion produced by a prophet, as is the sense of "prophecy of scripture" (v. 20). The subject, then, is the same as that of II Timothy 3:15-17, treated above. There have been various views of "no prophecy of the scripture is of any private interpretation." This writer is persuaded that it refers to the fact there is no magical or "spontaneous" generation. The word "is" renders the Greek *ginetai*, more properly "came to pass" or "became." The word for "interpretation" (*epilusis*) and its verbal cognate (*epiluo*) mean essentially to set free, release, and only by extension, to interpret. In fact, the word occurs only here in the whole New Testament. The word "private" means essentially "its own." Now join these together: "No prophecy of the Scripture came to pass of its own release." It sounds much like denial of any spontaneous power of books to publish themselves. Perhaps Peter is elaborating the earlier denial of any connection between "fables" and the Scripture. At any rate, in spite, strangely, of most of the English translations, old and recent, many of the most authoritative commentators agree that this verse has no reference to interpretation by readers of the Bible but to the *origin* of it, as indeed the next verse (21) clearly states.

Verse 21 is the nearest to a statement of the divine method in using the human writers to be found in the Bible. "Men spake [or wrote, as context proves] from God, being moved by the Holy Spirit" [ASV, which follows the better Greek text]. The divine work is more than supervision or guidance, though they are included. "Being moved" is a Greek word meaning "being borne along." It is the word usually translated to bring. Interpreters seeking to explain the work of the Holy Breath [Spirit] on the prophetic writers of Scripture point out how that twice (Acts 27:15, "were driven" and 17, "were driven," ASV) this word *fero* is used of the action of a ship moving by the force of the wind. All the peculiarities of the ship are imparted to its motion, but it is nevertheless completely in the grasp of the wind. This comparison must not be pressed too far, but it is helpful.

So, if II Timothy 3:16 lets us know that the Scriptures are divinely created, II Peter 1:21 qualifies the knowledge with information that God's method was to work through Spirit-borne men.

Now, obviously, these verses refer to the divine creativity as working in a more concrete and definite way than in God's general providence. For these verses are intended plainly by their authors to explain the peculiar authority and power of the Scriptures — authority and power that other books do not have. There is unique working of God in and through man producing a unique book with unique power and authority.

The third text is a portion of a verse in the heart of a section (John 10:22-39) reporting a hot extemporaneous debate between Jesus and "the Jews" as He walked in the portion of the Jewish temple called Solomon's porch (John 10:23). Of interest to us at this juncture is that Jesus cited Psalm 82:6 (v. 34) to support His argument. Then, addressing Himself to them on the basis of their common opinion (His and theirs, *argumentum a concessu*), He states "the scripture cannot be broken" (v. 35). The word "broken" here is the common one for breaking the law, or the Sabbath, or the like (John 15:18; 7:23; Matt. 5: 19), and "the meaning of the declaration is that it is impossible for the Scripture to be annulled, its authority to be withstood or denied." Note that what Jesus had quoted was a rather casual sounding sentence, "Ye are gods." Yet this was held to be quite as binding as if God had sounded seven mighty trumpets first, as in Chapter 11 of the Book of Revelation.

In summary, the three representative texts just discussed tell us three things about the idea of inspiration, three qualifications or refinements of the affirmation that "God inspired the Bible." Firstly, according to II Timothy 3:16, the Bible was created by God. Secondly, the Lord produced it through the work of ancient men called prophets who were specially empowered and controlled for their task of writing Scripture. Thirdly, these Scriptures, interpreted according to the intention of their divine Author, declare the undeniable truth of God without any error.

The above passages are sufficient to establish the Bible's teaching concerning its own inspiration. There are many more texts. Furthermore, the doctrine can be amplified.

This we shall do shortly. But it must be iterated that for anyone convinced of the unity of the Bible, the above texts are sufficient, and as among the plainest, definitive. As a famous theological writer puts it, Biblical testimony to its own inspiration and inerrant authority is not a single stone or two. It is an avalanche! One may dodge a stone or two on a hillside but not an avalanche.

An important feature of this subject, often overlooked, is the expressed testimony, direct and indirect, of our Lord Jesus Christ with regard to the Scriptures, both the Old and New Testaments.

We will consider first His testimony to the Old Testament. It is hardly necessary to establish that the Bible of Jesus was our Old Testament. This was the Bible of the Jews of His day and Jesus was a Jew. With this Bible He was very familiar, for He was constantly referring to it. One can find references to every major period of the Old Testament in His reported words and never look outside the book of Matthew. He frequently quoted the Old Testament and more frequently alluded to it. Many of the leading ideas of His public and private discourses were drawn from the Old Testament, as, for example, "the kingdom of heaven" (Matt. 4:17; cf. Dan. 2:22), and "the Son of Man," His favorite name for Himself (Matt. 26:64; cf. Dan. 7:17).

Not only did Jesus know the Old Testament; He believed it implicitly. This is borne out not by a few isolated, obscure statements but by His entire private and public life and ministry. For example, He referred to most of the great miracles of the Old Testament and accepted the Biblical reports of them as true — even the ones that seem most preposterous to skeptical persons. The story of the great flood (Luke 17:26, 27), the destruction of Sodom, with the unlikely story of Lot's wife's unhappy end (Luke 17:28-32) and the very remarkable experience of Jonah in the belly of a fish, together with Jonah's success in inducing national repentance at Nineveh (Matt. 12:40, 41) are only a few examples of the many that could be cited from the Gospels. In the reference to Jonah, as also the others, Jesus refers to the miracle in such a manner that it is difficult, if not impossible, to take Him any way but literally; i.e., He accepts Jonah and the story of him as literal truth. He mentions the "queen of the south" and her visit to Solomon in the next breath, of whom there is no reason to suppose any but literal existence. The use of the men of Nineveh as a warning loses most of its force to His own generation if they are only imaginary men engaging in a fictitious literary repentance.

When Jesus uses the Scripture He does so in a circumstantial and natural way. There is nothing contrived or artificial, as if He were only playing to an audience which believed in the miracle and was speaking thus to please them.

Of special importance to Christians are these hearty endorsements of the divine origin, divine authority, and truthfulness of the Old Testament by Jesus. His testimony is the same after His resurrection as before — any alleged ignorance arising from His *kenosis* or "humiliation" is both irrelevant and untrue. When the Sadducees have wrong opinions about divine things, Jesus says, "Ye err, not knowing the Scriptures" (Matt. 22:29). When the Scripture speaks (i.e., reports with the author's approval), it is God who speaks (Matt. 19:4, 5; cf. Gen. 2:24 where the human author is commenting rather than quoting any spoken works of God). Jesus even went so far as to state that the Old Testament is incapable of failing in any way, down to the smallest letter of a word ("jot") and the smallest part of a letter ("tittle"; Matt. 5:17).

But Jesus did far more than *talk* of His endorsement of the Old Testament. By His life He demonstrated it. His was a life of obedience to its laws, even to the extent of supporting the temple rituals and traveling long distances to attend the festivals. It is of utmost significance that He

placed personal dependence on quotations from the Bible
(the book of Deuteronomy) in the hour of His temptation
by the devil, His time of greatest spiritual peril (Matt. 4:
4; cf. Deut. 8:3; Matt. 4:7; cf. Deut. 6:16; Matt. 4:40; cf.
Deut. 6:13; 10:20). In Jesus' dying hours the words of
Scripture were on His lips, and with its words He committed His soul to God (Luke 23:46; cf. Ps. 31:5).

Jesus' testimony to the New Testament must, in the nature of the case, be different. None of the New Testament
was as yet written when He ascended. Yet He did, by
way of prophecy to His apostles, in His last hours with
them, indicate that a new revelation, completing what He
had begun, would come into existence during the lifetime
of those very apostles. This is often missed by Bible readers
by reason of the fact that they ignore the basic rule that
interpretation of any text is governed in part by its connection with the immediate context. Thus, when our Lord addresses words to "you," though ordinarily coming under
the "umbrella" of "teaching them [disciples through the
centuries] to observe all things that I have commanded you
[apostles in His company and others then present, Matt.
28:20]," sometimes He means *only* the apostles, perhaps
two or three or even a single person present. (See examples:
Luke 19:29 ff., for two disciples only; Matt. 10:5 ff., for 12
apostles only; John 21:15 ff., for one person only).

It is an educational axiom that men understand answers
well only after they have asked related questions; i.e., education in certain areas cannot run ahead of personal development. Therefore it should be no surprise that on that
last night with the Twelve (and only the twelve, remember), He said to Peter that he was not yet ready to understand the significance of that striking feet-washing incident
in Chapter 13 of John (vv. 6, 7). Later in the evening
He said to them all (the Eleven), "I have yet many things to
say unto you, but ye cannot bear them now" (John 16:12).
Be reminded that no one questions that Jesus was saying

this to eleven men. Next, observe that He predicted a coming time when that unfinished revelation would be finished and delivered to the same eleven men. Before reading this in Jesus' words of the next verse, turn one leaf backward in your Bible to the last two verses of the preceding chapter. These verses furnish the indispensable contextual limitation on verse 13: "But when the Comforter is come, whom I will send unto you from the Father, even the Spirit of truth, which proceedeth from the Father, he shall testify of me: and ye also shall bear witness *because ye have been with me from the beginning*" (John 15:26, 27). Those who had been with Jesus from the beginning of His official ministry were the chosen witnesses; *to them* the Spirit was to have a unique ministry of revelation, as we now read in John 16:13. Let us read it with verse 12 again, to see the connection: "I have many things to say unto you [eleven], but ye cannot bear them now. Howbeit, when he, the Spirit of truth, is come, he will guide you into all truth" (Greek, all *the* truth).

This is a clear promise that a certain body of truth, the very divine revelation of the "Son" (Heb. 1:2) which the Son already had given, in part, to His chosen apostles, was to be completed after His ascension by the descended Holy Spirit. No one since those apostles may claim this promise, be he pope or peon, Mary Baker Eddy or Ellen G. White. The day of the "Son's" speaking ended with the apostles whom He had chosen.

To understand the unique authority of these men, it will be helpful to move on to Chapter 17 of John and, after first noting the contextual structure of our Lord's great prayer therein, to note what He said to God about these twelve (minus one, Judas) men. The chapter reports our Lord's "high priestly" prayer. As a good high priest He left out no intercessory responsibility. First He prayed for Himself. This part of the prayer ends at verse 5. He begins His prayer for the twelve apostles at verse 6 and ends it at verse 19. Verse 20 clearly indicates the transition to His prayer for the saved of all the ages since, evangelized and taught by the apostles' ministry, as follows: "Neither pray I for them [apostles] alone, but for them also which shall believe on me through their word."

Now let us discover what He told or asked the Father regarding the Eleven in verses 6 through 19. Twice He reminds the Father that He, the Son, had already given them God's words (v. 8, 14). Now note what that meant with regard to the authority of these Eleven, and the one, Paul, later added to their number. "As thou hast sent me into the world, even so have I also sent them into the world" (v. 18). This means that the apostles went to the world with a unique authority to speak for God. It is the "truth" that is involved here (vv. 17, 19). That truth was to be in their unique custody, the truth which we now call the New Testament. The world was to be reached "through their word" (v. 20), a promise that would never have been realized if they had not written that "word" in the books we call the New Testament.

An examination of the story of the call of the Twelve Apostles and their first commission (Matt. 10:1-20) will show that unique authority at its inception. For it would be a hardy claimer of "all the promises in the Book" who would want to claim all of this temporary commission. Yet the unique apostolic authority is there.

Furthermore, as the Lord promised *to* and *through* the apostles a further revelation, He indicated that it would be at a certain future time — "when he the Spirit of truth is come" (John 16:13); "thou shalt know hereafter" (John 13:7, a promise to Peter himself). The promise was fulfilled by the coming of the Spirit as described in the second chapter of the Acts.

Our Lord even went so far as to indicate the contents of this future revelation. There would be, first, a work of *recollection,* enabling the apostles and those under their aegis, to write the Gospel records of our Lord's words and deeds. "But the Comforter, which is the Holy Ghost, whom the Father will send in my name, he shall teach you all things, *and bring all things to your remembrance, whatsoever I have said unto you*" (John 14:26). Is this not the true solution of the so-called "synoptic problem"?

The doctrinal portions of the New Testament, wherein the facts of the Lord's redemptive and revelatory work would be interpreted and amplified, were within the range of Jesus' promise. For He went on to say, "And when he, the Spirit of truth, is come . . . he shall receive of mine and shall shew it unto you" (John 16:14). That is, as is repeated in verse 15, the Spirit would explain the meaning of Jesus to the apostles in a manner they were not, before Calvary, the empty tomb and the upper room, able to comprehend. This doctrinal revelation they were to tell and write. We have it mainly in Romans through Jude, the Epistolary section of the New Testament.

The predictive (including apocalyptic) portions were promised also. This is indicated in the simple statement, "He will show you things to come" (John 16:13).

It is also important to observe that Jesus put a limit both on the time of the revelatory epoch and the content of it. The Greek text of John 16:13, followed by all the important recent English versions (ASV, RV, RSV, NASB, NEB) reads, "He will guide *you* into *all the truth*." "The truth" in such a context is mainly of a spiritual sort — saving truth. No reference to the arts and sciences, of course, was intended. The apostles ("you") were to be guided into *all* the revelation God intends to give our epoch ("all the truth"). Revelatory activity came to an end with the Apostolic New Testament Scriptures. It was a finished book because God had no more to say! God is not now *speaking*; He *has spoken* (Heb. 1:1, 2). If one wants to know the will of God today, let him consult the Prophetic and Apostolic Scriptures. The Scriptures are complete and final.

We must conclude on this aspect of the subject by briefly treating another question: How far does this divine authority and guaranteed truthfulness extend — to *ideas* only or to the *words* of Scripture? The welter of contemporary objection to "verbal inspiration" might give the impression that the idea is *hard to find in Scripture.* It is instructive to find the same objections (and evangelical answers) in works now over 150 years old. As a matter of fact, verbal Scriptural inspiration is the only kind the Bible mentions at all.

Now, granting that the gospel does not need to be stated always in the same words, if it is a saving message, the words used must always convey the gospel truly. An angel promised Cornelius a human messenger "who shall tell thee *words* whereby thou and all thy house shall be saved." We have those "words" today in Acts 10:34-43.

This same emphasis on "words" is an emphasis in the Biblical representation of its own inspiration. On both the oral and spoken levels, which is to say, whether spoken or written, it was the prophet's "words" which were given by God: "I will put my *words* in his mouth . . . my *words* which he shall speak in my name" (Deut. 18:18, 19). It was the words which conveyed the thoughts! Wrong words convey wrong thoughts. Thus, revealed messages, in the Biblical sense, are conveyed by inspired words. Strictly speaking, the Bible knows nothing of inspired men but only inspired words. What was true of the prophetic Scriptures, as just noted, was true of the writings of Moses also (Exod. 4:10-12). Other Old Testament references to inspiration of the words of prophetic writers are to be found at Ezekiel 2:7; 3:4; Daniel 9:2; cf. v. 12; Jeremiah 1:6-9; II Samuel 23:1, 2; Amos 1:1; cf. 3:1; 7:10; cf. v. 16. The New Testament is no different. Paul claims to have received his message (shall we say his *ideas*) by revelation (Gal. 1:11, 12); yet he also claims that his *words* were divinely supplied by God as well, as he specifically claims. After introducing "the things . . . given to us of God," he adds, "which things also we speak, not in *words* which man's wisdom teacheth, but which the *Holy Ghost* teacheth" (I Cor. 2:12, 13). In another place Paul does not hesitate to call his own message "the word of God" and to assert that so it had been received by others (I Thess. 2:13).

Of equally impressive weight is the way the later apostles and prophets, and the Lord Jesus as well, use the earlier Scriptures. In addition always to assuring the truthfulness and divine authority of Scripture, over and over they base exegetical arguments on the turn of a phrase, the tense of a verb, or the number of a noun, etc. This is evidence of the most minute and circumstantial sort. Many pages might be cited here from both older and recent writers pointing these cases out and elaborating their importance as proof that the Biblical view of inspiration is *verbal* inspiration. A well-known example is Paul's basing an argument on the singular number of a noun in Genesis (Gal. 3:16; cf. Gen. 13:15). Another is Jesus' basing an argument on the syntax of a sentence which in the Hebrew has no verb (Matt. 22:32; cf. Exod. 3:6). There is never the slightest hint in any New Testament passage that the Old Testament it cites, quotes, and interprets is not truthful down to the least detail of its words. Remember, it was Jesus Himself who spoke of the imperishable authority even of jots and tittles.

VI. There is an important further step, however, in explaining the peculiar confidence Christians have always had in the Holy Scriptures. Granting the truth of all these affirmations about God's person and providence in making such a book at least possible, the preparation of chosen men for their tasks as organs of revelation, their certification to the people of God in their own day, the revelation of God's mind and the inspiration of the record, we still have full basis for no deeper conviction and appropriation of truth than had the hypocritical Pharisees of Jesus' time, or some licentious renaissance popes, nor of a host of nominal church-goers today who say, "Lord, Lord, and do not the things" the Bible says.

How some people "happen" to respond with faith to the Word of God and others do not is never fully explained in the Bible. There is, nevertheless, something significant to be said about it. The answer, insofar as we know it, is that aspect of doctrine known as *Illumination*.

Man as he exists apart from the special saving power of God is "dead in trespasses and sins" (Eph. 2:1). The preaching of the cross is foolishness to him (I Cor. 1:18). "The natural man receiveth not the things of the Spirit of God: for they are foolishness unto him; neither can he know them" (I Cor. 2:14). Of their rational faculties another text states they have "the understanding darkened, being alienated from the life of God through the ignorance that is in them, because of the blindness of their heart" (Eph. 4:18).

Even regenerate disciples do not always understand and obey the Word of God. This explains our Lord's sharp rebuke when He, after His resurrection, called certain disciples "fools and slow of heart to believe all that the prophets have spoken" and why shortly thereafter he "opened their understanding that they might understand the scriptures" (Luke 24:25, 45). This fact finds further elaboration in the fact that Paul prayed most earnestly that the Ephesians might be "enlightened, that ye may know" (Eph. 1:18).

Even when a man is convinced that the Bible is a truthful report, it remains for him only a good history book, law book, or something of the sort, until God enables him to have deeper insights by giving him a new spiritual understanding. This is stated in many different ways in the Bible. It is a teaching found in several very suggestive contexts. When, on a certain occasion, men had rejected his message, Jesus assigned full responsibility for it to their own wicked hearts. After the feeding of the Five Thousand many would have made Him their king (John 6:15). But

Jesus rebuked this shallow response (vv. 2, 27). Then, after further evidence of their unbelief, Jesus said, "He that cometh to me shall never hunger, and he that believeth on me shall never thirst. But I said unto you, That ye also have seen me and believe not" (John 6:35, 36). There was no attempt at excusing their unbelief or of offering extenuating explanations. Then He went on to say, "All that the Father giveth me shall come to me" (v. 37), and later, "No man can come to me except the Father which hath sent me draw him" (v. 44). Similar expressions occur in verses 45 and 65. Of course, the doctrines of election and calling are involved here. But there is also the work of God's Spirit in the sinner's heart, enabling him to believe that the warnings and promises of Scripture are true *for him* and causing him to desire to turn to God.

This preliminary work in the sinner's heart is what is often called "illumination" by the theologians. Since God's work of salvation in man is one capable of analysis and distinction but not of separation, it is no surprise that such an enlightening work continues. In fact, the experience of conversion (or regeneration) is called an illumination (Heb. 10:32; cf. 6:4, as well as Col. 1:13; Eph. 5:8; II Cor. 4:4-6). When Peter was enabled to perceive more fully than certain others the full depth of Christ's person, he was told by Jesus that no mere human understanding had brought it about but Jesus' own Father (Matt. 16:15 ff.). It is this spiritual enlightenment carried on to perfection in regeneration and progressive sanctification that makes possible spiritual discernment and growth in grace (I Cor. 2:14–3:1).

This work of enlightenment (or illumination) is called by various theological terms. One of the greatest of the Reformers, John Calvin, who devoted several pages to discussion of it, with full Scriptural proof, in his *Institutes of the Christian Religion,* called it by the pregnant name "the testimony of the Holy Spirit." This, in Calvin and others, is not precisely the testimony of the Spirit to our sonship found in certain passages (Rom. 8:15, 16; I John 5:10), but the self-certifying work of the Bible in our heart through the Holy Ghost, convincing the hearer (or reader) of its truth objectively as well as subjectively for him and enabling him thus to trust in Christ through the word.[26] "Faith cometh by hearing, and hearing by the word of God" (Rom. 10:17).

VII. Closely related to the work of illumination is the work of *interpretation* of the Bible. Though both this and the last previous topic are allied to the division of theology called Soteriology, or Salvation, their place in connection with the doctrine of Holy Scripture may not be wisely overlooked.

As a matter of fact, though the Bible is "perspicuous," as the Reformers said, that is, capable of being plainly understood by plain people with only the Holy Spirit's aid, the beginning of that understanding usually, we would almost say, normally, takes place through human aid. The important passage here is the well-known account of the evangelist-deacon Philip and the Ethiopian eunuch (Acts 8:26-40). The eunuch was equipped with a good copy of the Bible, or at least an important portion of it (Isaiah) and was reading the heart of the gospel as set forth in Chapter 53 when Philip joined him. Said Philip, "Understandest thou what thou readest?" Whereupon the eunuch responded, "How can I, except some man should guide me?" The remainder of the story is well known. The human messenger of the gospel joined the eunuch in his chariot, explained the Scripture, thus leading him to faith in Christ and confession of the same in Christian baptism. After that the eunuch went on his way rejoicing, no doubt later to read the rest of the Bible, finding it, when read, interpreted and obeyed, in company with other believers, sufficient for life and godliness (See II Tim. 3:17).

This story is an example of how the Holy Spirit usually helps beginners in Bible study to interpret the Bible — with good human aids! It was an angel who took Philip away from a very successful missionary effort and sent him off for the unlikely mission field on a desert highway (Acts 8: 26). It then was the Spirit who directed Philip to the eunuch and his chariot (v. 27) and it was the same Spirit who brought the message home to the eunuch and enabled him with faith to say, "I believe that Jesus Christ is the Son of God" (v. 37), for "No man can say that Jesus Christ is Lord but by the Holy Ghost" (I Cor. 12:3).

The office of pastor-teacher in the church is God's means of continuing human help for men in interpreting the Word of God. The fourth chapter of Ephesians and numerous texts in I and II Timothy, Titus, and the Epistles of Peter, are the New Testament authority and explanation for this statement. Let the man who disdains the help of these Spirit-appointed men look steadily at the following verses:

"And account that the longsuffering of our Lord is salvation; even as our beloved brother Paul also, according to the wisdom given unto him, hath written unto you; as also in all his epistles, speaking in them of these things; in which are some things hard to be understood, which they that are unlearned and unstable wrest, as they do also the other scriptures, to their own destruction. . . . But grow in grace, and in the knowledge of our Lord and Saviour Jesus Christ" (II Peter 3:15, 16, 18).

A summary will now bring this study of the Christian doctrine of Holy Scripture to a close.

Christians have always believed that in a unique way the Bible is the Word of God, conveying to them the Truth, the will of God, without any admixture of error. This has been true in all the ages of the church and among all bodies of Christians. They have received this conviction by the same means and in the same manner they have received all other common doctrinal convictions; that is, the Holy Scriptures have taught it to them in plain passages. Even in modern times when convictions based on authority of any kind, even divine authority, have been out of fashion, no recognized church body has yet abandoned this conviction. They find this intellectual commitment supported in the heart with convictions prompted by the Holy Spirit.

Upon close examination of the Scriptures it is discovered that this teaching of the Bible about itself is capable of analysis. The Christian God is the almighty Ruler of the world in all its working. Nothing is beyond His providential control, including the acts of both good and evil men. Such a God is able to direct pious men in such a way as to produce a book that perfectly records divine revelation. The actual stages in conveying God's message to human hearts are several. God prepared the writers by nature and training; He certified them as accredited messengers to the godly people of their times, choosing men of the Hebrew nation to speak in His name, accompanying their message with the prophetic gifts and wonders of divine power. On their part they remained faithful to the Mosaic revelation with which the Scriptures began. God also revealed Himself and His Truth to them in a variety of ways, the last and highest being the personal revelation in His Son. A record of this revelation by the undefined, but real, work of inspiration gave men a Bible in which human instruments and divine authorship perfectly meet, giving mankind a faithful "enscripturation" of all that is "profitable" for doctrine, for reproof, for correction, for instruction in righteousness. This record, as originally written and interpreted according to the Author's intention, is without error. Yet to produce a response of faith there must be a work of illumination of the Bible's meaning in the hearer's (or reader's) heart. Accompanying the divine work of illumination there is usually an accompanying initial human work of interpretation, assisting the believer in his first steps and thereafter as the Christian has need. This will usually take place in that fellowship of believers called the church.

Notes

1. This sentence is a reflection of Josephus' striking expression of Jewish belief in the authority of the Bible (*Against Apion*, I, 8). Josephus wrote during the second half of the first century of the Christian era.

2. Since the official statements coming from the Reformation era are not readily accessible to present-day readers but are basic to the beliefs of most of the churches of which present-day Christians are members, and, are very important to definition of beliefs today, several of the more important standard statements are quoted herewith. To these we add one or two more recent statements. The Lutheran document, *The Formula of Concord* of 1576, devotes its introductory article to Scripture. Beginning, "We believe, confess, and teach that the only rule and norm, according to which all dogmas ought to be esteemed and judged, is no other whatsoever than the prophetic and apostolic writings both of the Old and of the New Testament," the article goes on to say that "a clear distinction is retained between the sacred Scriptures of the Old and New Testaments, and all other writings; and Holy Scripture alone is acknowledged as the [only] judge, norm, and rule, according to which as the [only] touchstone, all doctrines are to be examined and judged, as to whether they be godly or ungodly, true or false" (Philip Schaff, *The Creeds of Christendom*, Vol. III, pp. 93-97). The *Second Helvetic* [Swiss] *Confession* of the earliest "Reformed" confessions (A.D. 1566). The section on Scripture is first and fills most of four pages in the original Latin. A few lines will furnish the flavor of this document: "We believe and confess the Canonical Scriptures of the holy prophets and apostles of both Testaments to be the true Word of God, and to have sufficient authority of themselves, not of men. For God himself spake to the fathers, prophets, apostles, and still speaks to us through the Holy Scriptures" (*Ibid.*, p. 832). *The French Confession of Faith*, 1559 (prepared mainly by Calvin) devotes Articles II, III, IV and V to the doctrine of Scripture. The fifth reads: "We believe that the Word contained in these books [canonical books of the two Testaments] has proceeded from God, and receives its authority

from him alone, and not from men. And inasmuch as it is the rule of all truth, containing all that is necessary for the service of God and for our salvation, it is not lawful for men, nor for angels, to add to it, to take away from it, or to change it. Whence it follows that no authority, whether of antiquity, or custom, or numbers, or human wisdom, or judgments, or proclamations, or edicts, or decrees, or councils, or visions, or miracles, should be opposed to these Holy Scriptures, but, on the contrary, all things should be examined, regulated, and reformed according to them. And therefore we confess three creeds, to wit: the Apostles', the Nicene, and the Athanasian, because they are in accordance with the Word of God" (*ibid.* p. 362). The *Belgic Confession,* mainly for Flanders and The Netherlands, in use from 1561 and endorsed by the Synod of Dort, 1619 devotes the third through seventh articles to Scripture. The fifth says, "We receive all these books, and these only, as holy and canonical, for the regulation, foundation, and confirmation of our faith; believing without any doubt, all things contained in them, not so much because the Church receives and approves them as such, but more especially because the Holy Ghost witnesses in our hearts they are from God, whereof they carry the evidence in themselves" (*Ibid.* pp. 381-389). The *Thirty-Nine Articles of the Church of England* 1571, devotes Articles VI and VII to Scripture and Canon, agreeing fully with the previous creeds cited here. It is also agreed (i.e., with *Belgic Confession*) that the reason for accepting the ancient ecumenical creeds is that they agree with Scripture (*Ibid.* 489-492). The great English Puritan statement of 1647, known as the *Westminster Confession,* used widely by Congregational churches and by the Presbyterian Church to the present time is incomparably clear, Biblical, and persuasive. The first chapter, containing ten numbered paragraphs of varying length, is "Of the Holy Scripture" (*Ibid.* 600-606). Though perhaps the greatest purely human document relating to this subject, it is fairly accessible to general readers. We therefore quote here only Paragraph IV: "The authority of the holy Scripture, for which it ought to be believed and obeyed, dependeth not upon the testimony of any man or church, but wholly upon God (who is truth itself), the Author thereof; and therefore it is to be received, because it is the Word of God." In America, the Baptists, though not regarding any statement of faith outside the Bible as a *creed,* as such, nor as binding on all members, have widely used *The New Hampshire Confession* of 1833.

The first article reads, "We believe that the Holy Bible was written by men divinely inspired, and is a perfect treasure of heavenly instruction; that it has God for its author, salvation for its end, and truth without any mixture of error for its matter; that it reveals the principles by which God will judge us; and therefore is, and shall remain to the end of the world, the true center of Christian union, and the supreme standard by which all human conduct, creeds, and opinions should be tried" (*Ibid.* p. 742). The *Methodist Articles of Religion,* 1784, Article V, agrees in all essential particulars with the Lutheran, Reformed, etc., confessions above. We close this lengthy paragraph with "The Basis of Union" of the United Church of Canada, 1925. Article II: "We believe that God has revealed Himself in nature, in history, and in the heart of man; that He has been graciously pleased to make clearer revelation of Himself to men of God who spoke as they were moved by the Holy Spirit; and that in the fulness of time He has perfectly revealed Himself in Jesus Christ, the Word made flesh, who is the brightness of the Father's glory and the express image of His person. We receive the Holy Scriptures of the Old and New Testaments, given by inspiration of God, as containing the only infallible rule of faith and life, a faithful record of God's gracious revelations, and as the sure witness to Christ" (*Ibid.* 935).

3. In November 1893, Pope Leo XIII issued an Encyclical, "Providentissimus Deus" which contained a lengthy section on the study of Holy Scripture. It was largely in wholesome reaction against the destructive "higher criticism" of the time. In the main all orthodox Protestants would agree with it, with the exception, chiefly of his renewing of the decision of the Council of Trent that it is the privilege of the Roman Church alone to interpret Scripture and the acceptance of the Apocrypha as Scripture. The following excerpts are important: ". . . it would be entirely wrong either to confine inspiration only to some parts of Sacred Scripture, or to concede that the sacred author himself has erred. . . . The books, all and entire, which the Church accepts as sacred and canonical, with all their parts, have been written at the dictation of the Holy Spirit; so far is it from the possibility of any error being present to divine inspiration, that it itself of itself not only excludes all error, but excludes it and rejects it as necessarily as it is necessary that God, the highest Truth, be the author of no error whatsoever. This is the ancient and uniform faith of the Church" (Henry Denzinger, *Enchiridion*

Symbolorum, Translated by Roy J. Defarrari as *The Sources of Catholic Dogma.* St. Louis, Mo.: B. Herder Book Co., 1957).

4. "But the catholic faith is this, that we worship one God in trinity, and trinity in unity. Neither confounding the persons nor separating the substance" (The Athanasian Creed" (H. Denzinger, *Ibid.,* 15; Paul T. Fuhrman, *An Introduction to the Great Creeds of the Church.* Westminster Press, 49; Charles Hodge, *Outlines of Theology,* p. 117.

5. Gen. 36:1-43; I Chron. 1:43-54.

6. Gen. 47:31; Heb. 11:21.

7. Matt. 27:37; Mark 15:26; Luke 23:38; John 19:19.

8. The theological method of Biblical-Evangelical Christianity approved in this chapter is given very unfair treatment in the usual "critical" modern treatment. An older example is "How to Form True Notions of Inspiration" — the fifth chapter in *How God Inspired the Bible,* J. Paterson Smyth, 1892. He says of his own method, "I have . . . no way of finding out except by examining the phenomena presented by the Bible itself" (p. 64). C. H. Dodd, *The Authority of the Bible,* 1929, employs Smyth's method throughout his lengthy and widely read book. Contrariwise, that the theological method employed for the rest of Christian doctrines must be applied to Scripture also is ably defended by Edward J. Young, *Thy Word is Truth,* 1957. All agree that the "phenomena of Scripture" are important and merit attention. The question is, Do we accept what God has clearly said the Bible is and adjust our interpretation of the phenomena to that, (as has the church for 18 centuries) or decide what the Bible is by treating it as any other book, without reference to its clear claims for itself? An unusually perceptive article by Dr. Millard J. Erickson, "A New Look at Various Aspects of Inspiration" has just appeared in *Bethel Seminary Journal* (Vol. XV, No. 1, Autumn, 1966). Dr. Erickson surveys the options open for evangelicals in handling the phenomena of Scripture and comes to some solid conclusions.

9. The Apostle Paul treats this issue and traces our certainty in "the things that were freely given to us of God" to the fact that God's Spirit who "searcheth all things" has revealed them to the hearts of those whom "God hath chosen" and "called" (I Cor. 1:26, 27; 2:10-16). This inward testimony of the Holy Spirit is "the mind of Christ" (I Cor. 2:16) producing spiritual discernment. The Reformed theologians as well as the early Protestant creeds emphasized this; viz., Calvin, *Institutes,* I. 7. 5; I. 8. 13; *Westminster Confession* I. 5; *Belgic Confession,* V.

See E. J. Young, *op. cit.*, chap. 8, esp. pp. 192, 193. "The Wheaton Position on Inspiration" of 1956, prepared by 16 professors of Wheaton College, of which the present author was one, treats this subject in its twelfth paragraph. My present feeling is that it is the weakest part of the "Statement" — mixing the basis of assurance of salvation with the basis for assurance of truth in Revelation, two related, but not identical, subjects. See the penetrating criticism by A. A. Hoekema in *Torch and Trumpet*, Vol. VII, No. 5, Oct. 1957.

10. J. O. Buswell, *A Systematic Theology of the Christian Religion,* Vo. I, p. 5.

11. A. H. Strong, *Systematic Theology*, p. 52.

12. Matt. 10:29.

13. A. H. Strong, *Ibid.*, 421-443; Exod. 12:36; I Sam. 24:18; Ps. 33:14, 15; Prov. 16:1; 19:21; 20:24; 21:1; Jer. 10:23; Phil. 2:13; Eph. 2:10; James 4:13-15; II Sam. 16:10; 24:1; II Thess. 2:11, 12.

14. Acts 21:39; 22:3.

15. Phil. 3:5.

16. Acts 26:5.

17. Acts 16:37, 38; 22:25, 26, 27, 29; 23:27.

18. Acts 22:3.

19. W. H. Green, *General Introduction to the Old Testament: The Canon*, 1898, 1926 presents a full discussion of this proposition, as do also standard conservative works of Systematic Theology, e.g., A. H. Strong, *op. cit.*, 117-141.

20. E.g., Adolph Saphir, *The Divine Unity of Scripture*, 1892, still a classic.

21. The Historical Books point back to the Pentateuch as furnishing explanation for the varying fortunes of the Hebrew people. The nation prospered when obedient to the Mosaic Law, became spiritually, morally and otherwise depressed when disobedient. The Poetical Books sing the praise of the Law. The Prophetical Books call the people back to the Law. See G. Ch. Aalders, *A Short Introduction to the Pentateuch*, pp. 111-138; W. H. Green, *op. cit.*, pp. 11-18.

22. The Biblical view is ably expounded and defended by B. B. Warfield, "The Biblical Idea of Revelation" in *The Inspiration and Authority of the Bible*. See the article "Revelation" by the same author in *International Standard Bible Encyclopedia;* also the excellent chapter "The Authority of the Bible," Kenneth S. Kantzer, *The Word for This Century,* Ed. M. C. Tenney.

23. This is the view of Karl Barth, announced in his early work,

Romerbrief (Commentary on Romans) and in his later *Dogmatics,* especially the first two books of the series (Vol. I, Part I, Part II). Emil Brunner's similar views on the nature of Revelation were given currency in America through his *The Mediator,* now on the market in English for over thirty years and certainly one of the most influential books in theology ever written. His recent three-volume *Dogmatics* is widely used in theological seminaries of the English-speaking world. The late Paul Tillich's idea that "revelation is the manifestation of the depth of reason and the ground of being" — expounded in a manner similar to that of Barth and Brunner — has been given currency through the multitude of his books and addresses, especially, *Systematic Theology,* Vol. I. For a complete favorable discussion of the "neo-orthodox" doctrine see *The Idea of Revelation in Recent Thought* (1956) by John Baillie. It is the most prevalent view outside of evangelical circles today, even making inroads into Roman Catholic thinking. Recently, however, the shifting interest of theologians not definitely rooted in evangelical Biblical theology has shifted to other topics. Theologians of the world like the students of ancient Athens, have leisure for "nothing else but either to tell, or to hear some new [newer] thing" (Acts 17:21).

24. The category of divine Mystery and related terms — dialectic, contradiction, antinomy, and paradox are given very helpful treatment by J. R. Packer in his *Evangelism and the Sovereignty of God* (Chicago: Inter Varsity Press, 1961), pp. 18-25.

25. The student will find more technical discussion of the meaning of *theopneustos* in context of II Tim. 3:16 in Warfield, *The Inspiration and Authority of the Bible,* Chap. VI; article, "Inspiration" by the same author in *International Standard Bible Encyclopedia;* Edward J. Young, *op. cit.,* chap. 1.

Chapter III

PRESENT-DAY PRACTICES OF SEARCHING THE SCRIPTURES

The following examples and recommended practices pertaining to methods of searching the Scriptures were sent to the authors by the individuals noted. They are from men and women in many different walks of life and may therefore be helpful to the average reader who is eager to discover practical ways of searching the Scriptures both for his own spiritual growth and in order to equip himself for "handling aright" the word of truth in his relation to others to whom he desires to communicate the message of the Bible.

A Radiologist. Charles F. Smith, M.D., Howard Community Hospital, Kokomo, Ind.:

"Since the Christian life is really Christ living His own life through me, I must receive daily sustenance from Him. I must partake of Him daily if I am to live a healthy Christian life. When I partake of physical food, I can no longer direct that the nourishment go only to one arm or one leg. Just so, when I partake of Jesus Christ and assimilate Him, it nourishes and affects my whole life.

"The Word of God is God's revelation of Himself to man. God revealed Himself to His creation through the prophets and apostles, and this record was preserved in written form. Jesus Christ took on human flesh and dwelt among us to embody in His flesh the message that had been revealed through the written Word.

"I study the Word of God that I might know Jesus Christ. This study of the Scriptures is not an end in itself, but that it might introduce me to the Person Jesus Christ. He is the key to knowing God, for God's whole purpose in letting me know Him was that He might possess me and make me into the image of His Son. This means that my ultimate purpose in studying His Word is so that He can transform my life into that which is pleasing to Himself.

"Bible study first became meaningful and exciting to me when I weaned myself from crutches (devotional books) and "canned" notes (commentaries) and started really digging into the Word for myself with the indwelling Holy Spirit as my Teacher. By the use of notebooks in my Bible study, I have been able through the years to build my own set of personal commentaries.

"I find personally that the most effective method for me to use to get real help from personal Bible study is to ask myself questions just as I would if I were leading a group Bible study. I have found those used by Inter-Varsity Christian Fellowship students for many years to be especially helpful:

Is there an example for me to seek to follow by God's help?
Is there a command to be obeyed?
Is there a sin for me to avoid or forsake?
Is there a promise for me to claim? If so, what are its conditions?
What does this passage teach me about Jesus Christ, God, myself, His will for my life?
Is there something in this passage which should be my prayer for today?

(From *His*)

"Certain books of the Bible are full of promises and others contain numerous admonitions. I find it useful to list these in my notebook. I also like to add other key questions, depending on which book I am studying. For example, in studying one of the Gospels, I ask myself questions such as:

What does this passage teach me about Jesus Christ — His person and work?

What specific claims did Jesus Christ make?

What shows the authority of Jesus Christ — and in what areas?

What brought this person to Jesus Christ?

What specific need did Christ meet in this life?

What did various witnesses think of Jesus Christ?

What is there about this Person that attracts me or might attract my friends to Jesus Christ?

What practical difference does knowing Jesus Christ make in one's life?

"In studying the Book of Acts, I ask myself general questions such as:

What individual needs did God meet in the everyday lives of Christians or seekers?

What principles were employed in witnessing?

What characterized the early Christians?

What were some of the characteristics of the early church — its qualities, purposes and methods?

What guiding principles can I get from the formation and operation of the early church?

What was God's method of dealing with the early church?

What is the work of the Holy Spirit?

What are the principles of church extension — Missions?

What are the enemies of the church?

What are the things God uses to bring about spiritual and numerical growth?

What life principles should I emulate if I am to be the kind of person God uses?

"One can easily make his own list of questions concerning the things he feels he should look for as he embarks on any particular topical or book study.

"I think that it would be well for someone less experienced in studying the Scriptures for himself to start with a more simple method, such as the one used successfully by Bible students for years:

What does it say?
What does it mean?
What does it mean to me?

"I personally think that it is helpful to add a fourth question: What can it mean to others? This causes us to study not only with the thought of feeding our own spiritual lives but also of sharing what we learn with others.

"These basic questions can be worded in another way:

What is God saying to me here?
What would God have me to learn here?
What would God have me to be and do?

I must confess that I spent many years studying the Scriptures largely to gain knowledge and had built up an extensive set of notebooks jammed with facts, outlines, lists, questions, etc., before I came to my present realization of the singular importance of personal application in all of Bible study. How really futile it is to accumulate volumes of facts if this does not issue in a transformed life.

"Only recently did I adopt the ABC method that has been strongly advocated by the Navigators for so long. I have found that — at least in my study of several Old Testament books — it is the most rewarding method I have ever used in getting me to commit myself to really do something about those things in my life of which the Lord speaks to me through the printed page of His Word. In this method I first write out a short analysis of the passage or chapter. Then I select the best verse. This leads me to the crucial point of the whole study: my Contract with God; i.e., what I am going to do about it?

"I would be the last to say that my methods of Bible study are the last word and that they would be the best methods for everyone else. I merely present them as suggestions for others to try to vary their Quiet Time, hoping that they will find them as effective as they have been in my own life.

"No method will 'work' if there is not a real openness toward God, a sense of expectancy, and a determination to obey at all costs. It is only as we approach God's revelation with such an attitude that He can fill us with Himself and give that outward glow that is evidence to the world that we have been with Jesus."

A Grocery Company Executive. Howard Butt, Jr., Vice President, H. E. Butt Grocery Company, Corpus Christi, Texas:

"No phase of the Christian experience is more critically important than the devotional life. I prefer to set aside the first part of the morning for Bible study and prayer because I feel that evening is a worn-out time, that one is not as alert in the evening as in the early part of the day.

"This period of Bible study I usually spend in my study. The length of time which I spend each morning studying God's Word usually depends on my daily schedule. However, no matter how pressed I might be, I find it imperative to spend some portion of time with God to begin my day, studying His Word and in prayer.

"I also close my day by reading a chapter or so from the Bible before I retire, though my main time for real study is in the morning. I carry a pocket Testament which I can read at odd moments throughout the day, but I do not believe that we should rely on this as the sole means of reading God's Word.

"Personally, I like to use different versions of the Bible in my study. Besides the King James Version, I use the Montgomery translation of the New Testament, the Phillips New Testament translation and others. However, for memory work I believe there is no substitute for the Authorized version.

"As to method of study, I believe that it should be somewhat systematic. I have never believed it beneficial to open the Bible at random each day and study the particular verse or passage which catches my eye. I like to study book by book, taking a chapter or more a day. Also, especially helpful to me is a topical study, using a concordance for Scripture references on particular subjects.

"Above all else, I believe that it is important to study the Bible prayerfully, asking for and relying upon the guidance and enlightening of the Holy Spirit.

A Christian College President. Dr. Bob Cook, President, King's College, Briarcliff Manor, New York:

"The following constitutes my personal method of Bible study:

"*The quiet time*: Read until the passage says something to you. Write it down. Pray it back until your soul gets hot with the truth. Share it with someone else as soon as possible.

"*The systematic study of great doctrines*: Read all passages that teach the doctrine directly and all illustrative material that throws light upon it indirectly. Correlate these Scriptures in the form that means something to you in terms of its relationship to God and His eternal purpose, life, and its problems.

"*Character study*: Follow the life and ministry of great characters of the Bible, their personal characteristics, whims, faults, foibles, etc.

"*Prophecy*: Great prophecies and their fulfillment."

A *Missionary Statesman.* George M. Cowan, missionary
to the Mazateco Indians in Mexico under the Wycliffe
Bible Translators:

"I was first invited to systematic Bible reading by my
father, who both encouraged me to do it and set me an
excellent example. He started me on the 'three chapters
every weekday and five on Sunday' method which takes
one through the entire Bible in almost exactly a year. I
had thus traversed the Scriptures in their entirety about
five times before I actually came to trust the Saviour as
my own. This method I believe laid the foundation for an
appreciation of the Scriptures as a whole which made later
seminary and private study in detail much more profitable.
Even as an unsaved teen-age boy I *enjoyed* reading and
re-reading the Word of God in this way.

"Later, when other Bible study methods were used and
keeping up the daily system above did not work out, I found
it very profitable to read the Bible through each year, reading each book through at one sitting. This gave a grasp of
each individual book that was quite stimulating and enlightening. I believe this can be done quite profitably by
reading and re-reading the same book several times, until
one is saturated with the message of the book and has the
over-all outline of the development of the theme of the
book well in mind while one reads. For the young Christian, succinct synopses of the books are very helpful, reading along with the book itself. For the mature Christian,
making his own synopses is one of the most profitable dis-
ciplines in order really to master the contents. This method,
and the previous one, I feel are too often neglected by
Christians to their detriment, for are they not the way we
read any other book worth reading? The 'dip and skip'
method is not generally used in our other reading and has
the disadvantage, I feel, of taking things too often out of
context. Once the larger context is in mind, then the care-

ful study of limited portions, preferably taken consecutively, is much more profitable and contributes to a knowledge of doctrine as a whole on all points.

"The study method which emphasizes a limited portion — finding key verses, writing summaries, and making personal applications — has proved of great blessing. The human tendency to let down is such, however, that the encouragement of a checkup by others, either individually or in small groups, is most profitable. I have been greatly stimulated and blessed, on occasions, by the Inter-Varsity recommendations which caused me to consider some passage, asking myself the questions they suggest: Is there any example for me to seek to follow by God's help? Is there a command to be obeyed? Is there a sin for me to avoid or forsake? Is there a promise for me to claim; if so, what are its conditions? What does this passage teach me (by illustration or statement) about Jesus Christ, God, myself, His will for my life? Is there something in this passage which should be my prayer for today?

"One thing of which I am convinced and that I recommend on every possible occasion is that to get the most out of the Scriptures one needs to know all he possibly can about the life and times and local setting of the people to whom the Scriptures were first directed. Books on Bible background and Bible customs have been of tremendous help. So much of the English Bible is simply not understood in full force because it is a translation and the English words bring English associations to mind (this is largely inevitable, of course, in any translation), failing to give the force and distinctive point to the truth which it had when first given, and which was, in fact, the teaching of the passage at that time."

A Writer and Former College President. Dr. V. Raymond Edman, Chancellor, Wheaton College, Wheaton, Illinois:

"The Bible is an exhaustless treasure. I read it daily for study purposes to determine the content of each book, then of each chapter, and then the meaning of each verse and word. Apart from this concentrated study of the Word, I read it also for devotional purposes. It is my practice, early in the morning, to read a portion taken consecutively from book to book in the Bible, and read it as indeed it is, God's personal message to me. Thus I find light for the problems of the day, and encouragement to face its difficulties, rebuke for shortcomings and disobedience, warning against self-will, humbling of heart before the Most High. The devotional reading is not for any set length of chapters or verses; rather, the reading may be shorter or longer, dependent upon the message from the Word itself. I find that this devotional reading of the Word leads into prayer and praise; and not infrequently what I have learned from the Lord in the early morning devotional study of His Word is needed by some other heart before the setting of that day's sun."

A Radio Broadcaster. Dr. Charles E. Fuller, Director, The Old Fashioned Revival Hour Broadcast:

"I seek to understand the meaning of a given passage by noting structure, repetition, and the progress of its various parts. The *Companion Bible* gives me a great deal of help in determining structure, although I do not follow it in all its teachings.

"Three basic steps are to be carried out, I feel, in all Bible study. (1) The smallest thought-units (independent clauses and sentences) must be understood first of all. (2) The relationship between successive clauses must be grasped, usually by noting the connectives that introduce each clause. (3) We must seek to determine the function or the relationship between the larger thought-units, until an entire book is seen as composed of successively larger units.

"But after all is said and done, it is the illumination of the Holy Spirit that we must depend on for coming to a proper interpretation of the Word. Prayer is and always will be the main means of determining the meaning God intends in His Word."

A Theological Seminary President. Dr. Vernon C. Grounds, President, Conservative Baptist Theological Seminary, Denver, Colorado:

" 'As newborn babes, desire the sincere milk of the word, that ye grow thereby.' Nothing, apparently, could be easier than that! In order to grow we must merely imbibe the Word of God. We must read the Bible. We must engage in a meditative study of the Bible. And as we do that we will, according to the apostolic guarantee, grow and keep on growing.

"We read the Bible wrongly when we read it *compulsively.* (The psychologist refers to any act as a compulsion when a person feels himself under pressure to perform it with meticulous precision and regards himself as guilty and hence as susceptible to punishment if he violates his ritualistic habit.)

"Again, we read the Bible wrongly when we read it *pharisaically.* (This means to reduce man's God-relationship to a business proposition. It is to accumulate merit, hypothetically, and create a sense of smug self-righteousness by the performance of certain duties.)

"Once more, we read the Bible wrongly when we read it *magically.* (We fancy that our compulsive Bible study has chalked up some credit to our account and hence we can demand God's favor and blessing. Yes, by reading the Bible we can even compel God to bless us.)

"Suppose, now, turning from the negative to the positive side of this matter, we consider how to read the Bible rightly.

"To read the Bible profitably, which is the result of reading it rightly, we must read it *daily*. We must be like the Christians in the old city of Berea to whom Luke pays this high compliment: 'These were more noble than those in Thessalonica, in that they received the word with all readiness of mind, and searched the scriptures daily, whether those things were so' (Acts 17:11).

"To read the Bible profitably, which is the result of reading it rightly, we must read the Bible *prayerfully*. After all, this Book differs from any other book in the world precisely because it is the Word of God, inspired by the Holy Spirit; and, accordingly, it yields its meaning and truth only under the Spirit's illumination.

"We must read it *believingly*. In Hebrews 4:2 a reason is assigned for the spiritual failure which marked the Israelites whom Moses led out of Egypt. 'The word preached did not profit them, not being mixed with faith in them that heard it.'

"We must read the Bible *expectantly*. Psalm 119 will prove of vital help. Observe verse fourteen: 'I have rejoiced in the way of the testimonies, as much as in all riches.' And verse twenty: 'My soul breaketh for the longing that it hath unto thy judgments at all times.' And verse forty-seven: 'I will delight myself in thy commandments, which I have loved.' And observe, in addition, verse 135: 'I opened my mouth and panted, for I long for thy commandments.' The psalmist read the Bible expectantly.

"We must read the Bible *reflectively*. Once more Psalm 119 will be of immense suggestiveness. Think of verse fifteen: 'I will meditate in thy precepts, and have respect unto thy ways.'

"It is better by far to read three or four verses, store them away in the memory, and bring them to the focus of consciousness again and again — better by far to do that than to gallop through five or ten chapters, keeping nothing in memory and never reflecting upon what has been read.

"We must read the Bible *attentively*. We must do as Paul admonishes in II Timothy, chapter two and verse fifteen: we must study the Bible, and study demands attention, diligence, and alertness.

"We must read the Bible *obediently*. A willingness to do God's will, not merely to know it as a matter of idle curiosity, brings with it a revelation of God's will.

"In other words, we are to read the Bible *personally*. We are to view Bible reading as an encounter between ourselves and God. We are to consider this Book not as a dead book but as the voice of the living God addressing our own souls, disclosing to us in the depths of our beings exactly what it is that He wishes us to do. And we are to listen with our hearts bowed, humbly beseeching, 'Speak, for thy servant heareth' (I Sam. 3:10)."

A *Magazine Editor*. Dr. Harold Lindsell, Associate Editor, *Christianity Today*:

"I read through the entire Bible once a year. I do not always do this consecutively. I may read in both Old and New Testaments at the same time.

"I like to read devotionally one book at a time and may re-read that book a number of times. Normally I stay with one book until it is finished. I like to read a minimum in this category of three chapters a day.

"Often I pursue a topical study of the theme in which I happen to be interested at the moment. Thus recently I have been re-studying the sections of the Bible relating to the rapture of the church. In a few weeks time I have read parts of Matthew, Mark, Luke, the Revelation, Daniel, and I and II Thessalonians a number of times in pursuit of the theme.

"I teach a Sunday-school class and in this class make it a

practice to engage in book study. Right now we are in II Corinthians. I take a given section each week and expound this. This is in addition to and apart from other use of the Bible.

"I often read the Psalms devotionally and at random or select particular ones relevant to a problem I may have at the time.

"Time is not the most important factor in my opinion. Neither is it important whether one decides to do his reading at one sitting or in several. Personal factors enter.

"I always try to engage in some Bible and other devotional reading prior to bedtime. I like to stay up late. I think it well to begin the day with Bible reading and prayer but I do not think it necessary to insist that the major part of such reading be engaged in either at the beginning or end of the day. Let the individual heart be satisfied.

"I gladly share my major problem with you and with others. I use the Bible professionally a great deal. I average three or four outside speaking engagements a week during the year. I am often tempted by this to allow the professional and technical use of the Scriptures to take the place of pure devotional use of the Bible. I am confident that I use the Bible professionally more than most people use it devotionally, but I do not believe that professional use should take away from time spent devotionally."

A Novelist and Housewife. Francena H. Arnold, well-known writer of Christian fiction:

"I know of no investment of time and effort that will pay higher dividends for life than that spent on Bible study. I am more thankful than I can say that during the years when memorization was easy, and when permanent impressions were being made, I was led into a systematic study of the Scriptures.

"My first course was a simplified survey course in which I learned the names and locations of the different books and a brief, concise statement of the content of each. That was a most valuable first step. The ignorance of the average young person in these fundamental facts of the Bible comes as a shocking surprise to those who are trying to teach them.

"The next course was a verse-by-verse study of the entire Bible, taken with a class of friends. We were six years on that study, and I finally finished it alone. I found it a most worthwhile and interesting experience. I finished it with a feeling of having acquired a knowledge of the factual content of the Bible, and an understanding of its message and cohesion that I would never lose.

"Since then I have used various methods: Bible doctrine, prophecy, chapter analysis, and many others. From each one I get new truths and a new light on an old Book. The one that yields to me the richest returns is what I call a *topical study.* In my daily reading I find some thought that I want to develop further. Or in my life I feel a need that can only be filled by God's provision. I turn to the Bible, and with the aid of my concordance I go from one passage to another until my soul is filled and satisfied with the immeasurable riches I find.

"For instance, at one time in my life I was called upon to wait many months for an answer to an urgent need. I began to think upon the waiting periods that make up so much of our life span. I wondered what God's Word had to say on the matter. The word 'wait' proved a veritable treasure trove of promises. It led me to another rich find, the study of the word 'patience.' From that I advanced to 'trust,' and now, many years later, I am still exploring those depths. Just a few weeks ago I learned of the salvation of one for whom I have been praying for over fifty years. How valuable the lessons of patiently waiting and trusting have been during that time!

"There are so many other topics that I have worked on that I cannot recall them all now. Here are a few: fear, seek, work, believe, friends, trials, affliction, gifts, and patterns. It seems that every time I open my Bible I find new lines of truth. They cross and recross at times, but they always lead to treasure.

"All of these methods of study have been needed and have proved profitable. As long as I live I expect to be enjoying the fruits from them."

A Representative of the Navigators. Dawson Trotman, late president of The Navigators:

"Down through the years I have used many different types of Bible study. As I see it now, the plan which has proved the most practical has been the one which I was able to share most easily with others. In other words, simplicity is the order of the day, both for my own personal life, busy as it is, and for others with whom I share. I don't want my Bible study to be limited to what I can find for myself or even share with others from the Scriptures; rather I want to set the pace for them and teach them how to study so they can feed themselves directly from the Word in the days and years to come.

"The most profitable plan I have found is that of studying a book of the Bible straight through, taking it in portions such as a chapter or half-chapter a week, depending on the length and content. When the days are busy and there is little time for study, we use what we call the Search the Scriptures plan which includes four basic things to find. We have thought of this as the 'least common denominator' for the study of any portion of Scripture. First, what does it say? Second, what does it say that I don't understand? Third, what does it say elsewhere in the Word of God to clarify this portion? Fourth, what does it say to me personally?

"Here's how I do it:

1. It is only reasonable to believe that before we attempt to interpret what a portion of Scripture means, we should consider what it says. I used to ask one of my favorite Bible teachers what certain portions meant. He would say, 'What does it say?' After reading it I would again ask, 'Now what does it mean?' to which he would reply, 'What does it say?' I would read it again. 'That's it,' he would tell me, 'it means just what it says.' Often with this simple approach it seemed that the truth just jumped out at me. I discovered that I had thought each portion had to be interpreted, rather than taking it at face value. So I begin my study by writing a brief summary of the contents of the portion in my own words.

2. I find it only right to face the difficulties the portion presents and so I look at each verse and write down for present or future study any questions or problems raised by the verse.

3. Because Scripture is the greatest interpreter of Scripture and sheds light upon itself, it seems necessary to find out what else the Word says on the various truths referred to in the portion. So I look for parallel passages to cross reference each verse.

4. Being told to be a doer of the Word and not a hearer only, I then write what the Word of God is saying to me (using the personal pronoun I or me). It may be a challenge from one or two verses or the whole portion from which I make personal application to my own life.

Such a simple plan makes possible a regular, consistent, and systematic study through a book at a time. If you have more time to devote to your study, add other things.

5. Give a title to the portion.

6. Take some doctrinal truth or spiritual principle referred to in the portion and enlarge upon it, gathering

data from other portions of the Word and adding illustrations if desired, much as you would if you were to speak on
the subject.

7. Instead of just listing personal difficulties, list two
types: (1) personal difficulties which I need to study; (2)
possible difficulties which do not trouble me but which
would be good to examine in view of helping others.

8. Then write two personal applications: (1) one which
deepens your devotion to the Lord and enables you more
adequately to glorify Him; (2) one which applies to your
relationship with other people.

9. The initial study includes a summary of what the
chapter says, and I feel the best way to put it into a
usable form is to outline the portion. Sometimes the process
is reversed and the outline made before other portions of
study are done.

"Variety is stimulating, so from time to time I change
my method of study and use a fresh approach in digging
into God's precious Word."

A Representative of Inter-Varsity. C. Stacey Woods, General Secretary, Inter-Varsity Christian Fellowship:

"I began as a child with the Scripture Union. (I suggest
you write to the Scripture Union, 30 St. Mary Street, Tor-
onto, Ontario, Canada, for their complete listing of Bible
study materials, which represents one of the most complete
series in the English language.) I commenced, first of all,
with the Junior Scripture Union and then went on to the
Adult. This involved reading a portion of Scripture at the
beginning of about ten verses a day increasing to about
eighteen verses a day of the adult portions. There was a
prayer to be used at the beginning of each day's reading.
Then followed a booklet of explanatory, expository notes
geared to the age-group concerned, and, as one developed
in that sort of thing, questions requiring answers.

"It was my practice to spend a little time every evening in such Bible reading, followed by prayer. When I was somewhat older, seventeen or eighteen, came the practice of 'quiet time' with some fifteen to thirty minutes devoted each day. The evolution of this was toward the use of a notebook and a number of questions I asked myself, putting pen to paper.

"Today, my personal Bible study takes two forms: first, the habit of reading a portion of Scripture each day, without a good deal of study attached to it; second, the meditation on one or two verses at greater length. While this is not with a view to the preparation of a message, frequently something of this nature is the result.

"One last word: in addition to all this, now I find it helpful to take two or three hours off at a time, on occasion, to study a whole book.

"The single most important part of Bible study, having taken care of the objective reading and study, is the personal application. Each time we read the Bible, a personal decision is called for, and the end of each time of Bible study should be a personal meeting with the Lord Jesus Christ."

A Representative of the Pocket Testament League. Glenn Wagner, Foreign Secretary, Pocket Testament League:

"My daily preparation and meeting with the Lord has kept me in the Psalms, first of all, covering a number of chapters, then on to other books.

"For study later on I have found help in using the King James Version first and writing down the actual text in my own words. Then, with the American Standard Version, I have been helped in the adding of additional notes to the margins of the Bible.

"For word study, the *Greek Text, International Standard*

Bible Encyclopedia, concordances, and *commentaries* have been used to explain the English Bible.

"Continual memorization of certain passages as they leap out of the King James Version has been invaluable. Staying with the Word itself in continual reading has allowed the Lord to get to me. It is His Word, and before trying to talk with Him I find it best to let Him tell me what He wants to say. After all, it is 'that I may know him . . .' (Phil. 3:10)."

A Lawyer. Jack C. Brown, Indianapolis, Ind., former United States Attorney for the Southern District of Indiana:

"The great Apostle Paul admonished young Timothy, 'Study to show thyself approved unto God, a workman that needeth not to be ashamed, rightly dividing the word of truth.' The Greek word for 'study' has a meaning of 'giving diligence,' which emphasizes the importance of careful study in equipping ourselves to 'handle aright' the Word of God.

"It is important to have proper materials for our study. In ascertaining the meaning of the Hebrew and Greek words used in Scripture, I have found the following volumes especially helpful to me: *The Expository Dictionary of New Testament Words,* by W. E. Vine; *Englishman's Greek Concordance,* published by Samuel Bagster; *The Amplified Bible;* a good concordance; and a good Bible dictionary.

"To me it is important to know the meaning of the words of Scripture, for we are told, '*All* scripture is given by inspiration of God' (II Tim. 3:16), and '*Every word* of God is pure' (Prov. 30:5), and 'holy men of God spake as they were *moved* by the Holy Ghost' (II Peter 1:21). The Greek word for 'moved' used here is *phero,* meaning that they spake as they were borne along by the Holy Spirit, not expressing their own thoughts but the mind of God in *words* provided and ministered by Him. Since every word of God is pure, every word of God is important and every word of God must be properly understood.

"I find, however, that it is also essential that there be some comprehension of the entire Bible and of how each one of the 66 books fits into the whole. As I grasp the contents as a whole I find it easier to study the individual words in a verse.

"As I search the Scriptures I give much emphasis to the matter of word study. The importance of this is demonstrated when we realize that, although there are a little more than 6,000 different English words in Scripture, there are 14,388 different Hebrew and Greek words used. Our English language is inadequate, and only as we go to the underlying languages can we hope properly to understand the blessings which the Holy Spirit has for us if we will but study diligently."

An Insurance Company Director. Harold J. Wilson, Christian Mutual Life Insurance Co.:

"Each time I open the Bible I repeat the Psalmist's prayer — 'Open my eyes that I may see the wonders of thy Word' (Ps. 119:18).

"An ancient peril still threatens Bible students. We may read the words and miss the wonders.

"The primary educational requirement for the Scribes and Pharisees was verbatim memorization of the Word of God. They searched the Scriptures but they missed the Christ. His condemnation stabs us wide awake — 'seeing, they see not. . . .'

"The closed mind misses revealed truth. The closed life robs the Word of its healing, helping power. The closed eyes never see the wonders.

"Nearly a half-century ago, William Lyons Phelps, Dean of Yale University, shared the personal values of his Bible study with his students, enriching and strengthening their faith.

"In an article in a national magazine he revealed the secret of his early acquaintance with the Word. In his boyhood days Phelps' mother required that he read one chapter of the Bible daily, and draw a picture representing the content. He recalled the difficulties, but he also acknowledged that the resulting familiarity with the Word of God was invaluable.

"In my Bible study I endeavor to become an active participant in every revelation of Divine power and providence.

"Approaching the Word with a prayer for open eyes, I have discovered that the text leaps into life.

"I ask myself, 'If I had been on the scene, what would my reactions have been to that which I was observing?'

"Only as I endeavor prayerfully to see the event as it happened, can I appreciate the human, every-day, intimately personal values.

"The synagogue incident of Mark 3 provides an illustration of my method of Bible study.

"Forgetting that I am a student, I become a participating observer. I stand in the synagogue — Jesus in the center — the man with the withered hand in the crowd.

"All the accumulated testimony of the centuries to the power of Jesus Christ, which is our heritage and inheritance, is at that moment in the synagogue, still future.

"Standing by Christ and looking at the man's paralysis, I protest the command, 'Stretch forth thine hand.' Jesus is mocking his impotence. It is impossible and therefore unreasonable. But I can say that only while my eyes are fastened on the man's paralysis.

"Moving to the side of the cripple I can almost feel the struggle in the helpless man's mind. I can see him look into the eyes of Christ and say, 'I can't. . . . I can't. . . . I CAN!! There it is — 'whole as the other.'

"This is not imagination. It is proven by the context.

"For the moment I become the man with the paralysis. How many times I have attempted to overcome my disability — a spiritual paralysis. All the effort has ended in heart-sickening failure. But I cannot look into His eyes, and hear His voice and not say, 'I will,' even though all the devils in hell thunder in my ears, 'You cannot.'

"How swift is the step from the synagogue to my life. He is with me. All power is His, in heaven and just where I am. It is within His power to make my life whole — and it is within my desire to let Him change my paralysis into power.

"My spiritual life is deepened, strengthened, and broadened by what I have seen in that synagogue.

"Instead of anaemic sentimental religion, the Christ I see and hear in the Word offers full-blooded, robust, strenuous Christianity which will lift the world and bless it.

"The Apostle Paul itemizes the 'wonders of the Word' in Ephesians 1:18, '. . . that the eyes of your heart being enlightened, you might know the hope of His calling; the riches of His glory; and the exceeding greatness of His power.'

"This method of Bible study in which the Spirit of God helps me to see and share the incident is infinitely worthwhile."

A Radio Producer and Writer. Eugenia Price, writer of Christian radio programs and widely known author:

"When I first became a Christian, in the year 1949, I didn't know the front from the back of the Bible! This did not stop Jesus Christ from reaching me for Himself, however. In fact, He used my very ignorance of His written Word to bring me to the place of surrender to Him. If this sounds fantastic to you, it is told in my autobiography, *The Burden Is Light!* and for our present purposes this much will suffice: from the very beginning the Holy Spirit seemed to apply what I read in the Bible to my own personal life. This startled me no end. You see, I had not yet read that Jesus promised us the Spirit of truth: '. . . the Comforter, which is the Holy Ghost . . . shall teach you all things, and bring all things to your remembrance. . . .'

"My mind was tired when I was converted. And so was I. But this didn't stop the Holy Spirit from lighting up just the passages I needed to 'see by' in order to see myself a sinner pathetically in need of a Saviour! Since my conversion I have found that the Spirit of truth brings all the things I need to know when I need to know them as I read. In other words, He is still applying the Bible to my life for me.

"Let me confess that I had to pray and keep on praying for two or three years to want to read His Holy Word at all! So, if the Bible bores you, don't kick yourself around. One of the questions most young people ask me is, 'How can I ever learn to like to read the Bible?' If you will follow along now for a few lines while I show you how I have managed to open myself to what God has to say to me in my Bible reading, I think you will discover at least one way whereby you can learn to like to read the Bible.

"The translation that has most increased my interest in the New Testament is the *Berkeley* version of the New Testament. Let us take the first letter of Peter, the one I read just this morning. I began reading the 'letters' a few days ago, usually reading an entire letter at a time, and to-day I Peter came up.

"I thought of you readers and what I would say to you in this book when I came to chapter two and read, 'So, *as you lay aside* all vice and all deceit, all pretenses, envies and slanderings, *you will, like newborn babes, be thirsty* for the unadulterated, thought-nourishing milk [the Word of God] so that by its use you may grow up to salvation . . . *presuming you have tasted how helpful the Lord is.*'

"I have italicized the words which hit me particularly.

Why did they? All right, look now — right off, we're told that as long as we are blocking God by vice, deceit, pretense, envy, etc., we block *our own desire* to go on with Him to maturity in our Christian lives. But, if we 'lay aside' these blocks we will 'like newborn babes, *be thirsty* for the unadulterated, thought-nourishing milk,' the Word of God. And no one doubts that when a newborn babe is thirsty, he's thirsty! Nothing is blocking that thirst and he lets us know it. The baby is alive and that is reason enough to cry for nourishing milk.

"When we have been born again by the invasion of the Spirit of God into our lives at the time of our conversion to Jesus Christ, we are also thirsty for 'thought-nourishing milk,' *if* we lay aside whatever would spoil our appetites. Once we have experienced Christ's life entering ours, our appeties are whetted for more and more of this life. The Bible tells us we can have all we need and more *if* we 'lay aside' the things that block Christ from becoming our Master.

"We have to keep our date with the Lord each day, with our Bibles open, ready to receive. The Bible was not written to entertain us. God gave it to us to live by. His instructions are there. He knows how we work. We don't. He never tries to mix us up.

"'. . . the Comforter, which is the Holy Ghost, whom the Father will send in my name, he shall teach you all things, and bring all things to your remembrance, whatsoever I have said unto you.'

"The Bible is all because of Jesus Christ. We have His word that God is not trying to confuse us. He is promising to make it clear. And if we can't believe Jesus Christ, whom can we believe?"

A Seminary Professor and President Emeritus. Dr. Charles W. Koller, Trinity Evangelical Divinity School professor and former President, Northern Baptist Theological Seminary:

"A devout carpenter, reverently opening his Bible for the morning devotions, was heard to say, 'Speak to me, Word of God, and tell me what my Lord has to say to me today.' This is the spirit with which we must come to the Scriptures. There must be reverence, humility, and scrupulous honesty in the search for truth.

"The first requirement for fruitful Bible study is not technical, but spiritual. In addition to the dedication of heart and mind, there are practical helps which greatly expedite the study of the Scriptures.

"(1) *The speaker.* Who is speaking — God; a prophet; an apostle; a saint; a fool; or the devil? What is the character of the speaker; his age; his experience; his condition?

"'For the good that I would, I do not: but the evil which I would not, that I do. Oh, wretched man that I am! . . .' (Rom. 7:19, 24). It may be surprising to discover that this is not the outburst of a new convert struggling with the old Adam or meeting the first counterattacks of Satan, but of a mature saint with perhaps a quarter of a century of unparalleled Christian experience. It may be similarly surprising to find that Daniel, when thrown into the lions' den, was not a stripling, as he is often represented, but a man of about ninety years of age.

"(2) *The addressee.* Many errors of interpretation may be avoided by noting whether the particular message is addressed to devout believers, or to backsliders, or unbelievers; to groups, or to individuals as such.

"There are innumerable verses of Scripture to support a missionary appeal, without misapplying to such use the words with which God rebuked Cain, the murderer: '. . . thy brother's blood crieth unto me from the ground' (Gen. 4:10).

"(3) *The time.* Many good Bibles carry in the margins

the approximate dates of incidents recorded. While these dates cannot be established with finality, they nevertheless help to make the Scriptures live.

"Thus it is interesting to note that while Daniel was bearing his witness in the royal court of Babylon, Ezekiel was ministering to the wretched captives 'by the River of Chebar,' and Jeremiah was comforting the sorrowing survivors among the ruins of Jerusalem. And the closing heartbroken appeal of Hosea (Hos. 14) takes added force from the fact that it came only about three years before the judgment of God descended.

"(4) *The place.* Where was Paul when he wrote to the Ephesians about being blessed '. . . with all spiritual blessings *in heavenly places*' (Eph. 1:3)? He was in his Roman imprisonment, hounded and persecuted for the 'crime' of preaching the gospel, not knowing whether he would ever draw another breath as a free man. Here the importance of place looms large. Similarly, many incidents of Scripture become more significant in the light of other incidents with which they may be related in time and place.

"(5) *The occasion.* The circumstances which called for the message in the first instance may well suggest the point of contact with a modern audience.

"(6) *The subject.* To be sure of the meaning of a particular verse, it may be necessary to know the subject of the entire passage. Unless the context be taken into account, a particular verse may be made to mean almost anything; and this certainly is not the divine intent.

"(7) *The aim.* All Scripture aims to make men '. . . wise unto salvation . . .' and '. . . furnished unto all good works' (II Tim. 3:15-17); but in every passage there is a specific aim which must be discerned, lest we stray into bypaths and errors of misinterpretation.

"Let the Bible student first be sure of his facts; then, he

may with confidence proceed to principles and their application to life."

A Dentist. Robert O. Hansen, D.D.S., chairman, Board of Directors, Trinity College and Trinity Evangelical Divinity School, Deerfield, Illinois:

"There is no book ever written or published about which so many other books have been written. Guides for Bible reading and Bible study abound, at least in our country, and are available to anyone who needs help in 'searching the Scriptures.' It is necessary to select from among the many commentaries and Bible study books those which best meet the particular need of the individual or group coming to the Book. There are helps available in preparation for the teaching of a Sunday school class; guides for the cultivation of the devotional life, and specific helps for those who may desire to engage in personal evangelism or some other form of Christian service, or for those who may be seeking guidance in the solution of a particular problem.

"My inclination is to use as many helps and as many methods of Bible study as possible rather than to limit myself to any one approach.

"A method I have used and one which I commend is a systematic comparison of versions. Some versions may be better than others, but English-speaking people are blessed with an abundance of good translations, and by comparing one with the other it is possible to arrive at insights not obtainable in any other way except by scholars who are familiar with the original languages of Scripture. When a new translation comes into one's possession, he is often challenged to read long portions of Scripture, chapter after chapter and book after book, just because the language is different and less familiar. Perhaps a 'method' that is too often neglected is just the careful and continuous and consecutive *reading* of the Word.

"Some of the daily devotional books, such as *Our Daily Bread,* are helpful, especially for family devotions. There is a suggested portion of Scripture to be read, a brief but practical comment, with perhaps a good illustration, short devotional poem, and a thought for the day. If there are children in the family, there are devotional books especially adapted to the capactiy and need of the children.

"My own testimony is that I have not used any one method of Bible study for an extended period but have varied the method from time to time to meet some particular need. I am grateful to all those servants of God who have given me a greater appreciation of and a greater insight into that Word about which God Himself has said, 'So shall my word be that goeth forth out of my mouth: it shall not return unto me void, but it shall accomplish that which I please, and it shall prosper in the thing whereto I sent it' (Isa. 55:11)."

Chapter IV

SPECIFIC METHODS OF SEARCHING THE SCRIPTURES

BIBLE STUDY OF BIBLE BOOKS

INTRODUCTION

The Bible is a library of sixty-six separate books, each adding its contribution to the full orbit of truth. Satisfying Bible study ultimately must bring one to an understanding of the particular argument or theme of each individual book.

To accomplish this, two processes are necessary, one analytic and the other synthetic. It is impossible to separate completely these two processes, but the usual procedure will be to make an initial synthesis by determining the central theme and purpose of the book, then a more or less detailed analysis of the book, developing or correcting this original estimate (and a complete analysis may involve all the methods outlined in this book), and finally arriving at a mature and thorough synthesis which fixes the book's main argument in your mind.

I. EXPLANATION OF BACKGROUND STUDY

1. Discover the main theme of the book. This should be in the form of a title or phrase. Decide upon your own theme after having read the book and then compare it with those given in books of Bible introduction.

2. Learn what you can about the writer — reflections of the author's personality and biography found in the book. List these, giving chapter and verse reference for each.

3. Where was the book written? If possible, this should be determined through a reading of the book itself. Give the chapter and verse which you use as a basis for your conclusion. If there is no indication within the book, then check a work on Bible introduction.

4. When was this book written? Give chapter and verse references from the book which indicate definite points of time. Locate the time of the writing of the book within the life span of the author.

5. Who were his hearers — to whom was this book written? Give chapter and verse reference if there is internal evidence. Otherwise, check an outside source.

6. What problems in their lives made the book necessary — what emergency was the book designed to meet? Give evidences of this emergency found within the text and elaborate by using material from at least one outside source.

7. List by chapter and verse any peculiar or repeated terms. When terms appear to be outstanding due to the number of times they are repeated, count them and give the number. Peculiar terms are those which attract your attention while reading, which seem to be unique to this particular book.

8. What does the book teach concerning the Godhead? List the chapter and verse of each reference to the Father, Son, and Holy Spirit.

9. List any references which may indicate major divisions in the structure of the book. These may be in the form of repeated phrases, abrupt changes of subject, person, or rhetorical form.

II. EXEMPLIFICATION

1. *The main theme of the book*: James, "Epistle of Good Works," or "Christian Faith in Action."

2. *Reflection of author's personality and biography found in this book*: Authorship uncertain: Probably James, the Lord's brother.

   a. James, surnamed "the just," shown by doctrine of good works in this book.
   b. A very strict Jew, addressed book to Jews (1:1), called them brethren (1:2), was leader in Jerusalem.
   c. Servant of God (1:1).
   d. Jewish in style and spirit, refers to the law (2:10).

3. *Where was book written?* Probably Jerusalem. How did environment of author affect contents? As of Jerusalem, James was acquainted with Jewish problems, and the difficulties of the Jews there affected his directions to Jews "scattered abroad."

4. *When was this book written?* Near the close of James' life after a thirty-year pastorate of Judean church, around A.D. 60 Halley; A.D. 45-58 Thiessen, before many Gentiles became Christians. It was possibly the first New Testament book to be written.

5. *To whom was the book written?* Jewish Christians living outside the Holy Land. Circumstances of recipient affecting content: epistle seems to have been occasioned by outward experiences, spiritual state, and doctrinal misconceptions of the Jewish Christians in the dispersion.

6. *Emergency the book was designed to meet*: They endured for a while (1:1-12). Then they began blaming God (1:13-18), and they had apparently "let down" in their own living (1:19; 5:20) and there were strife and division in the churches, wrong attitudes toward God (1:13), unbridled speech (3:15), worldly spirit, many

acting as if by knowing the truth they were sufficient, as if faith without works met all the requirements (1:21 ff.).

7. *Any peculiar or repeated terms*:

Faith   fifteen times
Works   eleven times
Patience   five times
Law   five times
Wisdom   five times
Rich   five times
Brother (cognates) fourteen times

8. *What does the epistle teach concerning God and Christ?*
   a. Jesus, Lord of glory (2:1)
   b. Jesus was not a respecter of persons (2:1)
   c. Jesus was God's Son (1:1)
   d. God gives wisdom liberally to those who ask (1:5)
   e. God gives crown of life (1:12)
   f. God cannot be tempted with evil (1:13)
   g. God does not tempt man (1:13)
   h. God gives every perfect gift (1:17)
   i. God's righteousness (1:20)
   j. God chooses poor to be rich in faith (2:5)
   k. One God (2:19)
   l. Men made after similitude of God (3:9)
   m. God's wisdom (4:17)
   n. World's friend is God's enemy (4:4)
   o. Lord will lift up the humble (4:10)
   p. Lord's coming draweth nigh (5:8)
   q. Lord is pitiful, of tender mercy (5:11)
   r. Lord shall raise sick in answer to prayer (5:15)

9. *List any references indicating major divisions in the structure of the book*:

1:1-18   Endurance of trials
1:19-27 Hearing and doing of God's Word
2:1-13   Respect of persons

2:14-26	Relation between faith and works
3:1-12	Control of the tongue
3:13-18	Earthly and heavenly wisdom
4:1-17	Wickedness of strife, wordliness, and evil speaking
5:1-11	Sins of the rich, comfort and counsel for patient sufferers
5:12-20	Oaths, power of prayer, blessedness of converting others

III. EXPLANATION OF CONTENT STUDY

1. Read the book through to find:
   a. The main theme of the book
   b. The key verses of the book
2. Trace the development of the main theme in the light of:
   a. The problems presented
   b. The general tone of the book (argumentation, exhortation, instruction)
   c. Types of reasoning employed
   d. Unique expressions employed
   e. Outstanding affirmations which are set forth
   f. Grammatical peculiarities
3. Establish an outline. In doing this, take special note of possible hints given by the author, repeated phrases, abrupt changes of subject, persons, and rhetorical form. It is suggested that you follow the text by paragraphs.
4. Compare three outlines of the book to determine the thematic segments. Check three good books of Bible introduction for the purpose of comparing their outlines. For example, note where each author suggests the first break for the introduction to the book. Use the unanimous or majority decision of these writers to determine the outstanding points of division within the outlines.

5. Compose a list of the most common thematic segments to cover the content of the book.

6. Apply one or both of the two sets of study guide questions to thematic segments:

Study Guide I

(1) Suggest a theme for each thematic segment
(2) Outline the contents of the passage
(3) List the words and phrases which need definition
(4) Show differences between the King James Version and one other version

Study Guide II

(1) *Who* — Personal. List and summarize the material in the passage pertaining to each character listed
(2) *Where* — Locational. Locate geographically each place referred to; list important incidents that have taken place at this location
(3) *When* — Temporal. Locate this passage as to time in light of the immediate context, and also in respect to the writer's life span
(4) *What* — Definitive. Explain words needing definition. Establish a thematic analytical outline of the passage
(5) *Why* — Rational. What was the purpose behind the presentation of this passage in the Bible?
(6) *Wherefore* — Implicational. List the conclusions gathered from the passage as they pertain to:
    (a) Theology
    (b) Daily experience

7. Formulate a list of study projects which will lead you into further specific research within the book. For example, in the study of the Epistle of James, the following projects might be formulated:

a. A subject chart
b. A key words chart
c. A comparison between the Epistle of James and the Epistle of I Peter
d. A comparison between the Epistle of James and the Sermon on the Mount
e. A study of God in the Epistle of James
f. A listing of the imperatives
g. A correlated study of faith and works
h. A comparison of versions for one thematic segment

IV. EXEMPLIFICATION

1. *Read the book through to find*:

   a. *The main theme of the book*:
      "The works for Christian living"
   b. *The key verse of the book*:
      2:26: "Faith without works is dead"

2. *Develop the main theme as to*:

   a. *Problems presented*:
      The main problem is that man by his own lust falls into sin and becomes unstable, self-deceived, double-minded
   b. *General tone*:
      James is at first encouraging, but he is later forced to reprove and correct quite severely
   c. *Types of reasoning employed*:
      (1) Direct declaration forms the largest part
      (2) Interrogation: 2:4, 5, 6, 7, 20; 3:11, 12; 4:1, 4, 5, 12, 14
      (3) Illustration: 2:2-4; 2:15, 16; 2:21-23; 2:25; 3:5; 3:6-12; 5:10, 11, 17
      (4) Analogy: 1:22

   d. *Unique expressions employed*:
      1:2: "Count it all joy"; 1:8: "A double-minded man";
      1:17: "The Father of lights"; 3:13: "the meekness of
      wisdom"; 3:18: "the harvest of righteousness"; 5:16:
      "effectual fervent prayer"; 5:17: "a man of like pas-
      sions." James has a "knack for a good phrase."
   e. *Affirmations that are set forth*:
      1:13: "God cannot be tempted with evil"
      1:17: "Every good and perfect gift comes from
             above"
      2:5   "God has chosen the poor of this world, rich
             in faith"
      2:26: "Faith without works is dead"
      4:6:   "God opposes the proud, but gives grace to
             the humble"
      4:17: "Whoever knoweth to do good, and doeth it
             not, to him it is sin"
      5:16: "The effectual fervent prayer of a righteous
             man availeth much"
   f. *Grammatical peculiarities*:
      Exclamation: 3:5
      James has a very epigrammatic style of expression.

3. *Establish an outline*:

   a. Salutation (1:1)
   b. The implications of temptation (1:2-18)
      (1) The endurance of temptation
      (2) The tempter
   c. Practical Christian living (1:19–5:18)
      (1) Be doers of the Word
      (2) Have no respect of persons
      (3) Do not break the law
      (4) Have faith plus works
      (5) Control the tongue
      (6) Seek the wisdom of God

(7) Seek God's grace to supercede one's own lust
(8) Remember man's Giver of life
(9) Beware of the results of sin
(10) Be patient
(11) Practice prayer

d. The victory over temptation (5:19, 20)

(1) One of Christ's
(2) A soul winner

4. *Compare three outlines of the book to determine the thematic segments:*

The Pulpit Commentary	Thiessen, *Introduction to N.T.*	Blackwood, *Preaching from the Bible*
1:1 Salutation	1:1 Salutation	1:1 The apostle of applied Christianity
1:2-18 The subject of temptation	1:2-18 In his attitude toward trials and temptations	1:2-4 Joys of enduring temptation
		1:5-8 Cause of unanswered prayer
		1:9-11 Fading joys of the rich man
		1:12-18 The practical workings of temptation
1:19-27 Exhortation: (1) To hear rather than speak (2) Not only to hear, but to do	1:19-27 In his reception of the Word	1:19-27 Practical meaning of religion

The Pulpit Commentary	Thiessen, *Introduction to N.T.*	Blackwood, *Preaching from the Bible*
2:1-13 Warnings against respect of persons	2:1-13 In his impartiality toward others	2:1-13 The sin of snobbishness in church
2:14-26 Warnings against mere barren orthodoxy	2:14-26 In his credentials of faith	2:14-26 The practical meaning of faith
3:1-12 Further warnings against over-readiness to teach, leading to general remarks on need of governing tongue	3:1-12 In the use of the tongue	3:1-12 The perils of the tongue
3:13-18 Further warnings against jealousy and faction	3:13-18 In his attitude toward true wisdom	3:13-18 The secret of harmony among men
4:1-12 Rebuke of quarrels arising from pride and greed	4:1-10 In his amiableness, unworldliness, and humility	4:1-10 The cause of strife among men
	4:11, 12 In his considerateness of his fellows	4:11, 12 The folly of the fault-finder
4:13-17 Special denunciation of overweening confidence in our own plans and ability to carry them out	4:13—5:6 In his business affairs	4:13-17 The folly of counting on tomorrow
5:1-6 Special denunciation of rich sinners		5:1-6 The woes of the idle rich

The Pulpit Commentary	Thiessen, *Introduction to N.T.*	Blackwood, *Preaching from the Bible*
5:7-11 Concluding exhortations to patience and longsuffering	5:7-12 In his patience and endurance	5:7-12 The patience of the Christian hope
5:12 Against swearing		
5:13-20 With regard to behavior in health and sickness	5:13-18 In his conduct in affliction	5:13-18 The healing of the sick through prayer
	5:19, 20 In his effort in behalf of an erring brother	5:19, 20 The joys of the soul winner

5. *Compose a list of the most common thematic segments to cover the content of the book:*

1:1	4:1-10
1:2-15	4:11, 12
1:16-27	4:13-17
2:1-13	5:1-6
2:14-26	5:7-12
3:1-12	5:13-18
3:13-18	5:19, 20

6. *Apply one or both of the two sets of study guide questions to the thematic segments:*

Each study guide is adapted to a specific type of content. The Bible student should scan the passage on which he is going to work, and select either study guide I or study guide II. If the passage is basically narrative in form it would be wise to select study guide II, because greater stress is placed on such factors as time, places, persons, and activities.

If the passage is basically nonnarrative in form, it would be wise to select study guide I, because its greatest emphases are on outline and version comparison. In the following example we have chosen to use study guide I because of the doctrinal nature of the Epistle of James. The student will find an exemplification of study guide II under Bible Study of Bible Paragraphs, since the basis of study in that section is the Gospel of Mark.

The Epistle of James

1:1-12

(1) *The Theme*: The enduring of temptation

(2) *The Outline*

    A. Introduction

        1. James speaking
           Servant of God and of the Lord Jesus Christ

        2. The tribes scattered abroad heeding

    B. Temptation

        1. Count it all joy

        2. Place of faith and patience in temptation

           a. Trying of faith works patience

           b. Patience brings perfection and if perfection is reached, nothing is lacking

           c. Through faith, man can ask of God and be given wisdom

               1) God gives to all men liberally

               2) God upbraids not

               3) Do not merely think you will receive it, but be single-minded and stable

           d. Examples

               1) The brother of low degree can rejoice in that he is exalted

               2) The rich can rejoice in that he is made low, for the rich man fades away in his ways

        3. Results of endurance
           The crown of life

(3) *Words and Phrases Needing Definition*
  (a) The twelve tribes scattered (v. 1)
  (b) Divers temptations (v. 2)
  (c) The crown of life (v. 12)
(4) *Differences between the King James and the Berkeley Versions*

(a)	To the twelve tribes scattered abroad (v. 1)	To the twelve tribes in the Dispersion (v. 1)
(b)	When ye fall into divers temptations (v. 2)	When you get involved in all sorts of trials (v. 2)
(c)	The trying of your faith worketh patience (v. 3)	The testing of your faith brings out steadfastness (v. 3)
(d)	That ye may be perfect and entire wanting nothing (v. 4)	That you may be completed and rounded out with no defects whatever (v. 4)

1:13-18

(1) *The Theme*: Man, his own tempter
(2) *The Outline*
  Exhortations
    1. Do not say we are tempted of God
      a. God cannot be tempted
      b. God does not tempt
      c. Man is his own tempter
        (1) Drawn away of his own lust
        (2) Brings sin
        (3) Brings death
    2. Do not err
      a. Good and perfect gifts come from God
      b. God begat us with the Word of truth

(3) *Words and Phrases Needing Definition*
     A kind of firstfruits (v. 18)
(4) *Differences between the King James and the Berkeley Versions*

Then when lust hath conceived, it bringeth forth sin: and sin, when it is finished bringeth forth death	Then, when the passion has conceived, it gives birth to sin, and the sin, when it reaches maturity, produces death

1:19-27

(1) *The Theme*: A religion of doing
(2) *The Outline*
     Strengthening protectors against temptation
     1. Be swift to hear
     2. Be slow to speak
     3. Be slow to wrath
     4. Lay apart filthiness and superfluity of naughtiness
     5. Receive meekly the Word
     6. Be doers of the Word
        a. A hearer forgets
        b. A doer is not forgetful
     7. Bridle the tongue
     8. Visit fatherless and widows, which is pure religion
     9. Keep self unspotted from the world
(3) *Words and Phrases Needing Definition*
     The engrafted Word (v. 21)
(4) *Differences between the King James and the Berkeley Versions*

(a) For the wrath of man worketh not the righteousness of God (v. 20)	For man's anger does not promote God's righteousness (v. 20)

(b) Wherefore, lay apart all filthiness and superfluity of naughtiness (v. 21)

So, get rid of everything vile and the outgrowth of evil (v. 21)

(c) But be ye doers of the Word and not hearers only, deceiving your own selves (v. 22)

But become doers of the Word, and not deluders of yourselves by merely listening (v. 22)

2:1-9

(1) *The Theme*: Have no respect of persons

(2) *The Outline*

A. Persons
 1. Rich man
  a. Gold ring
  b. Goodly apparel
 2. Poor man
  Vile raiment

B. Man's evil judgments
 1. Rich man to sit in good place
 2. Poor man to stand or sit on footstool

C. The poor
 1. Chosen of God
 2. Rich in faith
 3. Heirs of the kingdom

D. The rich
 1. Oppress
 2. Judge
 3. Blaspheme that worthy name

E. Conclusion
 1. Love thy neighbor as thyself
 2. Have no respect of persons

(3) *Words and Phrases Needing Definition*
None

(4) *Differences between the King James and the Berkeley Versions*

(a) Have not the faith of our Lord Jesus Christ, the Lord of glory, with respect of persons (v. 1)

Do not combine faith in Jesus Christ our glorious Lord with partiality (v. 1)

(b) Do not men oppress you, and draw you before the judgment seats? (v. 6)

Do not the rich domineer you and personally drag you into the courts? (v. 6)

(c) Do not they blaspheme that worthy name by the which ye are called? (v. 7)

Do not they slander the noble name by which you are distinguished? (v. 7)

2:10-13

(1) *The Theme*: Do not break the law
(2) *The Outline*
   A. Penalty of the law
      A breaking at one point brings guilt
   B. Statements of the law
      1. Do not commit adultery
      2. Do not kill
   C. Penalty of the law re-given
      A breaking at one point brings guilt
   D. Judgment
      1. Live as if you were to be judged by the law
      2. No mercy to those who have no mercy
(3) *Words and Phrases Needing Definition*

So speak ye, and so do,
as they that shall be

judged by the law of
liberty (v. 12)

(4) *Differences between the King James and the Berkeley Versions*

(a) So speak ye, and so do, as they that shall be judged by the law of liberty (v. 12)

Speak and act in such a way as befits people who are to be judged by the law of liberty (v. 12)

(b) For he shall be judged without mercy, that hath shewed no mercy; and mercy rejoiceth against judgment (v. 13)

For the judgment is merciless to those who have practiced no mercy (v. 13)

2:14-26

(1) *The Theme*: Have faith plus works
(2) *The Outline*
   A. Faith without works
      1. Man's faith cannot save a man
      2. Man must give physical things to a needy man
      3. Is dead
   B. Faith with works
      1. Abraham offered Isaac
      2. Rahab, the harlot, received the messengers
(3) *Words and Phrases Needing Definition*
   Imputed (v. 23)
(4) *Differences between the King James and the Berkeley Versions*

(a) What doth it profit though a man say

What is the use for anyone to say he has faith, if he fails

he hath faith, and have not works? Can faith save him? (v. 14)	to act on it? His faith cannot save him, can it? (v. 14)
(b) Seest thou how f a i t h wrought with his works, and by works was faith made perfect? (v. 22)	You see how his faith cooperated with his works and how faith reached its supreme expression through his works? (v. 22)
(c) Ye see then how that by works a man is justified, and not by faith only (v. 24)	You see that a person is pronounced righteous due to his works and not on account of faith alone (v. 24)

3:1-12

(1) *The Theme*: Control the tongue
(2) *The Outline*
   A. A teacher's responsibility
      1. Shall receive greater condemnation
      2. A man offends unless he is perfect
         a. To control a horse a bit is used
         b. To control a ship a governor is used
   B. Dangers of the tongue
      1. A fire
      2. A world of iniquity
      3. Defiles whole body
      4. Sets on fire the course of nature
      5. Is set on fire of hell
      6. No man can tame it
      7. An unruly evil
      8. Full of deadly poison
   C. Activities of the tongue

      1. Blesses God
      2. Curses man

  D. Illustrations
      1. Fountain cannot send forth bitter and sweet
      2. Fig tree cannot bear olive berries
      3. A vine cannot bear figs
      4. Fountain cannot yield salt water and fresh

(3) *Words and Phrases Needing Definition*
None

(4) *Differences between the King James and the Berkeley Versions*

(a) My brethren, be not many masters, knowing that we shall receive the greater condemnation (v. 1)

Not many of you should become teachers, my brothers, for you know we are assuming the more accountability (v. 1)

(b) For in many things we offend all. If any man offend not in word, the same is a perfect man, and able also to bridle the whole body (v. 2)

Because we all make many a slip. Whoever makes no slip of the tongue is certainly a perfect man, able as well to control his entire body (v. 2)

(c) Even so the tongue is a little member, and boasteth great things. Behold, how great a matter a little fire kindleth! (v. 5)

Just so the tongue is a small organ and can talk big. Think how great a forest an ever so small spark sets on fire (v. 5)

(d) And it is set on fire of hell (v. 6)

While it is kindled by Gehenna (v. 6)

3:13-18

(1) *The Theme*: Seek the wisdom of God
(2) *The Outline*
  A. A man of heavenly wisdom
    1. Endued with knowledge
    2. A good conversation shows his works
    3. Meekness of wisdom
  B. A man of earthly wisdom
    1. Has bitter envying and strife in heart
    2. Glories
    3. Lies against the truth
    4. His wisdom is sensual, devilish
  C. Results of earthly wisdom
    1. Envy
    2. Strife
    3. Confusion
    4. Every evil work
  D. Heavenly wisdom
    1. Pure
    2. Peaceable
    3. Gentle
    4. Easy to be intreated
    5. Full of mercy and good fruits
    6. Without partiality
    7. Without hypocrisy
    8. Fruit of righteousness is sown in peace.
(3) *Words and Phrases Needing Definition*
  None
(4) *Differences between the King James and the Berkeley Versions*

  (a) . . . let him show   . . . let him show by his
  out of a good con-   good behavior that his ac-
  versation his   tions are carried on with un-

| works with meekness of wisdom (v. 13) | obtrusive wisdom (v. 13) |
| (b) And the fruit of righteousness is sown in peace of them that make peace (v. 18) | And the harvest, which righteousness yields to the peacemakers, comes from a sowing in peace (v. 18) |

4:1-12

(1) *The Theme*: Seek God's grace to supercede own lust
(2) *The Outline*
   A. Man's ways
      1. Lusts
      2. Killing
      3. Fighting
      4. Warring
      5. Does not ask of God
   B. God's decisions
      1. Does not give unless asked
      2. Does not give unless asked rightfully with the proper motive
   C. Because man: Because God:
      1. Is friend of the world   1. Is enemy of man
      2. Has lusting spirit   2. Gives grace
      3. Is proud   3. Resists him
      4. Is humble   4. Gives grace
   D. Exhortations
      1. Submit yourself to God
      2. Resist the devil and he will flee
      3. Draw nigh to God
      4. Cleanse your hands
      5. Purify your hearts

6. Be afflicted and mourn and weep
7. Humble yourselves in the sight of the Lord
8. Speak no evil of one another
   a. If one speaks evil of his brother and judges him, he:
      (1) speaketh evil of the law
      (2) judgeth the law
   b. If one judgeth the law, he is:
      (1) not a doer of the law
      (2) a judge
   c. There is one judge and lawgiver who can save and destroy

(3) *Words and Phrases Needing Definition*
Resist the devil and he will flee from you (v. 7)

(4) *Differences between the King James and the Berkeley Versions*

(a) From whence come wars and fightings among you? (v. 1)	Where do conflicts and fightings among you originate? (v. 1)
(b) Humble yourselves in the sight of the Lord and he shall lift you up (v. 10)	Take a low position before the Lord and he will set you high (v. 10)

4:13-17

(1) *The Theme*: Remember man's Giver of Life
(2) *The Outline*
   A. Man's thoughts
      1. We will go to a city for a year
      2. We will buy and sell and make money
   B. God's thoughts
      1. Can take life of sinful man

      2. Man's life is a vapor that comes and then vanishes
   C. Man's correct thoughts
      1. If the Lord wills we shall live
      2. If the Lord wills we shall do
   D. Admonitions
      1. Do not rejoice in boastings
      2. Boasting is evil
      3. Since you have been taught these things, if you continue in them, you sin

(3) *Words and Phrases Needing Definition*
    None

(4) *Differences between the King James and the Berkeley Versions*

Therefore to him that knoweth to do good, and doeth it not, to him it is sin (v. 17)	So, then, to the person who knows enough to do right and fails to do it, to him it is sin (v. 17)

5:1-6

(1) *The Theme*: Be aware of the results of sin
(2) *The Outline*
   A. Results of sinful living
      1. Rich men weep and howl
      2. Riches are corrupted
      3. Garments are moth-eaten
      4. Gold and silver is cankered and rusted
      5. Laborers cry for proper wages
   B. Causes for this calamity
      1. Living in pleasure
      2. Being wanton
      3. Nourishing hearts
      4. Condemning and killing the just

(3) *Words and Phrases Needing Definition*
    (a) and shall eat your flesh as a fire (v. 3)
    (b) been wanton (v. 5)
    (c) and he doth not resist you (v. 6)

(4) *Differences between the King James and the Berkeley Versions*

| (a) and shall eat your flesh as it were fire. Ye have heaped treasure together for the last days (v. 3) | As fire that you have stored up against the last days, it will consume your flesh (v. 3) |
| (b) Ye have lived in pleasure on the earth and been wanton; ye have nourished your hearts, as in a day of slaughter (v. 5) | You have been living a soft life in the land; you have given yourself up to pleasures; you have fattened your hearts for the day of slaughter (v. 5) |

5:13-18

(1) *The Theme*: Practice prayer

(2) *The Outline*

A. Circumstance   Solution
    1. Affliction   Prayer
    2. Merry   Sing psalms
    3. Sick   Prayer and anointing

B. The prayer of faith for one another
    1. Saves the sick
    2. The Lord will raise the sick
    3. The Lord will forgive his sins
    4. Heals

C. Example of the prayer of faith
    1. Elias prayed for no rain — it did not rain
    2. Elias prayed for rain — it rained

(3) *Words and Phrases Needing Definition*
None

(4) *Differences between the King James and the Berkeley Versions*

(a) The effectual fervent prayer of a righteous man availeth much (v. 16)

The earnest prayer of a righteous person has great force (v. 16)

5:19-20

(1) *The Theme*: The promised blessing of Christian living
(2) *The Outline*
The conversion of a soul
  1. Saves from death
  2. Hides a multitude of sins
(3) *Words and Phrases Needing Definition*
None
(4) *Differences between the King James and the Berkeley Versions*

(a) Brethren, if any of you do err from the truth, and one convert him (v. 19)

My brothers, in case one of you strays from the truth and someone brings him back (v. 19)

(b) Let him know, that he which converteth the sinner from the error of his way shall save a soul from death, and shall hide a multitude of sins (v. 20)

Let him be assured that he who turns a sinner back from the wanderings of his way does save his soul from death and covers up a great number of sins (v. 20)

7. *Formulate a list of study projects*

(1) Subject Chart

| | ───── Chapters ───── | | | | |
Subjects	1	2	3	4	5
Temptation	2-3, 12-16				
Patience	3-4				7-11
Wisdom	5		13-18		
Prayer	5-8			2-3	13-18
Faith	6-8	14-26			
Vanity of riches	9-11	1-13		1-10, 13-17	1-6
Sin	14-15				
The Christian's birth	17-18				
Tongue	19-20, 26		1-18	11-12	12
Doers of Word	21-25	14-17			
Pure religion	26-27				
Respect of persons		1-13			
Faith and works		14-26			
Singing					13
To win a soul for Christ					19-20
Origin of wars				1-2	
Double-mindedness				4-10	
Self-sufficiency				13-17	

(2) Key-words Chart

Chapter	Faith	Works	Brothers	Law	Wisdom	Rich (or rich man)	Temp-tation	Patience
1	2	1	4	1	1	3	5	2
2	12	11	2	4		2		
3		1	3		3		1	
4			3	3		2		2
5	1		3					

(3) A Comparison between the Epistle of James
and the Epistle of I Peter

a. In many important points the order of the epistles is the
same:

James		*I Peter*
1:2-4	Manifold temptations and the proof of faith	1:6, 7
1:12	The reward of faith: praise and honor: the crown of life	1:7
1:21	The salvation of your souls	1:9
1:22 ff.	Children of obedience: doers, not hearers only	1:14
1:26, 27	Putting away evil speaking, bridling the tongue, pure religion	2:1-5
2:1-13	Religion and conduct with others	2:11—3:8
3:1-12	The tongue	3:9, 10
3:13-18	Peacemaking, especially as touching religion	3:11-17
4:4-6	Friendship with the world	4:2-4
5:7-11	The end of all things, judgment, persecutions	4:7-19
5:14 ff.	Elders	5:1 ff.

b. Note:
   1. Verbal similarities
   2. To whom addressed
   3. Things taught by James but not Peter
   4. Things taught by Peter but not James

(4) A Comparison between the Epistle of James
and the Sermon on the Mount

a. Comparative references:

James 1:2	Matthew 5:48
James 1:4	Matthew 5:10-12

James 1:5; 5:15	Matthew 7:7-12
James 1:9	Matthew 5:3
James 1:20	Matthew 5:22
James 2:13	Matthew 6:14, 15; 5:7
James 2:14	Matthew 7:21-23
James 3:17-18	Matthew 5:9
James 4:4	Matthew 6:24
James 4:10	Matthew 5:3, 4
James 4:11	Matthew 7:1-5
James 5:2	Matthew 6:19
James 5:10	Matthew 5:12
James 5:12	Matthew 5:33-37

b. Note:

1. Fill in the comparison between James and Matthew.
2. On what points is there the most similarity?
3. Was James like Christ in the light of the above contexts? Explain their likenesses or differences. The word "just" may suggest one likeness.

(5) A Study of God in the Book of James

God is used seventeen times in James:
Lord (or God the Father), 5:10
Father of lights, 1:17
Lord of Sabaoth, 5:4
Lord (or Christ), 1:7, 12; 4:10, 15; 5:7, 8, 11, 14, 15
Lord Jesus Christ, 1:1; 2:1
Lord Jesus Christ, Lord of Glory, 2:1

(6) Imperatives

a. *Chapter 1*

Let patience have (v. 4)
Let him ask (v. 5)
Let him ask (v. 6)

b. *Chapter 2*

Hearken (v. 5)

c. *Chapter 3*

Behold (v. 3)
Behold (v. 4)
Behold (v. 5)

Let him not think (v. 7)
Let rejoice (v. 9)
Let say (v. 13)
Let be (v. 19)
Be doers (v. 22)

d. *Chapter 4*

Submit (v. 7)   Humble (v. 10)
Draw nigh (v. 8)   Speak (v. 11)
Be afflicted (v. 9) Go to now (v. 13)

e. *Chapter 5*

Go to now (v. 1)   Be patient (v. 8)   Behold (v. 11)
Behold (v. 4)   Grudge (v. 9)   Confess (v. 16)
Be patient (v. 7) Take (v. 10)   Let know (v. 20)

(7)   A Correlated Study of Faith and Works

Comparative references

FAITH	*WORKS*
Trying of faith works (produces) patience, i.e., steadfastness (1:3)	Let patience have her perfect work (full effect) (1:4)
Ask in faith (1:6)	The doer of the work shall be blessed in his deed (1:25)
Have not the faith of our Lord Jesus Christ with respect of persons (partiality) (2:1)	
Poor of this world are rich in faith (2:5)	
A man says he has faith; can faith save him? (2:14)	He does not have works (2:14)
Faith is dead being alone (by itself) (2:17)	If it does not have works (2:17)
Thou hast faith	I have works

I will show you my faith
Show me thy faith (2:18)
Faith is dead (2:20)
Faith wrought
Faith was made perfect
(2:22)
Not by faith only (2:24)

Faith is dead (2:26)

By my works
Without works (2:18)
Without works (2:20)
With his works
By works (2:22)

By works a man is justified
(2:24)
Without works (2:26)
Wise man, let him show by
his life his works with meekness (3:13)

Prayer of faith shall save the
sick, and the Lord shall raise
him up; and if he has committed sins, they shall be for-
given him (5:15)

(8)   A Comparison of Versions for One Thematic Segment

Comparative References   James 3:1-11

King James Version	*Berkeley Version*	*Williams Translation*
My brethren, *be not many masters,* knowing that we shall receive the greater condemnation.	Not many of you *should become teachers,* my brothers, for you know we are assuming the more accountability.	*Many of you,* my brothers, *should avoid becoming teachers* because you know that we teachers are going to be judged with stricter judgment than other people.
For in many things we offend all. If any man offend not in word, the same is a *perfect man,* and able also to bridle the whole body.	Because we all make many a slip, whoever makes no slip of the tongue is certainly a *perfect man,* able as well to control his entire body.	For we all make many a slip. If any one never slips in speech, he is a *man of maturity;* he can control his whole body, too.
Even so the tongue is a little member, and *boasteth* great things. Behold, how great a	Just so the tongue is a small organ and can *talk big.* Think how great a forest an *ever*	So the tongue, too, is a little organ but can *boast* of great achievements. See how *a spark so tiny*

matter a *little fire* kindleth!

And the tongue is a fire, a world of iniquity: so is the tongue among our members, that it *defileth the whole body,* and setteth on fire the *course of nature;* and it is set on fire *of hell.*

But the tongue can no *man* tame; it is an *unruly evil,* full of deadly poison.

So can no fountain both yield salt water and fresh.

so small spark sets on fire.

The tongue also is a fire, a word of wickedness. Among the members of our body the tongue is situated where she *taints the whole body* and sets on fire the *whole machinery of existence,* while it is kindled *by Gehenna.*

But no *human being* is able to tame the tongue, this *undisciplined mischief* so full of deadly poison.

Neither can salt produce fresh water.

can set a vast forest on fire!

And the tongue is a fire, and takes its place among the parts of our bodies as a world of evil; it *soils the whole body* and sets on fire the *circle of man's nature,* and it is set on fire *by hell.*

But the tongue no *human being* can tame. It is an evil *incapable of being quieted,* full of deadly poison.

And a salt spring cannot furnish fresh water.

BIBLE STUDY OF BIBLE CHAPTERS

INTRODUCTION

The Bible, as it was originally written, had no chapter and verse divisions, but in A.D. 1250 Cardinal Hugo introduced chapter divisions which form fairly satisfactory groupings of content and which enable us to locate and identify various passages.

There are 1189 chapters in the Bible, many of them, like the Twenty-third Psalm or I Corinthians 13 have been favorites of Christians for generations. Since these divisions exist, they form suitable units for study, and one of the goals of a Bible student should be to be able to think his way, chapter by chapter, through the various books and identify the contents of each chapter.

The following suggestions will indicate some suitable beginning chapters and provocative questions which will help you to analyze and master the contents of any particular chapter.

Suggestions for Young Christians — Begin by studying

1. Psalm 1
2. Psalm 23
3. Psalm 90
4. Mark 10
5. Luke 15
6. John 11
7. John 15

8. Romans 1
9. I Corinthians 12
10. Ephesians 2
11. I Thessalonians 1
12. II Timothy 2
13. Titus 2
14. II Peter 1

15. I John 1
16. Ecclesiastes 12
17. Jonah 3
18. Psalm 73
19. Isaiah 55
20. Isaiah 53

Suggestions for Mature Christians — Begin by studying

1. Genesis 3
2. Genesis 22
3. Exodus 12
4. Exodus 20
5. Exodus 32
6. Leviticus 16
7. Leviticus 23

8. Deuteronomy 32
9. Joshua 1
10. I Samuel 7
11. I Samuel 15
12. II Kings 5
13. Psalm 32
14. Psalm 51

15. Matthew 5
16. John 17
17. Romans 6
18. Philippians 2
19. I Corinthians 2
20. Colossians 3

I. EXPLANATION

1. What is the theme of the chapter?
   Read the chapter in its entirety in one sitting and put into a phrase what you consider to be the main thought of the chapter.

2. Which is the best verse in the chapter?
   Make your selection on the basis of the verse which has special appeal for you from the standpoint of practical and spiritual refreshment.

3. What personages are mentioned? What information is included regarding each one mentioned?

Make a tabulated list of the people and information giving the reference for each.

4. What are the commands which we should obey?
List these in tabulated form giving the reference for each.

5. What are the promises which we should claim?
List these in tabulated form giving the reference for each.

6. What are the lessons which we should remember?
List these in tabulated form giving the reference for each.

7. Which words and phrases did you like best?
List these in tabulated form giving the reference for each.

8. Which words kept recurring throughout the chapter?
Count the number of times these words recurred and give a statement for each as to its meaning and pertinence to the general thought of the chapter.

9. Which words were not clear as to their meaning?
List these giving chapter and verse and check the meaning in a concordance or Bible dictionary.

10. What *logical* reason can you detect for the inclusion of this chapter in the Bible?
Note what would be missing from the general biblical account if this chapter had been omitted by divine decree.

11. What are the errors of living which we should avoid?
Be specific in your statement of each error and give the reference for each.

12. What does this chapter teach about God?
List each reference to the Father, the Son, and the Holy Spirit.

II. EXEMPLIFICATION
Ephesians 5

1. *What is the theme of the chapter?* The believer's walk.
   a. Walk in love (vv. 1-7)
   b. Walk in light (vv. 8-14)
   c. Walk in wisdom (vv. 15-21)
   d. Walk wisely in marital relations (vv. 22-33)

2. *Which is the best verse in the chapter?*
   "For ye were sometimes darkness, but now are ye light in the Lord: walk as children of light" (v. 8)

3. *What personages are mentioned? What information is included?*
   a. Children of God
   b. Christ
   c. God the Father
   d. Husbands and wives

4. *What are the commands which we should obey?*
   a. Be followers of God (v. 1)
   b. Walk in love (v. 2)
   c. Let no man deceive you with vain words (v. 6)
   d. Walk as children of light (v. 8)
   e. Have no fellowship with the unfruitful works of darkness, but rather reprove them (v. 11)
   f. Walk in wisdom (v. 15)
   g. Redeem the time (v. 16)
   h. Give thanks always to God for all things (v. 20)
   i. Wives, submit yourselves to your husbands (v. 22)
   j. Husbands, love your wives as you do your own bodies (vv. 28, 33)
   k. Wives, reverence your husbands (v. 33)

5. *What are the promises which we should claim?*
   a. Christ has given Himself as an offering and sacrifice to God for us (v. 2)

   b. A promise of inheritance in the kingdom of God
      (v. 5)
   c. Christ will give thee light (v. 14)

6. *What are the lessons which we should remember?*
   a. Walk in love (v. 2)
   b. Have no fellowship with darkness (v. 11)
   c. Redeem the time (v. 16)
   d. Give thanks always to God for all things (v. 20)
   e. Wives, submit yourselves to your husbands (v. 22)
   f. Husbands, love your wives (v. 25)

7. *Which words and phrases did you like best?*
   a. Walk as children of light (v. 8)
   b. Be filled with the Spirit (v. 18)
   c. The name of the Lord Jesus Christ (v. 20)
   d. For we are members of His body (v. 30)
   e. Mystery (v. 32)

8. *Which words kept recurring throughout the chapter?*
   a. Wives — nine times
   b. Christ — seven times
   c. Lord — six times
   d. God — six times
   e. Church — six times
   f. Husbands — five times
   g. Light — five times

9. *Which words were not clear as to their meaning?*
   a. A sacrifice to God for a sweet-smelling savor (v. 2)
   b. For we are members of His body, of His flesh, and
      of His bones (v. 30)
   c. Mystery (v. 32)

10. *What logical reason can you detect for the inclusion
    of this chapter in the Bible?*
      The church seems to be the theme of the epistle.
      In this chapter we note the characteristics which
      should mark the walk of the member of the church.

This chapter adds the emphasis upon conduct which should accompany the emphasis upon creed included in the first three chapters of the epistle.

11. *What are the errors of living which we should avoid?*
    a. Put away fornication, all uncleanness and covetousness (v. 3)
    b. Put away filthiness, foolish talking, jesting (v. 4)
    c. Be not drunk with wine wherein is excess (v. 18)

12. *What does this chapter teach about God?*
    a. Be followers of God (v. 1)
    b. Christ loves us and died for us (v. 2)
    c. Nonbelievers have no inheritance in the kingdom of God (v. 5)
    d. Wrath of God is upon the children of disobedience (v. 6)
    e. Christ shall give us light (v. 14)
    f. God deserves our thanks (v. 20)
    g. Christ is the head of the church (v. 23)
    h. Christ is the saviour of the body (v. 23)
    i. The Church is subject unto Christ (v. 24)
    j. Christ loves the church (v. 25)
    k. Christians are members of His body, of His flesh, and of His bones (v. 30)

BIBLE STUDY OF BIBLE PARAGRAPHS

INTRODUCTION

The Bible books, as they were originally written, did not contain paragraph divisions, but most English translations appear either in paragraph form with the appropriate sign marking off the verses into groups.

Each paragraph is a unit of thought, and for that reason it forms an ideal unit for serious and careful study. The object of such study is to master the contents of each paragraph and to give it a title, or record the gist of it.

Then one may proceed to the next paragraph, and after studying a chapter or more, compare the paragraphs to find structural relationships, such as similarity, contrast, progression, etc. Consider the paragraphs as individual building blocks from which to construct the interpretation of larger sections, and ultimately of entire books of the Bible.

In your study, be careful not to use a Bible which has the paragraphs titled. Reach your own conclusions as to paragraph content and meaning, and only after your own independent study should you compare your results with commentaries or reference Bibles.

I. EXPLANATION

1. Selecting

Determine the paragraph limitations within the book being studied by comparing the paragraphing as found in at least three versions.

2. Searching

Apply either study guide number I or study guide number II to each paragraph selected. This selection of a paragraph should be made on the basis of the most common paragraph breakdown within the versions studied.

II. EXEMPLIFICATION

A. *Selecting*

EPISTLE OF FIRST JOHN

Paragraph Number	Greek Testament	Revised Standard Version	Williams	Selected Paragraphs for Study
1	1:1-4	1:1-4	1:1-4	1:1-4
2	1:5—2:6	1:5-10	1:5	1:5—2:6
3	2:7-17	2:1-6	1:6-10	2:7-11
4	2:18-27	2:7-11	2:1-6	2:12-14

5	2:28—3:24	2:12-14	2:7-14	2:15-17
6	4:1-6	2:15-17	2:15-17	2:18-28
7	4:7-21	2:18-25	2:18-21	2:29—3:10
8	5:1-12	2:26-27	2:22-25	3:11-18
9	5:13-21	2:28-29	2:26-29	3:19-24
10		3:1-3	3:1-3	4:1-6
11		3:4-12	3:4-8	4:7-12
12		3:13-18	3:9-12	4:13-18
13		3:19-24	3:13-15	4:19—5:5
14		4:1-12	3:16-18	5:6-13
15		4:13-21	3:19-24	5:14-17
16		5:1-5	4:1-3	5:19-21
17		5:6-12	4:4-6	
18		5:13-17	4:7-10	
19		5:18	4:11-16a	
20		5:19	4:16b-21	
21		5:20-21	5:1-5	
22			5:6-12	
23			5:13-17	
24			5:18-21	

B. *Searching.* An application of study guide number I to the paragraphs in the Gospel According to Mark.

1:1-8

1. Who

   a. *Jesus Christ*: Son of God, heralded by John.

   b. *Isaiah*: quoted in his prophecy of Christ's herald.

   c. *John*: preached repentance in preparation for the coming of Christ.

   d. *Inhabitants of Judea*: came in great crowds for baptism.

   e. *Holy Spirit*: agent by whom Christ would baptize.

2. Where
   The wilderness along the Jordan River, near Jerusalem.

3. When
   At "the beginning of the gospel . . .," immediately preceding Jesus' entrance upon His ministry.

4. What

   a. *Words needing definition*:

      (1) *baptism of repentance*: how much understanding of God's redemption did this repentance imply, especially in view of the baptized disciples of John, found in Acts 19:1-5, who had apparently not experienced the new birth? John's baptism is apparently only a preparation for the further disclosure of the gospel through Christ.

      (2) *all the country*: obviously hyperbole.

      (3) *baptize*: distinction needs to be made between this external ritual and the baptism of the Spirit whereby believers are joined to Christ. (Cf. I Cor. 12:13; Rom. 6:3; Col. 2:12.)

   b. *Outline*: "The Saviour's Herald"

     I. Predicted (vv. 1-3)

     II. Preaching (vv. 4-8)
        1. Calling for repentance (vv. 4, 5)
        2. Exhibiting humility (vv. 6)
        3. Pointing men to Christ (vv. 7, 8)

5. Why

This paragraph is included in the narrative because Jesus' herald, predicted in prophecy, appears as an integral part of the story, adequately authenticated by his character and his ministry.

6. Wherefore

   a. *Conclusions for theology*:

      The baptism of John is here met for the first time, and its significance must be related to the earthly ministry of Christ as its proper call for repentance as a preparation.

b. *Conclusions for daily experience*:

> The gospel, which is the good news about Christ, almost always (as here) begins with someone other than Christ. We are brought to Christ by an "introducer." John might well be named "John, the Introducer," and all that we can learn from his humility and his faithfulness will enable us better to introduce Jesus to others.

1:9-11

1. Who
   a. *Jesus*: came to Jordan for baptism.
   b. *John*: baptized Jesus publicly.
   c. *The Holy Spirit*: descended on Jesus as a dove.
   d. *The Father*: attested His approval of Jesus by a voice from heaven.

2. Where

   In the Jordan River, where John was baptizing.

3. When

   At the same time as the preceding paragraph.

4. What
   a. *Words needing definition*:
      (1) *baptized*: what was the process involved, and its significance? These questions cannot be answered from this brief passage, but must be determined from an inductive study of all other relevant New Testament references.
      (2) *opened*: in what sense can heaven be said to be "open"? Probably we are to assume that spiritual perception, rather than a physical phenomenon, was granted our Lord.

b. *Outline*: "The Saviour's Attestation"
   I. The Baptism of John (v. 9)
   II. The Coming of the Spirit (v. 10)
   III. The Approval of the Father (v. 11)

5. Why

   Christ's ministry is preceded by His visible empowering by the Spirit and approval from the Father, obviously as spiritual preparation for the work ahead. Why He was baptized we cannot determine without reference to parallel passages in the other gospels. Surely He was not baptized for repentance from sin, as were the others who were coming to John. Matthew says that it was "to fulfil all righteousness," and it apparently was an act whereby Jesus identified Himself with the nation of Israel in its humbling.

6. Wherefore

   a. *Conclusions for theology*:

      There seems to be in this incident a coming of the Holy Spirit in new power on Christ in preparation for His ministry. This idea need not conflict with the realization of His deity, for Scripture makes it amply clear that He humbled Himself and made Himself subject to the Spirit in His incarnation. Perhaps this event was a time of new realization of His mission, since He grew and developed in His manhood while incarnating Deity. At least it was essential to the commencement of His preaching.

   b. *Conclusions for daily experience*:

      The act of humiliation brings God's blessing. Yieldedness (symbolized by Jesus' submitting to John's baptism) is the key to the Spirit's fullness and the Father's approval. No greater ambition can be ours than some day to hear the Father's "Well done."

1:12, 13

1. Who

   a. *The Holy Spirit*: forced Jesus into temptation.
   b. *Christ*: tempted forty days in the desert.
   c. *Satan*: spearheaded the temptation.
   d. *Angels*: protected Him.

2. Where

   The wilderness, a place *alone*.

3. When

   Just preceding Jesus' public ministry.

4. What

   a. *Words needing definition*:
      tempted: what was involved? Could Jesus have sinned? If not, was He truly tempted? Only a comparison with other passages, such as Hebrews 2:18; 4:15, can determine the issue.
   b. *Outline*: "The Saviour's Victory"
       I. The Preparation (the Spirit)
      II. The Temptation (Satan)
     III. The Ministration (angels)

5. Why

   Jesus' withstanding of temptation was an obvious demonstration of superiority over Satan and of victory over sin which qualifies Him for the work ahead of Him.

6. Wherefore

   a. *Conclusions for theology*:
      (1) The sinlessness of Christ is evidenced in a crucial testing, in personal combat with Satan himself.

(2) The distinction between God's perfect will and His permissive will can here be seen. God tempts no man, yet the Spirit expressly "drove" Him to the place of temptation. Satan was the active agent, but God the permissive superintendent.

b. *Conclusions for daily experience*:

(1) Temptation often precedes an important responsibility, as a spiritual preparation for it.

(2) The wilderness implies "aloneness," and all temptation ultimately must be faced by the soul alone, separate from all other men.

1:14, 15

1. Who

a. *John*: His mission arrested.

b. *Jesus*: His mission commenced.

2. Where

Galilee, where Jesus deliberately returned to begin His preaching.

3. When

As soon as John was removed from the scene.

4. What

a. *Words needing definition*:

(1) *Kingdom of God*: God's reign over men.

(2) *at hand*: because of the fulfillment of time, the rule of God over men is imminent.

b. *Outline*: "The Saviour's Announcement"

I. The Time (when John ceased to minister)

II. The Theme (the Kingdom of God)

III. The Terms (repentance and faith)

5. Why

   a. Jesus apparently waited until John's ministry was at an end to begin His, or perhaps John was providentially removed when Jesus was ready to act.

   b. The central theme of Jesus' preaching is announced at once, together with the terms of its acceptance.

6. Wherefore

   a. *Conclusions for theology*:

   This setting of the stage for the ensuing public ministry of Christ has immense implications. (1) It describes Him as beginning in the remote, despised region of Galilee from whence He mounted for an assault on the religious center of Jerusalem. (2) It describes His message as "good news," the rule of God in the hearts of men. (3) It describes the human responsibility as a two-sided one: repentance and faith.

   b. *Conclusions for daily experience*:

     (1) There is a right time for everything. As John's ministry had to precede that of Christ, there must be preparation in our lives for spiritual advance and conquest.

     (2) There was a forthrightness to Jesus' message that we should reproduce. He set the claims of God before men without equivocation, although it was still "good news." The good news of God still requires humbling through repentance and faith, in order to be appropriated.

1:16-20

1. Who

   a. *Jesus*: called men to be His followers.

b. *Peter and Andrew*: called from their boat.
c. *James and John*: called from their nets.
d. *Their father*: left behind.

2. Where

By the Sea of Galilee, to which Jesus returned after His baptism near Jerusalem.

3. When

No specific statement is made.

4. What

a. *Words needing definition*: none.
b. *Outline*: "The Saviour's Call"
   I. The Call of Peter and Andrew (vv. 16-18)
      1. Situation: casting their nets
      2. Separation: left their nets
   II. The Call of James and John (vv. 19, 20)
      1. Situation: mending their nets
      2. Separation: left their father

5. Why

Jesus evidently had in mind that at the heart of His ministry would be the training of individual men. Here He selects the men, and challenges them to the greatness of the mission that lies ahead.

6. Wherefore

a. *Conclusions for theology*:
   (1) This is the first episode in the formation of the group of disciples, and their first "classroom" experience with the greatest of all teachers.
   (2) The grace and wisdom of God is revealed in Jesus' choice of men. Who would expect a religious teacher to select Galilean fishermen for His inner circle? Evidently He intends to confound the wise and the mighty with the trans-

formation of such weak vessels as a testimony to His transcendent power and grace.

b. *Conclusions for daily experience*:

   (1) In order to follow Jesus it is necessary to "leave" all else: things with which we make our living, and loved ones as well. By "leaving" is implied the surrendering of those things to God, putting His interests first and subordinating all human possessions and relationships thereby.

   (2) The play on the word "fisher" suggests that whatever our present occupation, or our innate ability, God can sanctify it and use it for His own higher purpose.

1:21-28

1. Who

   a. *Disciples*: went with Jesus.
   b. *Hearers of His teaching*: amazed at His authority.
   c. *Scribes*: contrasted with Jesus.
   d. *Demon-possessed man*: healed.
   e. *Jesus*: taught and wrought with authority.

2. Where

   Capernaum, the seat of operations for much of Jesus' itinerant ministry in Galilee.

3. When

   On a Sabbath, the traditional time for teaching.

4. What

   a. *Words needing definition*:

      (1) *synagogue*: the place of local Jewish worship and instruction.

      (2) *scribes*: official interpreters of the Old Testament Scriptures.

   b. *Outline*: "The Saviour's Authority"
      I. His words (vv. 21, 22)
        1. Occasion: teaching in the synagogue
        2. Response: astonishment at His authority
     II. His works (vv. 23-28)
        1. Occasion: demon-possessed man healed
        2. Response: astonishment at His authority

5. Why

This passage seems to be included to show at the outset of Jesus' ministry His twofold authority in word and work, and to record the instantaneous reaction of the crowd. Here is the feeling that His ministry created on the listener.

6. Wherefore

   a. *Conclusions for theology*:

     (1) Jesus' lack of concern with Sabbath restrictions is revealed in the healing of the demon-possessed man, though we must wait for other such incidents for a record of the opposition this inspired in the Pharisees.

     (2) The contrast drawn by the crowd between the authority of Christ and the lack of it on the part of the scribes must be viewed as a strong element in the commencement of official opposition to Christ. Jealousy may well have been the motivating factor.

     (3) Jesus' power over the world of evil spirits is here documented, opening up a realm of truth about which Scripture says much, but about which we would know next to nothing otherwise.

   b. *Conclusions for daily experiences*

     (1) In a world of uncertainty and confusion we

find the One whose authority we must acknowledge in Jesus Christ.

(2) The world around us is looking for people who speak with authority, and we may well draw a personal challenge from this passage. In Jesus' denouncement of the scribes, recorded in Matthew, chapter twenty-three, it is apparent that the scribes' lack of authority grew out of the hypocrisy of their lives. It was not so much that they taught incorrect or uncertain doctrine, as that they failed to live a correspondingly righteous life. Our personal authority, then, will depend on the quality of our daily living.

1:29-31

1. Who
   a. *Jesus*: healed the sick woman.
   b. *Peter and Andrew*: their house is the scene.
   c. *James and John*: they attend.
   d. *Peter's mother-in-law*: healed of her sickness.

2. Where
   Peter's home in Capernaum.

3. When
   On the Sabbath, after healing in the synagogue.

4. What
   a. *Words needing definition*: none.
   b. *Outline*: "The Saviour's Healing"
      I. The Miracle
         1. Its Nature: spontaneous
         2. Its Means: lifted her by the hand

II. The Result
1. Immediate healing
2. Response by serving

5. Why

Jesus' power over the physical body, and His loving interest in individuals are clearly pictured.

6. Wherefore

a. *Conclusions for theology*:

The demonstration of Jesus' deity is seen in His healing works, of which this is but one of thousands. Here we see, by implication, that He did not perform "miracles for miracles' sake," but out of genuine love for the individual in need.

b. *Conclusions for daily experience*:

(1) It is encouraging to know that no human need escapes the attention of our Saviour. This is implied by the inclusion of this incident, quite casually, into the permanent record of His transcendent life.

(2) The natural response to God's grace is to serve Him as this dear woman did. Here the pattern of human response is set, not in theological terms, but in the record of everyday experience. Service for God includes service of others as well.

1:32-34

1. Who

a. *The sick*: brought to Jesus and healed.
b. *Jesus*: the great healer.

2. Where

Capernaum.

3. When
   Immediately following the healing of Peter's mother-in-law.

4. What
   a. *Words needing definition*: none
   b. *Outline*: "The Saviour's Mass Healings"
      I. Mass Movement (vv. 32, 33)
         1. The sick and demon-possessed
         2. The entire city of onlookers
      II. Many Healings (vv. 34)
         1. The miracle of healing
         2. The prohibition to speak

5. Why
   The record proceeds to show the natural response of the people to Jesus' display of power.

6. Wherefore
   a. *Conclusions for theology*:
      (1) Jesus' authority over demons is here re-emphasized.
      (2) An intriguing question is raised as to why the healed man was not permitted to speak. Perhaps it was because Jesus wanted to discourage the gathering of huge, but only idly curious crowds, with the results that actually followed the healed man's widespread announcement (cf. v. 45).

   b. *Conclusions for daily experience*:
      What a contrast there is between the crowds of curious folks and the few true disciples. We must not be deceived by mass movements, but realize that the way is narrow, and that of the many who are called, only a few are chosen.

1:35-39

1. Who
   a. *Jesus*: praying and preaching.
   b. *Peter and others*: trying to bring Him back for the crowd.

2. Where

   A lonely place, where Jesus went to pray; then all Galilee, where Jesus went to preach.

3. When

   Early morning, then an undetermined time span.

4. What
   a. *Words needing definition*: none.
   b. *Outline*: "The Saviour's Praying and Preaching"
      I. Prayer (vv. 35, 36)
         1. Practiced in a solitary place
         2. Urged by disciples to return to the crowd
      II. Purpose (vv. 37-39)
         1. Announced: a chance for every town
         2. Practiced: all Galilee visited

5. Why

   The incident reveals the Saviour's steadfast purpose to reach the whole of Galilee, and it shows the divine source of His authority.

6. Wherefore
   a. *Conclusions for theology*:
      (1) The prominence of prayer in Jesus' life emphasizes the voluntary subjection to which He submitted Himself in His incarnation.
      (2) The purpose of His ministry is declared to be the announcement of the imminence of the Kingdom of God to all the country.

b. *Conclusions for daily experience*:

(1) Here is a great challenge to pray. Jesus prayed early, and He prayed alone. If He needed to pray, as the Son of God voluntarily putting Himself in the place of dependence, how much more do we!

(2) From Jesus' example we learn to get our orders from God and not to allow men, even our well-meaning friends, to deter us.

(3) We learn here the danger of popularity. Jesus did not succumb to the temptation. We will need a strong sense of purpose, and true humility, to resist it if it comes.

(4) A pattern for evangelization is here set forth. We are to press on to the next place and see to it that men everywhere have an opportunity to hear.

1:40-45

1. Who

a. *A leper*: came seeking health and got it.
b. *Jesus*: healed the leper; was engulfed by the crowd.
c. *The crowds*: swarmed around Jesus.

2. Where

Somewhere in Galilee.

3. When

No specific identification.

4. What

a. *Words needing definition*: none.
b. *Outline*: "The Saviour's Popularity"
   I. Compassion (vv. 40-42)
       1. The miracle
       2. The motive

II. Command (vv. 43, 44)
   1. "Don't tell everyone"
   2. "Give legal proof to the priest"
III. Contradiction (vv. 45)
   1. Disobedience to the command
   2. Inability to enter the towns

5. Why

The Saviour's compassion for the most repulsive of human conditions is shown. A leper was one who had to be isolated from human society.

6. Wherefore
   a. *Conclusions for theology*:
      (1) Christ's character as one of extreme compassion is established.
      (2) Christ's concern for the valid requirements of the Mosaic law is implied.
      (3) His authority over sin, as it is typified by leprosy, is revealed.
   b. *Conclusions for daily experience*:
      (1) Faith is unreserved confidence in Christ in the presence of our personal helplessness to meet our need.
      (2) Witnessing is a spontaneous, undeniable overflow of gratitude for God's grace.
      (3) One man can cause a tremendous stir when he is truly enthusiastic over his salvation.

BIBLE STUDY OF MINUTE PARTS OF SCRIPTURE

INTRODUCTION

An understanding of the Bible's meaning often turns on the understanding of a single word or phrase. For that reason the student of the Bible must learn how to determine such meaning with precision and care.

Three areas will concern us here: the meaning of "non-routine" words (this term is borrowed from Mortimer J. Adler, *How to Read a Book.* The student would do well to read him at this point), the recognition and interpretation of figures of speech, and the meanings of the names of significant people and places.

I. HOW TO FIND THE MEANING OF NON-ROUTINE WORDS IN SCRIPTURE

A. *Explanation*

1. Check the root meaning of the word in a Bible dictionary or concordance.
2. Check the usage and meaning of the word in ancient extra-biblical Jewish (e.g., the Apochrypha) literature.
3. Check the occurrences of the word in the Bible by means of an exhaustive concordance.
4. Give attention to the Greek or Hebrew words from which this English word comes.
5. Give special attention to the location in Scripture where the word first occurs.
6. Check the usage of this word in the light of one particular book of Scripture.
7. Summarize your findings regarding this word in one paragraph.

B. *Exemplification*: a study of the word "tithe" or "tithing."

1. *The root meaning of the word.*
   Study of the word "tithe" or "tithing." A tenth part, or loosely a small part of some specific

thing paid as a voluntary contribution or as a tax to a superior for a public use, or the like, especially, as in British usage, a tenth part of the yearly increase arising from the profits of land, stock, or personal industry, paid in kind of money to the church or for religious or charitable uses; hence, any small ratable tax or levy (Webster).

2. *The usage and meaning in extra-biblical literature.* The custom of giving a tenth of the products of the land and of the spoils of war to priests and kings (I Sam. 8:17), was very ancient among most nations. That the Jews had this custom long before the institution of the Mosaic Law is shown by Genesis 14:17-20; Hebrews 7:4; Genesis 28:22, cf.

3. *Check the word in a concordance.* The following is from *Young's Concordance*: Tithe: to give, have pay, receive, take tithes to:
    (1) Deuteronomy 14:22
    (2) Nehemiah 10:37
    (3) Nehemiah 10:38

  b. To give away a tenth
    (1) Matthew 23:23
    (2) Luke 11:48
    (3) Luke 18:12
    (4) Hebrews 7:5

  c. To give a tenth
    (1) Hebrews 7:6
    (2) Hebrews 7:9

  d. Tithes, tithing:
    (1) A tenth
      (a) Genesis 14:20
      (b) Leviticus 27:30, 31, 32

    (c) Numbers 18:24, 26

    (d) Deuteronomy 12:6, 11, 17; 14:23, 28; 26:12

    (e) II Chronicles 31:5, 6

    (f) Nehemiah 10:37, 38

    (g) Amos 4:4

    (h) Malachi 3:8, 10

 (2) To give a tenth

    Deuteronomy 26:13

 (3) A tenth (part)

    Hebrews 7:8, 9

4. *Give attention to the Greek and Hebrew words.* (See *Young's Concordance*)

5. *Give special attention to the location in Scripture where the word is first mentioned.*

> First found in Genesis 14:20 when Abraham paid tithes to Melchizedek, king of Salem. Shows that even before Mosaic code of law tithes were given.

6. *Usage of this word as it is used in one particular book:*

> It seems to be found most in the Book of Deuteronomy (see above). However, it was contained throughout the entire Mosaic law. The article found in the *International Standard Bible Encyclopedia* Vol. IV on the "Tithe" is helpful.

7. *Summary:*

> The main emphasis seems to be in the Old Testament. However, the Christian should have some system of giving, and the tithe seems to be the best. The main emphasis, however, should not be on the system, but the attitude toward the Lord in giving. It was necessary for the Old Testament people of Israel to be hedged about with such a law of tithing that they would keep all

their activities God-centered, that a portion of all they gained would be given to the Lord. The believer of the New Testament serves the law, not by letter but by spirit. This means the person who really and truly loves the Lord will give all he possibly can, using the tithe of the Old Testament to guide him as a start. Thus increasingly he takes the Lord into his thoughts.

II. HOW TO RECOGNIZE FIGURES OF SPEECH IN THE BIBLE

A. *Explanation*

No attempt has been made to exhaust the figures of speech in the Bible, but only to exhibit the more prominent ones, so that the student will be aware of their presence and meaning.

B. *Exemplification*

1. Comparison (where the resemblance is shown between one thing and another).
   a. *Psalms 84:10:* "For a day in thy courts is better than a thousand. I had rather be a doorkeeper in the house of my God, than to dwell in the tents of wickedness."
   b. *Ephesians 1:19, 20:* "And what is the exceeding greatness of his power to us-ward who believe, according to the working of his mighty power, Which he wrought in Christ, when he raised him from the dead, and set him at his own right hand in the heavenly places. . . ."
   c. *Matthew 12:11, 12:* "And he said unto them, What man shall there be among you, that shall have one sheep, and if it fall into a pit on the sabbath, will he not lay hold on it, and lift it out?

How much then is a man better than a sheep?
Wherefore it is lawful to do well on the sabbath
days."

d. *James 3:3-6:* "Behold, we put bits in the horses'
mouths that they may obey us; and we turn
about their whole body. Behold also the ships,
which though they be so great, and are driven of
fierce winds, yet are they turned about with a
very small helm, whithersoever the governor list-
eth. Even so the tongue is a little member, and
boasteth great things. Behold, how great a matter
a little fire kindleth! And the tongue is a fire, a
world of iniquity: so is the tongue among our
members, that it defileth the whole body, and
setteth on fire the course of nature; and it is set
on fire of hell."

2. *Contrast* (where two things are designedly set in
opposition).

a. *Proverbs 11:1:* "A false balance is abomination to
the Lord; but a just weight is his delight."

b. *James 2:2-4:* "For if there come unto your assem-
bly a man with a gold ring, in goodly apparel,
And there come in also a poor man in vile raiment; and ye have respect to him that weareth
the gay clothing, and say unto him, Sit thou here
in a good place; and say to the poor, Stand thou
there, or sit here under my footstool: Are ye not
then partial in yourselves, and are become judges
of evil thoughts?"

c. *James 3:12:* "Can the fig tree, my brethren, bear
olive berries? either a vine, figs? so can no fountain both yield salt water and fresh."

d. *II Corinthians 3:5, 6:* ". . . our sufficiency is of
God; Who also hath made us able ministers of the

new testament; not of the letter, but of the spirit; for the letter killeth, but the spirit giveth life."

e. *Matthew 6:24:* ". . . Ye cannot serve God and Mammon."

f. *Romans 6:23:* "For the wages of sin is death; but the gift of God is eternal life through Jesus Christ our Lord."

3. *Simile* (where one thing is likened to another by direct statement).

a. *Psalms 103:11:* "For as the heaven is high above the earth, so great is his mercy toward them that fear him."

b. *Psalms 1:3:* "And he shall be like a tree planted by the rivers of water, that bringeth forth his fruit in his season; his leaf also shall not wither; and whatsoever he doeth shall prosper."

c. *Psalms 44:22:* "Yea, for thy sake are we killed all the day long; we are counted as sheep for the slaughter."

d. *Proverbs 25:25:* "As cold waters to a thirsty soul, so is good news from a far country."

e. *I Corinthians 13:1:* ". . . I am become as sounding brass, or a tinkling cymbal."

4. *Metaphor* (where one thing is likened to another by implication).

a. *Ephesians 2:20:* "And are built upon the foundation of the apostles and prophets, Jesus Christ himself being the chief corner stone."

b. *Colossians 1:18:* "And he is the head of the body, the church: who is the beginning, the firstborn from the dead; that in all things he might have the pre-eminence."

c. *John 15:5:* "I am the vine, ye are the branches: He that abideth in me, and I in him, the same bringeth forth much fruit: for without me ye can do nothing."

d. *John 10:9:* "I am the door: by me if any man enter in, he shall be saved, and shall go in and out, and find pasture."

e. *John 6:48:* "I am that bread of life."

f. *I John 1:5:* "This then is the message which we have heard of him, and declare unto you, that God is light, and in him is no darkness at all."

g. *Proverbs 20:27:* "The spirit of man is the candle of the Lord, searching all the inward parts of the belly."

h. *Psalms 23:1:* "The Lord is my shepherd; I shall not want."

5. *Allegory* (similar to a parable, only not, perhaps, capable of literal interpretation).

a. *Judges 9:7-15:* Jotham's allegory of the trees that sought a king.

b. *Psalms 80:8-16:* Israel spoken of as a vineyard.

c. *Isaiah 5:1-7:* Israel spoken of as a vineyard.

d. *Ezekiel 17:* Parable of two eagles and a vine.

e. *John 10:1-18:* Jesus as the shepherd.

f. *Revelation 17:* The harlot.

6. *Type* (where one thing supplies a suggestion or forecast of another).

a. *Romans 5:14:* "Nevertheless death reigned from Adam to Moses, even over them that had not sinned after the similitude of Adam's transgression, who is the figure of him that was to come."

b. *I Corinthians 15:45:* "And so it is written, The first man Adam was made a living soul; the last Adam was made a quickening spirit."

c. *Revelation 21:2:* "And I John saw the holy city, new Jerusalem, coming down from God out of heaven, prepared as a bride adorned for her husband."

d. *Revelation 22:17:* "And the Spirit and the bride say, Come. And let him that heareth say, Come. And let him that is athirst come. And whosoever will, let him take the water of life freely."

e. *Matthew 25:1:* "Then shall the kingdom of heaven be likened unto ten virgins, which took their lamps, and went forth to meet the bridegroom."

f. *I Corinthians 10:1-11:* Analogy drawn from experiences of Israel.

7. *Apostrophe* (where an absent or imaginary individual or attribute is addressed).

a. *Isaiah 51:9:* "Awake, awake, put on strength, O arm of the Lord. . . ."

b. *I Corinthians 15:55:* "O death, where is thy sting? O grave, where is thy victory?"

c. *Amos 4:1:* "Hear this word, ye kine of Bashan, that are in the mountain of Samaria, which oppress the poor, which crush the needy, which say to their masters, Bring, and let us drink."

8. *Hyperbole* (use of exaggerated terms for emphasis).

a. *Matthew 16:26:* "For what is a man profited, if he shall gain the whole world, and lose his own soul? . . ."

b. *Matthew 5:29:* "If thy right eye offend thee, pluck it out. . . ."

c. *John 21:25:* "And there are also many other things which Jesus did, the which, if they should be written every one, I suppose that even the world itself could not contain the books that should be written."

d. *II Chronicles 36:23:* "Thus saith Cyrus king of Persia, All the kingdoms of the earth hath the

> Lord God of heaven given me; and he hath charged me to build him an house in Jerusalem, which is in Judah. . . ."

9. *Metonymy* (where a thing is represented by one of its attributes or accompaniments).
   a. *Galatians 6:17:* ". . . I bear in my body the marks of the Lord Jesus."
   b. *Isaiah 59:1:* "Behold, the Lord's hand is not shortened . . . neither his ear heavy. . . ."
   c. *John 13:8:* "Peter saith unto him, Thou shalt never wash my feet. Jesus answered him, If I wash thee not, thou hast no part with me."
   d. *James 1:12:* "Blessed is the man that endureth temptation: for when he is tried, he shall receive the crown of life, which the Lord hath promised to them that love him."
   e. *Galatians 1:16:* ". . . I conferred not with flesh and blood."

10. *Synecdoche* (where a part is made to stand for the whole, or the whole for a part).
    a. *Romans 3:25:* "Whom God hath set forth to be a propitiation through faith in his blood. . . ." (For His completed work.)
    b. *I Corinthians 1:22:* ". . . the Greeks seek after wisdom." (For all the Gentiles.)
    c. *Revelation 1:11:* ". . . send it unto the seven churches which are in Asia. . . ." (For all local churches.)

11. *Litotes* (where a declaration is made by negation or by ironic understatement).
    a. *Acts 20:27:* "For I have not shunned to declare unto you all the counsel of God."
    b. *Acts 20:31:* ". . . I ceased not to warn every one. . . ."

    c. *Acts 21:39:* ". . . I am . . . a citizen of no mean city. . . ."

    d. *Acts 26:19:* ". . . I was not disobedient unto the heavenly vision."

III. THE MEANING OF THE NAMES OF SIGNIFICANT BIBLICAL PEOPLE AND PLACES

A. *People*

Abel—vanity

Abraham—father of a great multitude

Adam—red earth, ground, ruddy

Agrippa—wild olive

Amos—burden, burden-bearer

Anna—grace

Asa—physician

Barnabas—son of comfort

Benjamin—son of the right hand

Caleb—capable

Dan—judge

Daniel—judgment of God

David—well-beloved

Ebenezer—stone of help

Eli—height, high

Elijah—Jehovah is God

B. *Places*

Antioch—opponent

Arabia—desert, barren

Babel—confusion, gate of God

Beer-Sheba—well of the oath

Bethany—house of unripe dates, or house of misery

Bethel—house of God

Bethlehem—house of the fruitful, house of David, place of bread

Bethsaida—house of fishing

Cana—place of reeds

Canaan—low region, merchant

Capernaum—city of consolation, village of Nahum

Carmel—garden-land, fruitful place, or park

Eden—pleasantness, delight

Egypt—land of Copts, flack

Elisha—God is salvation
Elizabeth—God is an oath
Enoch—dedicated
Esau—tawny or shaggy, hairy
Esther—a star
Eve—life
Ezekiel—God strengthens
Ezra—help

Gideon—feller, hewer, he that cuts down

Hezekiah—strength of Jehovah

Isaac—laughter
Isaiah—salvation of Jehovah

Jonah—dove
Joseph—He will add
Joshua—Jehovah is deliverance

Matthew—gift of Jehovah

Emmaus—hot springs
Ephesus—permitted

Galilee—circuit, ring
Gilead—hill of witness, witness

Hermon—sacred

Jericho—a fragrant place
Jerusalem—founded in peace
Jordan—the descender, flowing downward
Judah—praised

Lebanon—to be white

Samaria—place of watch
Sinai—to shine, pointed

BIBLE STUDY OF BIBLE DOCTRINE

INTRODUCTION

The ultimate aim of Bible study is to understand its "doctrines" so that we may apply them to our lives. By doctrine we mean "that which is taught," the orderly statement of particular truths.

Whole sections of the Bible are pre-eminently doctrinal.

In them we find the direct setting forth of various doctrinal themes. In other sections (such as the narrative portions) doctrines are taught by illustration and implication, and must be deduced by the appropriate methods of study. In still other sections (such as the practical portions) doctrines are seen in their application to everyday situations and problems.

This distinction between doctrinal and practical passages is clearly seen in the division of the following New Testament books:

Romans: Doctrinal (1-11); Practical (12-16)
Ephesians: Doctrinal (1-3); Practical (4-6)
Colossians: Doctrinal (1-2); Practical (3-4)

A Tabulation of some of the Bible doctrines

Christ
Holy Spirit
Salvation
The Scriptures
Grace
Atonement
Faith
Baptism
Lord's Supper
Love
Blood (of sacrifices)
Death
Sanctification
Justification
Regeneration
Glorification
Christ's Second Coming
Punishment

Fall of Man
Joy
Miracles
Forgiveness
Liberty
Church
Holiness
Creation
Backsliding
Prayer
Temptation
Heaven
Hell
Resurrection
Obedience
Reverence
Demonology
Satan
Kingdom of God

Immutability of God
Original Sin
Sovereignty of God
Divorce
Marriage
Images
Virgin Birth
Election
Messiah
Repentance
Sacrifice
Inspiration
Knowledge of God
Existence of God
Attributes of God
Origin of Man
Reconciliation

Perseverance of	Israel	Adoption
Saints	Gentiles	Trinity
Revelation	Law	Rewards
Character of Sin	Dispensations	Providence
Judgment	Covenants	Anti-Christ
Priestly Office of	Predestination	Government
Christ	Works	Absolute Power
Prophetic Office of	Last Things	Eternity of God
Christ	Angels	Separation
Conversion	Nature of God	Ascension of
Sin Offering	Mystical Union	Christ
Circumcision	Chastity	Religious Reforms
Shekinah Glory	Humility	Righteousness
Names for Christ	Conscience	
Penitence	Eternal Life	

I. EXPLANATION

The study of a doctrine as it appears in the entire Bible is beyond the ability of most beginning students. It is preferable for the new Christian to study a doctrine in one particular book, and after reaching his conclusions from that book, to expand the study by going on to other books.

Begin by studying one of the following doctrines in a particular book: God, Christ, the Holy Spirit, Sin, Salvation, Christian Living, the Second Coming, Heaven, and Hell.

1. Collect all references to the doctrine. Trace this by the use of an analytical concordance, or topical Bible.

2. Define the doctrine, by comparing all Bible references, and by using such extra-biblical helps as necessary, and by formulating a concise, clear statement of its meaning. What do these statements have in common? Where do they differ?

3. Relate the references to their immediate context and the

total pattern of biblical truth. Study each reference in the light of its context, and evaluate the presence of this doctrine within the total pattern of the biblical revelation, cataloging them according to the various aspects of the subject they present.

4. Apply the doctrine to personal experience. Is this a doctrine for believers or unbelievers? In what way must it be applied to the lives of those to whom it is addressed?

5. Summarize the doctrine. Write a paragraph or more stating your conclusions, i.e., write a concise statement of its content and its importance.

II. EXEMPLIFICATION

A. *The New Testament Doctrine of Prayer*

	O.T.	N.T.	Total
1. The word "prayer" occurs	83 times	31 times	114 times
2. The word "pray" occurs	225	67	292
3. The word "prayed" occurs	31	34	65
4. The word "prayers" occurs	2	22	24
5. The word "prayeth" occurs	4	3	7
6. The word "praying" occurs	6	14	20
	351	171	522

7. The word "prayer" occurs the most in the Book of Acts, then in Luke and Matthew.

8. Place of prayer in the New Testament: Everywhere (I Tim. 2:8).

9. Time of Prayer in New Testament: Night and day (I Tim. 5:5): Without ceasing (I Tim. 5:17); Continue constant in (Rom. 12:12).

10. Postures in Prayer: Standing (Mark 11:25); Kneeling (Luke 22:41; Acts 20:36); Falling on face (Matt. 26:39); Lifting up hands (I Tim. 2:8).
11. Vain repetitions in prayer forbidden (Matt. 6:7).
12. Ostentation in prayer forbidden (Matt. 6:5).

B. *Definition of the doctrine*:
   1. Etymology of the New Testament word:
      a. Supplication for benefits either for one's self (form of petition) or for others (form of intercession).
      b. It is an act of worship which covers all the attitudes of the soul in its approach to God. Supplication is at the heart of it, for prayer always springs out of a sense of need and a belief that God is a rewarder of them that diligently seek Him (Heb. 11:6).
   2. Prayer consists of adoration, thanksgiving, confession, petition.
   3. Answers to prayer promised (Matt. 7:7); Christ gives answers (John 4:10; 14:14).
   4. Prayer in the New Testament is just as reverent as in the Old Testament, but far more intimate and trustful. Christ told His disciples that prayer was henceforth to be addressed to the Father in the name of the Son, and prayer thus offered was sure to be granted (John 16:23-26).

C. *Relation of references to the context or total pattern of biblical truth. Prayer is*:
   1. Commanded (Matt. 7:7; Phil. 4:6).
   2. To be offered to God (Matt. 4:10); through Christ (Eph. 2:18; Heb. 10:19); in power of the Spirit (Eph. 6, Rom. 8).
   3. To be offered up:

      a. In faith (Matt. 21:22).
      b. In submission to God (Luke 22:42).
      c. In holiness (I Tim. 2:8).
      d. In truth (John 4:24).

D. *Application of the doctrine to personal experience. How is personal faith related to this doctrine?*

  1. *Christ gives answers* (John 4:10; 14:14).
      a. Sometimes with delay (Luke 18:7).
      b. Sometimes differing from our desires (II Cor. 12:8).
      c. Sometimes beyond expectation (Eph. 3:20).
      d. Rewarded openly (Matt. 6:6).
  2. *Personal faith related to doctrines*
      a. Only those who have forsaken sin are authorized to draw nigh unto God in prayer. Those who have rebelled against the authority of God can approach Him only with renunciation of their rebellion and a petition for pardon.
      b. Your prayer should be offered with confidence in God (I John 5:14).

E. *Summerization of doctrines*

  1. Prayer is one of the most prominent doctrines in Scripture, being mentioned 522 times.
  2. We learn from a study of its definition that prayer presupposes an attitude of worship in approaching God. This attitude of worship springs from a sense of need and believes that God will hear and answer.
  3. The major elements of prayer are adoration, thanksgiving, confession, and petition.
  4. To pray with expectancy it is necessary to have a submissive attitude toward God.

BIBLE STUDY OF BIBLE BIOGRAPHIES

INTRODUCTION

Great fascination and profit will result from the study of the lives of various personalities in the Bible. There are 2930 such separate individuals, many of whom mirror in their experiences great spiritual lessons.

Such study leads to effective teaching and preaching since the lessons, far from being abstract, are concretized in a human life, and can be vividly portrayed and dramatized.

In studying a Bible character, be careful not to confuse different people who share the same name. (There are thirty Zachariahs, twenty Nathans, fifteen Jonathans, eight Judases, seven Marys, five Jameses, and five Johns.) Be careful, also, to identify the various names which may apply to one individual (such as Peter, Simon, and Simeon).

Young Christians might begin by studying Andrew, Barnabas, Daniel, Ruth, Peter, Timothy, Noah, Enoch, Simeon (Luke 2:25-32), or Ananias and Sapphira.

Mature Christians might well study John the Baptist, Saul, Abraham, Moses, Paul, Ezra, Job, David, Jonathan, or Mephibosheth.

Other biographies for study:

Christ	Joshua	Lot
John	Jonah	Philemon
Matthew	Elijah	Judas
Mark	Elisha	Rachel
Luke	Gehazi	Isaac
Joseph	Hezekiah	Samson
Samuel	Nicodemus	Solomon
Gideon	Stephen	Nathan
Adam	Aquila	Esther
Laban	Balaam	James

Isaiah	Caleb	Jacob
Jeremiah	Mary, the mother	Nehemiah
Ezekiel	of Jesus	Cain
Hosea	Deborah	Abel
Amos	Ishmael	Esau
Titus	Nahum	Sarah
Achan	Shem	Philip
Miriam	Bathsheba	Eli
Silas	Joel	Gamaliel
Bartholomew	Obadiah	Pilate
Herod	Eve	Uzziah
Barabbas	Aaron	Rebekah

I. EXPLANATION

1. What is the meaning of the individual's name? Check the individual's name in a good Bible dictionary, general reference Bible, or Bible encyclopedia. The meaning of the name will ofttimes give you a clue to the importance of the individual.

2. What is the ancestral background? By checking Bible helps and your Bible encyclopedia, trace the ancestral background of the individual being studied.

3. What significant religious and secular crises occurred in this life? List these including chapter and verse reference for each.

4. What advantages for personal development were enjoyed by this individual? Was he privileged to attend school? Did he have an opportunity to be exposed to wide cultural backgrounds?

5. What traits of character were manifested? List these and give chapter and verse reference for each.

6. What important friends did this person have? A person is ofttimes known by his friends. Who were the close companions of this Bible character?

7. What important influences did this individual exert? Did he influence other individuals, a church, or a nation?

8. What failures and faults occurred in this life? God had to use imperfect instruments. Tabulate these shortcomings and give chapter and verse reference for each.

9. What important contributions were made by this individual?

10. What one main lesson can be found within this life which is of special value to you?

11. What was the influence of the locality from the standpoint of geography, history, and culture upon this individual?

12. If this individual were in our present society, what would be his occupational status?

II. EXEMPLIFICATION

1. *What is the meaning of the individual's name?*
   a. Abraham — Etymology is difficult and vague; Abram probably meant "exalted father"; Abraham probably meant "father of a multitude."
   b. Peter — "rock" or "stone"; Simon — "hearing" (John 1:42).

2. *What is the ancestral background?*
   a. Abraham — A direct descendant of Noah through the line of Shem. His father, Terah, was originally from Ur of Chaldees.
   b. Peter — Son of John; brother of Andrew; from Bethsaida (Fish-town) (John 1).

3. *What significant religious and secular crises occurred in this life?*
   a. Abraham — Loss of his father shortly after leaving

his homeland; command to leave his family and country; lies concerning his wife; argues with his nephew, Lot; fights the kings; vision from God; has a child by Hagar and then family trouble; commanded to offer Isaac; death of Sarah (Gen. 11: 31-32; 12:1; 12:11-20; 13:8; 14:14; 15:1; chap. 22; 23:2).

b. Peter — Religious crises: His call to follow Jesus; testing of a faith that failed; confesses Christ as Messiah; denied Christ three times; disagreement with the Lord about ceremony rites; rebuked by Paul before Galatian church; restored to fellowship with Jesus. Secular crises: "Leaving all" (commercial life); in prison (Matt. 14:28-31; 16:16; 26:70, 72, 74; John 21:15-19; Acts 10:14; 12:4-8; Gal. 2:14).

4. *What advantages for personal development were enjoyed?*

a. Abraham — Close family ties; high culture and civilization; wealth; presence and promise of God (Gen. 11:29-32; 12:2, 3; 13:2).

b. Peter — Follower of Jesus; one of the twelve; one of the inner circle.

5. *What traits of character were manifested?*

a. Abraham — Trust, reverence, piety, generosity, fidelity, hospitality, compassion, self-respect, courage (Gen. 2:44; 12:8; 12:9; 14:14; 15:6; 18:1-8; 18:22, 23; 21:14; 23:4).

b. Peter — Impulsive, energetic, courageous, inconsistent, believing (Matt. 14:28; 16:16, 18; 16:22; John 18:10; Acts 2:14; Gal. 2:11-14).

6. *What important friendships did this person have?*

a. Abraham — Pharoah, Lot, Hagar, Abimelech, Eliezer, God (Gen. 12:15; 14:14; 16:1; 20:2; 24:1-67; James 2:23).

   b. Peter — Apostle John, John Mark, Silvanus, Paul,
      Christ (John 21:15-19; Gal. 1:18).

7. *What important influences did this individual exert?*

   a. Abraham — On Pharoah and Abimelech, on Isaac,
      on his descendants (Gen. 12:15; 22:8; 25:5).

   b. Peter — A leader of the early disciples; spokesman
      of the early church; apostle to the Jews of the dis-
      persion; first great preacher of the Christian church;
      first Jewish Christian to have converts among the
      Gentiles (Acts 2:1-47).

8. *What failures and faults occurred in this life?*

   a. Abraham — Lied twice concerning his wife; laughed
      at God; harkened to his wife rather than to God
      (Gen. 12:11; 20:2; 17:17; 16:2).

   b. Peter — Impetuous nature; doubted Jesus' power;
      rebuked Christ for telling of His death; denied
      Christ at His trial; resisted the vision of the Lord;
      changed face before the Jews at Galatia; tended
      to act first and think later (Matt. 14:28; 16:22;
      26:70, 72, 74; Gal. 2:11-14; Acts 10:14; Luke 22:
      61, 62; John 18:10).

9. *What important contributions were made?*

   a. Abraham — A lesson in faith; the beginning of the
      Jewish nation.

   b. Peter — Wrote two epistles.

10. *What one main lesson is there in this life for you?*

   a. Abraham — Believe God even when the future is
      unknown or when the problem seems to have no
      solution, for "God himself will provide" and "to
      believe God is to be accounted righteous."

   b. Peter — His life illustrates the power of Jesus to
      transform lives from instability to strength.

11. *What was the influence of the locality, geographically and historically?*
    a. Abraham — High culture in Ur; famine sent him to Egypt; land was conducive to semi-nomadic life.
    b. Peter — A rugged fisherman became a rugged preacher.
12. *If this man were in our present society, what would be his occupational status?*
    a. Abraham — A political and religious leader, perhaps in Israel (a pioneer).
    b. Peter — A missionary evangelist or great preacher and leader of men to Christ.

BIBLE STUDY OF BIBLE PRAYERS

INTRODUCTION

There are more than 500 references to prayer or one of its derivatives in the Bible. Great profit will be derived from studying not only the doctrine of prayer but the content of various prayers themselves, of which 100 or so are recorded.

The Old Testament particularly abounds with the prayers of God's people by which we are taken intimately into their relationship with God and whereby we may apply many important lessons to our own lives.

A partial classification of prayers in the Bible:

Old Testament Prayers

Aaron and the Priests	Numbers 6:22-26	Blessing for Israel
Abraham	Genesis 15:2	For a son
Abraham	Genesis 17:17	For Ishmael's acceptance
Abraham's servant	Genesis 24:12	Success in his mission
Agur	Proverbs 30:1	For moderation

Asa	II Chronicles 14:11	When entering battle
Daniel	Daniel 9:4-19	For restoration
David	II Samuel 7:18	To spare the nation
David	Psalm 51	For restoration
David	II Samuel 24:17	To spare the nation
David	I Chronicles 29:10	Thanksgiving
Elijah	I Kings 17:20	For restoration of life
Elijah	I Kings 18:36, 37	For vindication
Elijah	I Kings 19:4	For release from life
Elisha	II Kings 6:17	For vision
Ezekiel	Ezekiel 9:8	Intercession for the people
Ezra	Ezra 9:5-15	Confession for the people
Habakkuk	Habakkuk 2:1-20	For revival
Hannah	I Samuel 1:11	For a son
Hezekiah	II Kings 19:15	For protection
Hezekiah	II Chronicles 3:18	For healing
Hezekiah	II Chronicles 30:18	For pardon for his people
Israel	Deuteronomy 21:6-8	For forgiveness
Israel	Deuteronomy 26:5-10	Expiation for murder
Israel	Deuteronomy 26:13-15	For tithing
Jabez	I Chronicles 4:10	For divine blessing
Jacob	Genesis 32:9	For deliverance
Jehoshaphat	II Chronicles 20:6	For protection
Jeremiah	Jeremiah 14:7-9	For salvation
Jeremiah	Jeremiah 15:15-18	For comfort
Jonah	Jonah 2:2	For deliverance
Joshua	Joshua 7:7-9	Cry of distress
Levites	Nehemiah 9:5	Adoration
Manoah	Judges 13:8, 9	For divine guidance
Moses	Exodus 32:11-14	For forgiveness
Moses	Numbers 10:35	For protection
Moses	Numbers 11:11-15	For help to govern
Moses	Numbers 12:13	For healing
Moses	Numbers 14:13-19	For vindication
Moses	Numbers 27:15	For a successor
Moses	Deuteronomy 3:24	For entrance to the land
Nehemiah	Nehemiah 1:5-11	Confession and rebuilding
Nehemiah	Nehemiah 4:4, 5	For protection

Samson	Judges 16:28	For avenging
Solomon	I Kings 3:5-9	For wisdom to govern
Solomon	I Kings 8:22-53	Dedication of the temple

New Testament Prayers

Jesus	Luke 22:39-46	For courage
Jesus	Luke 23:34	For forgiveness
Jesus	Luke 23:46	For safekeeping
Jesus	John 17:1-26	For safekeeping
Disciples	Matthew 6:9-15	The divinely given pattern
Disciples	Luke 11:2-4	for prayer
Disciples	Acts 4:23-31	For boldness
Paul	Romans 1:9-12	For opportunity
Paul	Ephesians 1:16-23	For knowledge and prayer
Paul	Ephesians 3:14-21	For knowledge
Paul	Philippians 1:8-11	For maturity
Paul	Colossians 1:9-14	For fruitfulness

Suggestions for Young Christians — Begin by studying

Acts 4:23-31	Psalm 51:1-19
Matthew 6:9-15	Exodus 32:11-14
Philippians 1:8-11	I Kings 8:22-53

Suggestions for Mature Christians — Begin by studying

John 17:1-26	Nehemiah 1:5-11
Daniel 9:4-19	Genesis 18:23-33
Ezra 9:5-15	Luke 23:39-46
I Kings 18:36-37	Colossians 1:9-14

I. EXPLANATION

1. Note the one praying. Why was the prayer voiced?
2. Note the circumstances which led to the prayer.
3. Note the physical aspects involved in the prayer.

4. Note the word used to indicate the act of praying.

5. Note the one to whom the prayer is directed.

6. Note the general order of the prayer. Formulate an analytical outline, giving verse references for all major and minor points.

7. Note the main subject of the prayer. What elements does it contain (such as worship, thanksgiving, confession, or petition)?

8. Note the relation of the prayer to the promises of the Word of God. What specific promise of God was answered? Did the one who prayed have a right to expect an answer in the light of the biblical promises?

9. Note whether or not the prayer was answered, and how. When was it answered? Under what circumstances?

10. What was the final result of the prayer? What effect did it have on the one who offered it? On others? On those who heard it? What can this situation teach me personally?

II. EXEMPLIFICATION

A. *An Old Testament Prayer* — Daniel 9:4-19
   1. *Note the one praying.*
      Daniel.
   2. *Note the circumstances which led to the prayer.*
      There was a realization of the impending judgment of God because of sin (Dan. 9:2).
   3. *Note the physical aspects of praying*
      a. "Set my face unto the Lord" (9:3). (This could be figurative or it could mean that he was facing toward heaven or toward Jerusalem.)
      b. Fasting — Sackcloth — Ashes.

4. *Note the definite word used to indicate the act of praying.*

   "I prayed."

5. *Note the one to whom the prayer is directed.*
   a. The prayer is directed to "The Lord my God" (9:4).
   b. "O Lord, the great and dreadful God" (9:4).
   c. The God of covenant and mercy (9:4).
   d. God of righteousness (9:7).
   e. God of mercies and forgiveness (9:9).

6. *Note the general order of the prayer.*
   a. Confession (9:4-6).
   b. Adoration (9:7-9).
   c. Petition (9:10-19).

7. *Note the main subject of the prayer.*

   Confession and prayer for deliverance.

8. *Note the relation of the prayer to the promises of the Word of God.*

   Daniel claims mercy and forgiveness apparently on the basis of some foreknowledge of this attribute of God. He realizes that if his people had kept the law of God, this would not have befallen them.

9. *Note whether or not the prayer was answered, and how.*

   Gabriel descends, touches Daniel, and promises help, skill and understanding.

10. *What was the final result of the prayer?*
    a. Daniel received Divine aid.
    b. Daniel received deep prophetic insight.
    c. Daniel and his people received the assurance that while judgment is inevitable, deliverance will come.

B. *A New Testament Prayer* — Ephesians 3:14-21

    1. *Note the one praying.*
        A saint (the least of all saints: Eph. 3:8).

    2. *Note the circumstances which led to the prayer.*
        a. He was explaining to the Ephesians in a letter how the Gentiles are fellow-heirs with Christ (3:6).
        b. He was writing to them and praying for them lest they should faint (3:13).

    3. *Note physical aspects for praying.*
        He was in the kneeling position, which is the posture of humility.

    4. *Note the definite word used to indicate the act of praying.*
        a. "I bow my knees" (3:14).
        b. "As I live, every knee shall bow to me" (Rom. 14:11).

    5. *Note the one to whom the prayer is directed.*
        a. Directed to God.
        b. Title: Father.
        c. Attributes: "From whom every family in heaven and earth is named . . . according to the riches of glory . . . has the power to work within us . . . able to do more than we ask or think."

    6. *Note the general order of the prayer.*
        a. Adoration
        b. Petition and intercession.

    7. *Note the subject of the prayer.*
        a. That Christ may dwell in their hearts (3:17).
        b. Grant you to be strengthened (3:16).
        c. May have power to comprehend (3:18).
        d. May know the love of Christ (3:19).
        e. May be filled with all the fullness of God (3:19).

8. *Note the relation of the prayer to the promises of the Word of God.*

> The one interceding concluded with the words "Who is able to do far more than all that we ask or think." His confidence in the power and promises of God was strong.

9. *Note whether or not the prayer was answered, and how.*

> No answer to the prayer is recorded.

10. *What was the final result of the prayer?*

> There is no immediate result of the prayer noted. This church did grow and prosper, however, and exerted a strong influence for Christ.

BIBLE STUDY OF BIBLE MIRACLES

INTRODUCTION

Miracles are divine contraventions of the normal course of things and a special study of them in the Bible is valuable because they not only display God's power in some unusual character, but they point to some significant truth.

The language of Scripture reveals this threefold emphasis. In the Old Testament three classes of words are used to describe miracles. Some words emphasize their unusual character, others their display of divine power, and still others their purposeful design in revealing the character of God.

New Testament language carries on these distinctions. *Teras* and *Paradoxon* indicate the unusual nature or even incongruity of a miracle; *dunamis* refers to the power displayed; and *semeia* (the distinctive word in John's Gospel) points beyond the miracle itself to its purpose as a divine "sign."

A special value in the study of miracles will result from comparing the miracles in a certain section or book as to occasion, realm, means, and results. An example of such comparison at the close of this chapter may serve as a guide to such study.

Classification of Bible Miracles

1. There are sixty-two miracles in the Old Testament.
   a. Classified as to location:
      (1) Pentateuch — twenty-four
         a. Genesis — one
         b. Exodus — seventeen
         c. Numbers — six
      (2) Joshua — three
      (3) Judges — three
      (4) Samuel — three
      (5) Kings — twenty-six
      (6) Daniel — two
      (7) Jonah — one
   b. Classified as to direction:
      (1) Some from God to man.
      (2) Some from God through man.
      (3) All were from God.
2. There are thirty-eight primary miracles of Christ.
3. There are forty secondary miracles of Christ.
4. There are fifteen miracles by the Apostles.
5. Tabulation of the miracles in the Gospel of Luke:
   a. Number of miracles:
      (1) twenty-six primary
      (2) five secondary
   b. People who performed them:
      (1) The Lord
         4:28-30*; 4:31-37; 4:38, 39; 4:40, 41*; 5:1-11; 5:12-15; 5:17-26; 6:6-11; 6:17-20*; 7:1-10; 7: 11-15; 7:21; 8:2, 3*; 8:22-25; 8:26-39; 8:41,

42, 49, 56; 8:43-48; 9:11-17*; 9:37-43; 11:14-23; 13:10-17; 14:1-6; 17:11-19; 18:35-43; 22:50, 51; 24:1-7; 24:50, 51

(*Denotes secondary miracle.)

(2) Others:
    (a) Angel Gabriel   — 1:11-23, 57, 59
    (b) Holy Ghost   — 3:21, 22
    (c) God   — 9:28-37
    (d) Seventy Disciples — 10:17

c. Areas of activity:
  (1) Miracles of raising the dead — 7:11-15; 8:41; 42, 49, 56; 24:1-7
  (2) Miracles of exorcising devils — 4:33-37; 8:2-3; 8:26-39; 9:14-23; 9:37-43
  (3) Miracles of healing — 4:38, 39; 4:40, 41; 5:12-16; 5:17-26; 6:6-10; 6:17-20; 7:1-10; 8:43-48; 13:11-17; 14:1-6; 17:11-19; 18:35-43; 22:50, 51
  (4) Miracles over forces of nature — 5:1-11; 8:22-25; 9:11-17

6. Tabulation of the sixty-seven primary miracles of the New Testament. (When there is more than one reference given for a miracle, only the first is listed.)

Matthew	9:27	Matthew	15:21	Luke	4:30	John	9:1	Acts	9:36
	9:32		15:32		5:1		11:43		12:4
	8:2		17:14		7:11		21:1		12:21
	8:5		17:24		9:28	Acts	2:1		13:6
	8:14		20:3-		10:17		2:43		14:8
	8:26		21:18		4:33		4:16		16:18
	8:28	Mark	7:31		13:11		5:1		16:23
	9:2		8:22		14:1		5:12		19:11
	9:2-		6:7		17:11		5:17		20:9
	9:23		9:38		22:50		6:8		28:3
	12:10		1:23	John	2:1		8:6		28:7
	12:22		16:20		4:46		8:39		
	14:25	Luke	1:11		5:1		9:3		
	14:19		3:21		5:2-4		9:33		

7. Tabulation of the sixty-two Old Testament miracles.

Genesis	19:26	Exodus	16:15	II Samuel	24:15	II Kings	4:31-37
Exodus	3:2		17:6	I Kings	13:1-5		4:38-41
	7:8-12	Numbers	11:31		13:24		4:42-44
	7:19-25		12:10		17:6		5:14
	8:5-15		16:31-33		17:16		5:27
	8:16-19		17:8		17:17-23		6:6
	8:21-32		21:9		18:38		6:17-18
	9:1-7		22:28-30		19:5-8		7:1-6
	9:8-12	Joshua	3:15-17		19:11-13		13:21
	9:13-26		6:20	II Kings	1:9-16		19:35
	10:12-15		10:12-14		2:11		20:8-11
	10:21-23	Judges	6:21		2:14	Daniel	3:23-27
	12:29		6:36-40		2:21-22		6:22
	13:21		15:15-19		2:24	Joel	1:17
	14:21-22	I Samuel	5:3-5		3:20		
	15:23-25		12:16-19		4:3-6		

I. EXPLANATION

1. Make an outline of the miracle. This should follow the order of Scripture, with verse designations accompanying each major and minor division.

2. Note the term designating the miracle. Does it imply wonder, power, or purpose?

3. What does the miracle evidence regarding the human agent who performed it? (A study of the spiritual background of the agent would prove fruitful.)

4. What does the miracle reveal about the *nature* of God? (Which attributes are especially stressed?)

5. What does the miracle reveal about the *work* of God? (What is His normal means? What prompts Him to work in this unusual manner for His people?) What would those who watched have learned from it?

6. What command or prayer brought forth the miracle? (State this in Scriptural form.)

7. In the light of the total impact of Scripture, why do you think the miracle was recorded in Scripture? (See John

20:30, 31 for an overt expression of such purpose.) What one main truth does this miracle teach?

8. Construct a chart describing in parallel columns the realm, occasion, people, means, results, and reactions of the miracle. Where there are two or more miracles recorded in a passage, or where you desire to compare a number of miracles in a particular book, record these factors on the same chart and draw your conclusions.

II. EXEMPLIFICATION

First Draught of Fishes — Luke 5:1-11

1. *Make an outline of the miracle.*
   - I. Jesus preaches God's message (5:1-3)
     - a. Before pressing crowd (v. 1)
     - b. By Lake Gennesaret (v. 1)
     - c. Sees empty fishing boats (v. 2)
     - d. Enlists aid of Simon (v. 3)
   - II. Jesus commands fishermen to launch out again (5:4, 5)
     - a. Tells Simon to cast his nets (v. 4)
     - b. Simon submits to command (v. 5)
   - III. The resulting miracle (5:6, 7)
     - a. Huge catch (v. 6)
     - b. Nets break (v. 7)
     - c. Boats almost sink, so many fish (v. 7)
   - IV. Fishermen's awe (5:8-10)
     - a. Peter falls on knees (v. 8)
     - b. Others awe-struck too (v. 9, 10)
     - c. Jesus comforts them (v. 10)
     - d. Jesus commissions them (v. 10)

2. *Note the term designating the miracle.*
   No term for "miracle" is used in this passage, but the phrase ". . . he was astonished, and all that

were with him," (5:9) emphasizes its unusual character.

3. *What does the miracle evidence about the human agent who performed it?*

Jesus, who performed it, must have been endowed with supernatural powers.

4. *What does the miracle reveal about the nature of God?*

It reveals that if we trust God, He will supply us with more than enough to satisfy our needs.

5. *What does the miracle reveal about the work of God?*

God can work successfully in our lives only when we yield our wills to Him. The fishermen had to trust Him and launch out again after a wasted effort before realizing how God could work in their lives.

6. *What command or prayer brought forth the miracle?*

Luke 5:4 — "Launch out into the deep and let your nets down for a draught."

7. *In the light of the total impact of Scripture, why do you think the miracle was recorded in the Bible?*

To show in a metaphorical way that these fishermen will henceforth be fishers of men. Also gives further proof of His supernatural nature.

8. *Four miracles in Mark 4:35–5:43 compared.*

Conclusions: These four demonstrations of power covered four vast realms of human need. In each case there was no human hope. A perfect restoration resulted in each case, but the disciples, with all their privileges, reacted only in amazement or in sheer misunderstanding. Hearing the truth does not insure either grasping it or practicing it. Am I responding in faith to these demonstrations of God's miraculous power?

Miracle	Realm	Occasion	People	Means	Results	Reactions
a. The Storm 4:35-41	Nature	Helplessness (no hope of deliverance)	Experienced navigators, His disciples	Spoken word	Great calm	Amazement; "Who is this?"; Christ's rebuke
b. The Demoniac 5:1-20	Spirt world	Helplessness (chained among the tombs)	Demon possessed man	Spoken word	"Clothed and in his right mind"	Rebellion of the onlookers; faith of the healed man.
c. The Woman 5:24-34	Physical health	Helplessness (no help from doctor)	Woman with flow of blood	Touch of his garments	Healing	Disciples' lack of understanding; the woman's faith
d. Jairus' Daughter 5:21-24; 35-43	Physical death	Helplessness (no help from doctors)	Dead girl	Spoken word	Restoration to life	Amazement of disciples

BIBLE STUDY OF BIBLE PARABLES

INTRODUCTION

A parable is a form of argument. It teaches a spiritual truth by analogy from a natural situation. The word "parable" implies a "placing along side of" for purposes of comparison. It may or may not be a true story (which in itself is unimportant), since the essential element is the spiritual lesson to be taught.

Our Lord, in whose teachings parables are most frequent and prominent, explained that He taught in this manner so as to hide the truth from the idly curious, and to reveal it only to His sincere followers (Mark 4:11, 12), hence we need spiritual wisdom and perception in their interpretation.

Certain rules must be borne in mind. It is important to see the story against the background of the social customs of the time in which it was told. We must determine how much of the parable is interpreted by the speaker or by the context in which it is found.

Two dangers must be guarded against. Do not try to establish any doctrine on a parable. Be wary of any interpretation that does not square with the clear teaching of Scripture. Build on doctrinal passages, and use parables for what they were given to be, illustrations of the truth. Furthermore, be careful never to press a parable too far. No analogy can be pressed in *all* its details. Find the one central teaching of the story, and beware of reading into it any further meaning.

There are a few parables in the Old Testament, but the bulk of them occur in the teachings of Christ in the synoptic Gospels. (John omits all reference to them.) It would seem that many of them deal with the doctrine of the kingdom and with matters of eschatology, though matters of practical daily duty are not overlooked.

The following classifications will prove helpful in introducing the student to a fruitful line of personal study.

Outstanding Old Testament Parables

1. Judges 9:8-15
2. II Samuel 12:1-4
3. II Samuel 14:5-7

Major New Testament Parables

1. Contrasted Foundations (Matt. 7:24-27)
2. Sheep in the Pit (Matt. 12:11, 12)
3. The Creditor and the Two Debtors (Luke 7:41-43)
4. Sower, Seed, Soil (Matt. 13:3-23; Mark 4:3-20; Luke 8:5-13)
5. Tares and Wheat (Matt. 13:24-30)
6. Blade, Ear, Full Corn (Mark 4:26-29)
7. Mustard Seed (Matt. 13:31, 32; Mark 4:30-32; Luke 13:18, 19)
8. Leaven and Meal (Matt. 13:33; Luke 13:20, 21)
9. Hidden Treasure in the Field (Matt. 13:44)
10. Pearl of Great Price (Matt. 13:45, 46)
11. Dragnet (Matt. 13:47, 48)
12. Unmerciful Servant (Matt. 18:23-25)
13. Good Samaritan (Luke 10:25-37)
14. Good Shepherd (John 10:1-18)
15. Friend and Loaves (Luke 11:5-8)
16. Rich Fool (Luke 12:16-21)
17. Faithfulness of Stewards (Luke 12:35-48)
18. Barren Fig Tree (Luke 13:6, 7)
19. The Ambitious Guest (Luke 14:7-11)
20. Excuses for Nonattendance (Luke 14:12-24)
21. Lost Sheep (Luke 15:3-7; Matt. 18:12-14)
22. Lost Silver (Luke 15:8-10)
23. Lost Son (Luke 15:11-32)

24. Unjust Steward (Luke 16:1-8)
25. Rich Man and Lazarus (Luke 16:19-31)
26. Unjust Judge (Luke 18:1-8)
27. Pharisees and Publicans (Luke 18:9-14)
28. Laborers in the Vineyard (Matt. 20:1-16)
29. Servants and Pounds (Luke 19:11-27)
30. The Call to the Vineyard (Matt. 21:28-31)
31. The Wicked Husbandman (Matt. 21:33-43)
32. Marriage Feast (Matt. 22:1-14)
33. Servant and Fellow Servants (Matt. 24:45-51)
34. Wise and Foolish Virgins (Matt. 25:1-13)
35. Talents (Matt. 25:14-30)
36. Sheep and Goats (Matt. 25:31-46)

Minor New Testament Parables

1. New Cloth — Old Garments (Matt. 9:16; Mark 2:21; Luke 5:36)
2. New Wine — Old Bottles (Matt. 9:17; Mark 2:22; Luke 5:37-38)
3. Old and New Wine (Luke 5:39)
4. Blind Leaders (Luke 6:36; Matt. 15:14)
5. The Strong Man (Matt. 12:29; Mark 3:27; Luke 11:21, 22)
6. The Empty House (Matt. 12:43-45; Luke 11:24-26)
7. Householder (Matt. 13:52)
8. Things that Defile (Matt. 15:11-20)
9. Leaven of Pharisees (Matt. 16:6-12; Mark 8:15-21; Luke 12:1)
10. Servant and Master (Luke 17:7-9)
11. Fig Tree and Summer (Matt. 24:32; Mark 13:38; Luke 21:30)
12. Porter to Watch (Mark 13:34-36)

Classifications by Subject Matter (numbers refer to previous lists)

1. *Parables of the Kingdom*
   (No. 4, 5, 6, 7, 8, 9, 10, 11, 12, 17, 19, 20, 24, 28, 29, 31, 32, 34, 35, 36)
2. *Duties to God and Man*
   (No. 1, 2, 3, 13, 15, 16, 18, 25, 30)
3. *God's Attitude toward Men*
   (No. 14, 21, 22, 23, 26, 27, 33)
4. *Responsibility of Stewardship*
   (No. 7, 12, 17, 24, 26, 29, 30, 34, 36)
5. *Blessedness of Heart*
   (No. 7, 10 minor)
6. *Revealing Divine Character Attributes*
   (No. 13, 14, 33, 37) (No. 10 minor)
7. *Duty of Vigilance*
   (No. 11, 12 minor)
8. *Dealing with Money; talents, pounds, pence*
   (No. 28, 29, 36)

I. EXPLANATION

1. What occasion provoked the telling of this parable?
2. Note the details, customs, and practices which form the natural part of the parable. This involves gathering information on the manner of living referred to.
3. To whom was the parable told? What one lesson does it teach? Can you put yourself in their place and determine what they would have understood from it?
4. What other Bible passages teach the truth that this parable illustrates? Is the parable interpreted as a whole or in part anywhere in Scripture? If so, note the Scripture reference and the nature of the interpretation.
5. Are there clues for the interpretation of the parable in its immediate context?
6. What is its central teaching? Remember, that a parable must not be forced to "walk on all fours," but is given

to set forth one primary truth. How can you apply this truth to your own experience this very week?

7. Write a modern parable, using present-day situations and customs, to teach the same truth. This is a valuable test to see how well you comprehend the parable and how well you can adapt it to a modern setting.

II. EXEMPLIFICATION

The Lost Sheep (Matthew 18:10-14).

1. *What occasion provoked the telling of this parable?*
   Jesus' general teaching regarding God's concern for little children (see vv. 1-11).

2. *Note the details, customs, and practices which form the natural part of the parable.*
   a. A man owns a herd of sheep, a common thing in that locality.
   b. If he comes to the sheepfold and finds one missing, he goes in search of that one. (Must he not insure the life of one in order to gain the confidence of all? Does he not know them all and desire not to lose a single one?)

3. *To whom was the parable told?*
   The disciples. They must have seen God's love for every individual unfolded, and God's joy at the recovery of one who had strayed.

4. *Is the parable interpreted as a whole or in part anywhere in Scripture?*
   Verse 14 states Jesus' own interpretation, and other passages, such as II Peter 3:9 and Luke 15:7, 10, 24 reinforce it.

5. *Are there any clues for the interpretation of the parable in its immediate context?*
   The entire setting, the question in verse 1, and Jesus' specific statements in verses 3-6, 10, 14.

6. *What is its central teaching?*

To God, the lost sinner represents great value, great enough to warrant an intense search and great joy upon recovery. (If you speak of a thing as "lost" you imply its value; otherwise you simply refer to it as "misplaced," or "discarded.")

7. *Write a modern parable.*

A housewife could not find her wedding ring, so she turned the house upside down looking for it. Finally, in desperation, she searched through the incinerator. When she found it she called her family together to rejoice over what was "lost." But she never spoke of the garbage, in which it lay hidden, as lost.

BIBLE STUDY OF BIBLE POETRY

INTRODUCTION

Hebrew poetry possesses certain distinctive forms, and since a considerable portion of Scripture is set in poetic form, it is important to know its distinguishing features.

For the study of Bible poetry it is helpful to have a modern version in which the poetic structure is apparent. The versification in the King James version is an obstacle in this regard.

The distinguishing quality of Hebrew poetry is its *parallelism*, rather than any system of rhyme. Though there is no limit to the forms, and some are quite intricate and complex, we can get the sense of this parallelism by noting these basic forms:

A couplet:

> The Lord of Hosts is with us;
> The God of Jacob is our refuge.

Here the repetition of the thought forms a *synonymous* parallelism. But it could as easily be *antithetical* or *pro-*

gressive, contrasting one thought with another, or proceeding from it as from proposition to conclusion, from cause to effect, etc.

A *triplet*:

He maketh wars to cease unto the end of the earth;
He breaketh the bow, and cutteth the spear in sunder;
He burneth the chariots in the fire.

A *quatrain*:

    With the merciful
       Thou wilt show thyself merciful;
    With the perfect man
       Thou wilt show thyself perfect.

Here the thought alternates, line three repeating line one, and line four repeating line two. But this may be introverted with the outer two lines and the inner two lines corresponding.

Variations on these forms include interwoven couplets, double triplets, reversed double triplets, and the "envelope" figure in which two outer lines are equivalent and any number of intermediate lines amplify the thought.

These verse forms in turn are combined into various forms of stanzas, sometimes using several similar verse forms (such as four quatrains), sometimes alternating verse forms (Psalm one is constructed with a triplet, a quatrain, a double quatrain, a couplet, a quatrain, and a reversed quatrain), sometimes adopting various strophic and antistrophic combinations.

But in all these forms the basic parallelism (whether of words or of thoughts) is apparent, and it will be seen that an understanding of the literary form will aid in appreciation and interpretation.

Poetic Portions of Scripture Other than the Psalms

The books which are usually considered the poetical books are Job, Psalms, and Proverbs. Some add Ecclesiastes and the Song of Solomon. By the Jews, "they were designated by a mnemonic word 'Books of Emeth' (truth)," the word *emeth* being composed of the first letter of the names of each of the poetical books, thus *iov, meshallim, tehillim* (Job, Proverbs, Psalms), (Young, E. J., *An Introduction to the Old Testament*, p. 281). Besides these major books, there are also scattered poetical sections in the Old and New Testaments. Some of these portions are listed below.

Genesis 4:23, 24, Lamech to his wives
Genesis 49:2-27, Traditional oracle
Exodus 15:1-18, Song of Moses
Exodus 15:21, Song of Miriam
Numbers 21:27-30, Song of the Ballad Singers
Numbers 23:7-10, Song of Balaam
Numbers 24:3-9, 15-19, Traditional oracle
Deuteronomy 32:1-47, Song of Moses
Deuteronomy 33:1-29, Traditional oracle
Joshua 10:12-14, Song of Joshua
Judges 5:1-31, Song of Deborah and Barak
Ruth 1:16, 17, Song of Ruth
I Samuel 2:1-10, Song of Hannah
II Samuel 1:17-27, Lament of David for Saul and Jonathan
II Samuel 3:33-34, David's lament for Abner
II Samuel 7:10-16, Traditional oracle
II Samuel 22:2-51, David's song of victory
II Samuel 23:1-7, David's last words
I Chronicles 16:8-36, David's thanksgiving
Job 3:1—42:6, The epic of Job
Song of Solomon 1:1-9; 2:7, 8; 3:5, Collection of antenuptial songs

Song of Solomon 3:6; 5:1; 6:3, 4; 8:4; Wedding songs
Jeremiah 9:17-22, Dirge over the fallen nation
Lamentations 1, 2, 3, 4, 5, Dirges over the fallen nation
Ezekiel 27:25–28:23, Prophecies against Tyre
Ezekiel 19:1-14, Lamentation for Israel's princes
Hosea 2:1-15, The Chastisement of Israel
Habakkuk 3:1-19, Habakkuk's prayer
Matthew 10:24, Jesus (Synonymous parallelism)
Luke 1:46-55, Mary (Magnificat)
Luke 1:68-79, Zacharias (Benedictus)
Luke 2:10-12, Angels (Gloria)
Luke 2:29-32, Simeon (Nunc Dimittis)
Luke 6:41, Jesus (Antithetic form)
Luke 7:31, 32, Jesus (Mixed form)
Luke 9:23, Jesus (Synthetic form)

The Book of Psalms

1. Introduction

The Hebrew title of this book is "Praise," or the "Book of Praises," which indicates that the main contents of the book are praise, prayer, and worship. The early Christian fathers called the book the Psalter.

The Psalms is the national Hymnbook of Israel. Great men have made the following statements concerning the Psalms: Luther — "A little Bible." Spurgeon — "The Christian's map of experience." "Oh, to be shut up in a cave with David, to hear him sing!" Gladstone — "All the wonders of Greek civilization heaped together are less wonderful than the Book of Psalms" (Henrietta C. Mears, *Scripture Panorama Series*, p. 28).

2. Authorship

Almost all the information we have of the Psalms concerning the authors comes from the individual headings.

These "superscriptions" were furnished by the ancient Hebrew editors of the Psalm Book.

a. Psalm 90, attributed to Moses, is the earliest of the Psalms.
b. Psalms 72, 127, Solomonic.
c. Asaph wrote twelve Psalms.
d. Sons of Korah wrote eleven of the Psalms.
e. David wrote seventy-three Psalms.
f. Some are anonymous: Psalms 1, 2, 91, 100, 107, 119, 121, 137.

3. *Classification*

The Psalms may be classified and outlined in various ways.

a. Many feel this following fivefold division most helpful (the ancient Hebrew divisions).

   (1) Book 1 — Psalms 1:41:
       Man, his state of blessedness, fall, and recovery. Ends with doxology and a double Amen.

   (2) Book 2 — Psalms 42-72:
       Israel, her ruin, her Redeemer, and her redemption. Ends the same way, with slight addition.

   (3) Book 3 — Psalms 73-89:
       The Sanctuary, looking forward to its establishment in the fullness of blessing. Ends with Amen.

   (4) Book 4 — Psalms 90-106:
       The Earth, blessing needed, anticipated, and enjoyed. Ends with doxology, Amen, and hallelujah.

   (5) Book 5 — Psalms 107-150:
       The Word of God, ends with repeated hallelujahs.

4. *A Subject Classification*

    a. Prayer: 86, 90, 102, 142
    b. Praise: 8, 19, 81, 92, 95-100, 145-150
    c. Petition for deliverance: 6, 16, 38, 39, 41
    d. Confession of faith: 8, 33, 94, 104
    e. Confession of sin: 6, 32, 38, 51, 102, 130
    f. Instruction: 37, 45, 49, 78, 103-107
    g. Deprecation: 35, 59, 69, 105
    h. Intercession
       (1) For the king: 20, 21, 51
       (2) For Israel and the nations: 67
       (3) For the House of David: 89
       (4) For Zion: 121, 122, 132
    i. Meditation: 49, 73, 94
    j. Exaltation of the law: 19, 119
    k. Expectation of the Messiah: 16, 22, 24, 40, 68, 69, 110, 118 (G. Manley, *The New Bible Handbook*, pp. 197-198).

5. *Specific Classifications*

    a. Didactic Psalms:
       (1) On the character of good and bad men, their happiness and misery: 1, 5, 7, 9, 12, 14, 15, 17, 24, 25, 32, 34, 36, 37, 50, 52, 53, 58, 73, 75, 84, 91, 92, 94, 112, 119, 121, 125, 127, 128, 133
       (2) On the excellency of the divine law: 19, 119
       (3) On the vanity of human life: 39, 49, 90
       (4) On duties of rulers: 82, 101
       (5) On humility: 131
    b. Reflective and Didactic Psalms:
       (1) The lessons of Israel's history regarding Jehovah's character and demands: 77, 78, 81, 106, 127, 144
       (2) The value of the law: 19, 119

    (3) The prophetic standards of right and wrong: 15, 36, 50

    (4) The fate of the righteous and the wicked: 1, 14, 32, 34, 37, 49, 52, 73, 82, 91, 94, 112, 125, 128, 133

c. Psalms of praise and adoration:

    (1) Acknowledgment of God's goodness and mercy, and particularly of His care of good men: 23, 34, 36, 91, 100, 103, 107, 117, 121, 145, 146

    (2) Acknowledgment of His power, glory, and attributes generally: 8, 19, 24, 29, 33, 47, 50, 65, 66, 76, 77, 93, 95-97, 99, 104, 111, 113, 115, 134, 139, 147, 148, 150

d. Psalms of thanksgiving:

    (1) For mercy to individuals: 9, 18, 22, 30, 40, 75, 103, 108, 116, 118, 138, 144

    (2) For mercy to the Israelites generally: 46, 48, 65, 66, 68, 76, 81, 85, 98, 105, 124, 126, 129, 135, 136, 149

e. Devotional Psalms:

    (1) Expressive of penitence: 6, 25, 32, 38, 51, 102, 130, 143

    (2) Expressive of trust under affliction: 3, 16, 27, 31, 54, 56, 57, 61, 62, 71, 86

    (3) Expressive of extreme dejection, though not without hope: 13, 22, 69, 77, 88, 143

    (4) Prayers in time of severe distress: 4, 5, 11, 28, 41, 55, 59, 64, 70, 109, 120, 140, 141, 143

    (5) Prayers when deprived of public worship: 42, 43, 63, 84

    (6) Prayers for help in upright cause: 7, 17, 26, 35

    (7) Prayers in time of affliction and persecution: 44, 60, 74, 79, 80, 83, 89, 94, 102, 129, 137

    (8) Prayers of intercession: 20, 67, 122, 132, 144

   (9) Prayers for Jehovah's forgiveness and favor:
        38, 51, 85, 90
  (10) Petitions for deliverance from cruel, remorse-
        less foes: 5, 6, 7, 10, 12, 13, 17, 22, 25, 28, 31,
        40, 54, 55, 57, 64, 69, 71, 120, 140, 141, 142,
        143, 144
  (11) Petitions for deliverance from heathen oppres-
        sors: 44, 59, 60, 74, 79, 80
  (12) Petitions for vindication and restoration: 26, 27,
        41, 67, 86, 88, 102, 122, 123
  (13) Imprecatory Psalms: 35, 58, 83, 109, 129, 137
f. Hymns of praise and thanksgiving:
   (1) For Jehovah's just and gracious rule: 9, 33, 57,
        75, 92, 107, 113, 138, 145
   (2) Thanksgiving for Jehovah's guidance and care
        in Israel's past: 105, 111, 114, 117
   (3) Thanksgiving for recent national deliverances:
        18, 66, 68, 76, 124, 126, 118
   (4) Thanksgiving for Jerusalem and the Temple:
        48, 84, 87
   (5) Praise and thanksgiving for personal deliver-
        ances: 30, 66, 116
   (6) Liturgical hymns: 81, 100, 115, 134, 135, 136,
        146, 147, 148, 149, 150
g. Hymns of adoration and trust:
   (1) Jehovah's majesty and goodness revealed in
        nature: 8, 19, 29, 89, 104
   (2) Jehovah's loving provisions for man: 36, 65,
        103, 139, 144
   (3) The assurance of Jehovah's protection: 3, 4, 11,
        16, 40, 43, 56, 62, 63, 102, 121, 130, 131
h. Psalms eminently prophetical: 2, 16, 22, 40, 45, 68,
    69, 72, 97, 110, 118, mostly Messianic.
i. Historical Psalms: 78, 105, 106
j. The kingly and Messianic Psalms:

    (1) Petitions for King's welfare and success: 20, 21, 61, 72

    (2) The divine promises to David and his successors: 2, 89, 110, 132

    (3) The ideals of an upright ruler: 101

    (4) The rule of Jehovah the divine King: 22, 24, 47, 93, 95, 96, 97, 98, 99

6. *Further subdivisions of the books*

  a. Psalms of Korah, 42-49
  b. Psalms of Asaph, 73-83
  c. Michtam Psalms, 56-60
  d. Theocratic Psalms, 95-100
  e. Hallel Psalms, 113-118
  f. Psalms of Ascent, 120-134
  g. Hallelujah Psalms, 146-150

I. EXPLANATION

1. If you are studying a psalm, classify it as to type. What is the general tone of this poetic portion? Is it cheerful, repentant, hostile? Is it a song, a prayer, a meditation, a lesson?

2. What is the setting and background of the poetic portion? Sketch what you can of the author, the date, and the one to whom it was directed. Use outside helps, where necessary, to gather this information.

3. Is there a title? Find out what it means. Give the portion a title of your own in the light of its contents.

4. Read the passage at least five times, using several versions and noticing the differences.

5. List the words used most frequently, giving verse references for each.

6. Choose a key verse and memorize it, together with any other verses of special significance.

7. What is its main theme? Main appeal? Main purpose?
8. What predictive allusions are there to the New Testament? What allusions to other portions of the Old Testament?
9. What are the outstanding literary features of the poem? Can you discover the poetic form? What lines correspond to what other lines? Do they repeat, contrast, expand, or develop the previous thoughts?
10. What are the doctrinal teachings? The practical applications? What spiritual truths are taught here that will help you to lead a better Christian life?

II. EXEMPLIFICATION
Psalm 27

1. *Classify the psalm as to type*
   A devotional psalm, expressive of trust under affliction.
2. *The setting and background*
   David is the author, and the Septuagint suggests that he wrote it before one of his three anointings. It seems most appropriate before the anointing recorded in II Samuel 2:4. It was a private song of praise and petition.
3. *The title*
   No title is ascribed to the psalm, but we may well call it "A Confident Prayer for Deliverance."
4. *Note the difference in versions*

KING JAMES VERSION	REVISED STANDARD VERSION
When the wicked, even mine enemies and my foes came upon me to eat up my flesh, they stumbled and fell (v. 2).	When evil doers assail me, uttering slanders against me, my adversaries and my foes, they shall stumble and fall (v. 2).

Hear, O LORD, when I cry with my voice: have mercy also upon me, and answer me (v. 7).	Hear, O LORD, when I cry aloud, be gracious to me and answer me! (v. 7).
When thou saidst, Seek ye my face; my heart said unto thee, Thy face, LORD, will I seek (v. 8).	Thou has said, "Seek ye my face." My heart says to thee, "Thy face, Lord, do I seek" (v. 8).
When my father and my mother forsake me, then the LORD will take me up (v. 10).	For my father and my mother have forsaken me, but the LORD will take me up (v. 10).
I had fainted, unless I had believed to see the goodness of the LORD in the land of the living (v. 13).	I believe that I shall see the goodness of the LORD in the land of the living! (v. 13).
Wait on the LORD: be of good courage, and he shall strengthen thine heart: wait, I say, on the LORD (v. 14).	Wait for the LORD, be strong, and let your heart take courage; yea, wait for the LORD! (v. 14).

5. *List the words used most frequently*
    a. LORD (Jehovah) vv. 1, 1, 4, 4, 4, 6, 7, 8, 10, 11, 13, 14, 14 (thirteen times)
    b. Fear (or afraid) vv. 1, 1, 3 (three times)
    c. Evildoers (or adversaries, foes, enemies) vv. 2, 2, 2, 6, 11, 12 (six times)

6. *Key verse*
    Verse 4 expresses the innermost desire of David's heart.

7. *The main theme, main appeal, and main purpose*

   David wrote to express in song his deep feeling of confidence in God despite the hostility of his enemies. The preservation of the psalm in Scripture enables us to be challenged by David's example and to seek the same attitude.

8. *Allusions to other portions of Scripture*

   There are no predictive elements in the psalm. But the same sentiment of confidence finds expression in Psalms 46:1-3; 84:10-12; Isaiah 60:19, 20 and elsewhere.

9. *Outstanding literary features of the poem*

   The psalm is a series of poetic stanzas, with a distinct break between verses 6 and 7. Praise is followed by petition, which at the close turns again to praise.

10. *Doctrinal teachings and practical applications*
    a. Confidence grows out of relationship to God, v. 1
    b. There is singleness of purpose in desiring God's fellowship, v. 4
    c. Prayer is a response to God's desire, v. 8
    d. Confidence leads not to complacency, but concern, vv. 9-12

BIBLE STUDY OF BIBLE WRITERS

INTRODUCTION

This type of study views the Bible as a library to which each author has made his distinctive contribution, and seeks to analyze the particular contribution of each. It consists therefore of making an inductive study of the author's writings (and sermons) in regard to each division of theology and of drawing general conclusions.

It is especially recommended that such an approach be

applied to the New Testament. Begin by studying James or Jude, and then proceed to those writers who bulk larger in the amount of their writing.

Authors and Material

    James, The Epistle of James; Acts 15:13-21
    Jude, The Epistle of Jude
    Matthew, The Gospel according to Matthew
    Mark, The Gospel according to Mark
    Luke, The Gospel according to Luke; Acts
    Peter, I and II Peter, Acts 2:14-36, 38-40; 3:6, 12-26; 4:8-12, 19, 20; 5:29-32; 10:28, 29, 34-43, 47, 48; 11:5-18; 15:7-11
    John, The Gospel according to John; I, II and III John; Revelation
    An anonymous writer, The Epistle to the Hebrews
    Paul, Romans; I and II Corinthians; Galatians; Ephesians; Philippians; Colossians; I and II Thessalonians; I and II Timothy; Titus; Philemon; Acts 9: 20, 22; 13:10, 11, 16-41, 46-48; 14:15-17; 16:31; 17:2, 3, 22-31; 19:2-6; 20:18-35; 22:1-21; 23:1, 3, 5, 6; 24:10-21; 25:10, 11; 26:1-23, 25-27, 29; 27:21-26, 31, 33, 34; 28:17-20, 23, 25-28, 31

I. EXPLANATION

A. List all verses referring in any way to the following subjects: God (The Father), Christ, the Holy Spirit, Sin, Justification, Sanctification, and Future Things.

B. Organize these references into an outline which shows their relationships.

C. Summarize by (1) stating the distinctive characteristics of the writer's viewpoint on each division of theology, (2) listing any problems which you find incapable of solution, and (3) noting any unusual aspects of the writer's teaching.

D. The final step is to compare the theological contribution of the separate writers and to integrate them into an exhaustive Theology of the New Testament.

II.   EXEMPLIFICATION

A. *The Theology of James*

1. *Doctrine of God*
    a. *His nature*
        (1) Unity, 2:19 "God is one"
        (2) Personality
            (a) Abraham was His friend, 2:23; James is His servant, 1:1
            (b) Men are made in His likeness, 3:9
            (c) He is Father, 1:17; 3:9
        (3) Immutability, 1:17 "No variation or shadow due to change"
    b. *His character*
        (1) Impeccability, 1:13 "God cannot be tempted"
        (2) Righteousness, 1:20 "the righteousness of God"
            (a) He is the source of no evil, of all good, 1:13; 1:17
            (b) He expects pure and sacrificial living, 1:27
            (c) He is impartial 2:5, "chosen the poor of this world . . . heirs"
            (d) He opposes the world, 4:4
            (e) He hates pride, but rewards humility, 4:6
            (f) He is lawgiver and judge, 4:12
        (3) Mercy
            (a) He is generous and willing in meeting human needs, 1:5

        (b) He rewards faithful endurance, 1:12
        (c) He purposed our salvation, 1:18
        (d) He yearns for our friendship, 4:5
        (e) He awaits our turning to Him, 4:8

c. *His names*
    (1) God (seventeen times)
    (2) The Lord, 1:8; 3:9; 4:10; 4:15; 5:10, 11, 14, 15
    (3) Father of Lights, 1:17
    (4) Father, 3:9; 1:27
    (5) The Lord of Hosts, 5:4

2. *Doctrine of Christ*

  a. *His names*
      (1) Lord Jesus Christ, 1:1; 2:1
      (2) The Lord, 5:7, 8
      (3) The Lord of Glory, 2:1
      (4) The Judge, 5:9

  b. *His character*
      (1) He is glorious, "the glory," 2:1
      (2) He is preëminent, "The Lord," 1:1; 2:1
      (3) He is deity (by the ambiguity with which "The Lord" is used of the Father and of Christ)

  c. *His work*
      (1) He superintends Christians, 1:1 (James is His servant)
      (2) He is coming again, 5:7-9
        (a) Certainly
        (b) As a reward to the faithful
        (c) As a judge

  d. *Problems*: Christ is only mentioned five times in the entire epistle.
      Notable omissions: No reference to (a)

His earthly life (b) Messianic fulfillment (c) The atonement (d) His resurrection

3. *Doctrine of the Holy Spirit*

There is in this epistle no reference to the Holy Spirit, unless 4:5 be interpreted to speak of Him, rather than the human spirit. The context favors viewing this as the human spirit, since God is seen seeking "submission" and "humility," and the interplay seems to be between a yearning God and a stubborn human will.

4. *Doctrine of Sin*
   a. *Its nature*
      (1) Transgression of the law, 2:10
      (2) Wilfulness, 4:17 (knowing right but doing wrong)
      (3) Universality, 3:2 (there is no sinless perfection)
   b. *Its source*
      (1) God is never implicated, 1:13 (only good, never evil, comes from Him)
      (2) Man's inner nature is evil, 1:14; 4:1 (passions)
      (3) A dichotomy exists within man, 1:7; 4:8 ("double-minded")
          (a) Self-deception, 1:16, 22, 26
          (b) Results in hypocrisy outwardly, 2:14-17; 3:14; 4:1-4
      (4) The devil is implicated, 3:15; 4:7
   c. *Its results*
      (1) Judgment, 2:12, 13; 3:1; 4:12; 5:9
      (2) Sickness, 5:15
      (3) Death, 1:15; 5:20
   d. *Its expression*
      (1) Anger, 1:20

       (2) Filthiness, 1:21
       (3) Partiality, 2:4, 9
       (4) Adultery, 2:11
       (5) Murder, 2:11
       (6) Mercilessness, 2:12
       (7) Hypocrisy, 2:14-17; 3:14; 4:3
       (8) Uncontrollable tongue, 1:19, 26; 3:2-12; 4:11
       (9) Cursing, 3:10; 5:12
     (10) Jealousy, selfish ambition, disorder, etc. 3:16
     (11) Wars and fightings, 4:1
     (12) Enmity with God, 4:4
     (13) Pride, 4:6, 16
     (14) Evil speaking, 4:11
     (15) Complacency, 4:13–5:6
     (16) Grumbling, 5:9

  e. *Two observations*:

      (1) James emphasizes the dichotomy at a man's heart that produces self-deception, double-mindedness, hypocrisy.
      (2) The outward expression of sin emphasized is that of the tongue.

5. *Doctrine of Justification*

  a. There is a brief but precise mention of the new birth in 1:18. We are "brought forth" in fulfillment of God's will by the agency of the word of truth to be a kind of first-fruits of His creation.

  b. James' distinct contribution is his insistence on the genuineness of one's faith in God.

  c. James uses the unique word "religion" in 1:26, 27, but means by it the external aspect of one's faith, which fits well into the similar thoughts of chapter two on faith and works.

    d. James' emphasis is primarily *ethical*, rather than *evangelical*. (Rather strange in Apostolic age where primary witness was to the death and resurrection of Christ.) Solution: As intimated in Acts 15, James apparently took a mediating position, emphasizing the corresponding ethic.

6. *Doctrine of Sanctification*
    a. *The goal*
        (1) Spiritual maturity, 1:4
        (2) Future reward, 1:12
    b. *The standard*
        (1) Steadfastness, 1:2-4
        (2) Slowness to anger, 1:19, 20
        (3) Pure and undefiled religion, 1:26, 27
        (4) Impartiality, 2:1-13
        (5) Genuineness, 2:14-26
        (6) Controlled Speech, 3:1-12
        (7) Unselfishness, 3:13—4:3
        (8) Patience, 5:7-11
        (9) Dependence on God, 5:13-18
      (10) Concern for the wayward, 5:19, 20
    c. *The human quotient*
        (1) Inability to control one's self, 3:8
        (2) Instability (double-mindedness), 1:8; 4:1-8
    d. *The divine enablement*
        (1) Prayer
           (a) As a means to wisdom, 1:5-8
           (b) As a means to healing, 5:13-18
        (2) The Word of God
           (a) Preparation for its reception, 1:21
           (b) Attitude in its reception (meekness), 1:21; 3:13
           (c) Response to its reception, 1:22-25
        (3) Submission to God
           (a) Humility brings God's grace, 4:6, 10

(b) Resistance overcomes the devil, 4:7
(c) Drawing near brings God's response, 4:8
(d) True sorrow brings exaltation, 4:8b-10

(4) Expectation of Christ's coming
(a) Its time: imminent, 5:8
(b) Its effect: patience, 5:7-11

e. *Problems*:

(1) Neglect of the Holy Spirit's enablement in Christian growth.
(2) Frequency of reference to "the law" as the Christian's standard.
1:25, the perfect law; the law of liberty (2:12)
2:8, the royal law; "love thy neighbor as thyself"
2:9, convicted by the law
2:10, 11, failure in one point is violation of the entire law
4:11, judging the law

7. *Doctrine of Eschatology*
a. *References to judgment*
(1) God is judge, 4:12; 5:9
(2) Sin leads to death, 1:15; 5:20
(3) Unbelievers have no future, 1:10-12
(4) Future judgment awaits
(a) For Christians, 2:12
(b) For non-Christians, 5:1-3
(5) Future rewards await
(a) Crown of life to the faithful, 1:12
(b) Kingdom to those who love Him, 2:5
(6) The reality of hell (Gehenna), 3:6

   b. *References to Christ's second coming*
      (1) Cause for patient steadfastness, 5:7, 8
      (2) His coming is near at hand, 5:9

   c. *Observations:*
      (1) Most references seem very general. There
          appears here no clearly defined doctrine of
          judgment or the Second Advent. Conse-
          quently, there is no doctrine of a millennial
          kingdom, or the restoration of Israel, or any
          aspect pertinent to Premillennialism, except
          the imminence of Christ's return.

Chapter V

GENERAL METHODS OF SEARCHING THE SCRIPTURES

INTRODUCTION

This aid to Bible study brings together for comparison, contrast, and correlation existing outlines of material in a passage of Scripture or in an entire Bible book.

Comparison may be made between different versions of the same passage, between content outlines found in books of exposition, or between thematic, chronological, and geographical outlines of the same passage. Such study will bring greater comprehension of the passage, and will suggest many additional subjects for study.

I. *Comparison and Contrast of Versions*

The Epistle of James, Chapter 1

This presents a comparison and contrast of the *Goodspeed, Moffatt,* and Revised Standard versions. The paragraph limitations are given by noting the number of the verses included with a double line under each such paragraph limitation.

GOODSPEED	MOFFATT	REVISED STANDARD VERSION
v. 1	v. 1	v. 1
scattered over the world	dispersion	dispersion
sends greetings	greetings	greetings

		REVISED STANDARD
GOODSPEED	MOFFATT	VERSION

vv. 2-4

v. 2	v. 2	v. 2
You must find greatest joy	greet as pure joy	count it all joy
being involved in various trials	come across any sort of trial	meet various trials
v. 3	**v. 3**	**v. 3**
testing of your faith leads to steadfastness	sterling temper of your faith produces endurance	testing of your faith produces steadfastness
v. 4	**v. 4**	**v. 4**
steadfastness	let your steadfastness	let steadfastness
must have full play	be a finished product	have full effect
you must be fully and perfectly developed	you must be finished and perfect	you must be perfect and complete
without any defects	with never a defect	lacking in nothing

vv. 5-8

v. 5	v. 5	v. 5
deficient in	defective in	lacks
gives generously to everyone and does not reproach one with it afterward	gives to all men without question or reproach	gives to all men generously and without reproaching
he will give it to him	the gift will be his	it shall be given him
v. 6	**v. 6**	**v. 6**
He must ask	only let him ask	but let him ask

GOODSPEED	MOFFATT	REVISED STANDARD VERSION
without any doubt	with never a doubt	with no doubting
man who doubts	doubtful men	he who doubts
billowing sea	surge of the sea	wave of the sea
driven and blown about	whirled and swayed	driven and tossed
v. 7	v. 7	v. 7
such a man must not expect to get	that man need not imagine he will get	that person must not suppose . . . receive
v. 8	v. 8	v. 8
an irresolute person like him	double-minded creature that he is	double-minded man
who is uncertain about everything he does	wavering at every turn	unstable in his ways

vv. 9-11
===

v. 9	v. 9	v. 9
lowly brother	brother of low position	lowly brother
ought to be proud of his eminence	let exalt when he is raised	boast in his exaltation
v. 10	v. 10	v. 10
one who is rich ought to	let one who is rich	the rich in his
rejoice at being reduced in circumstances	exalt in being lowered	humiliation
Rich will disappear like a wild flower	rich will pass away like the flowers of the grass	like the flower of the grass he will pass away

GOODSPEED	MOFFATT	REVISED STANDARD VERSION
v. 11	v. 11	v. 11
heat	wind	heat
dries up the grass	withers the grass	withers the grass
flower withers	flower drops off	flower falls
all their beauty is gone	splendor of it is ruined	its beauty perishes
this is the way	so	so
rich men will fade and die in the midst of their pursuits	shall the rich fade away amid their pursuits	will the rich man fade away in the midst of his pursuits
vv. 12-18	vv. 12-19a	vv. 12-15
v. 12	v. 12	v. 12
endures trial	endures under trial	endures trial
stands the test	stood the test	stood the test
he will be given the crown	he will gain the crown	he will receive the crown
God has promised to them that love him	promised to all all who love him	promised to those who love him
v. 13	v. 13	v. 13
no one should think when he is tempted	let no one who is tried by temptation say	let no one say when he is tempted
that his temptation comes from God	my temptation comes from God	I am tempted by God
God is incapable of being tempted by what is evil	God is incapable of being tempted by evil	God cannot be tempted with evil
He does not tempt anyone	He tempts no one	He himself tempts no one

| | | REVISED
STANDARD |
GOODSPEED	MOFFATT	VERSION
v. 14	v. 14	v. 14
When anyone is tempted	everyone is tempted	each person is tempted
It is by his own desires that he is enticed and allured	as he is beguiled and allured by his own desire	when he is lured and enticed by his own desire
v. 15	v. 15	v. 15
then desire conceives	the desire conceives	then desire when it has conceived
and give birth to sin	and breeds sin	gives birth to sin
when it matures	while it matures	sin when it is full grown
it brings forth death	gives birth to death	brings forth death

vv. 16-18

v. 16	v. 16	v. 16
do not be misled	make no mistake about this	do not be deceived
my dear brothers	my beloved brothers	my beloved brothers
v. 17	v. 17	v. 17
every good gift	all we are given is good	every good endowment
every perfect present	all our endowments are faultless	every perfect gift
is from heaven	descending from above	is from heaven
comes down from the Father of the heavenly lights	from the Father of the heavenly lights	coming down from the Father of lights
about whom there	who knows no	with whom there is

GOODSPEED	MOFFATT	REVISED STANDARD VERSION
is no variation of changing shadow	change of rising and setting who casts no shadow on the earth	no variation or shadow due to change
v. 18 of his own accord he brought us into being	v. 18 it was his own will that we should be born	v. 18 of his own will he brought us forth
through the message of truth	by the word of truth	by the word of truth
so that we might be a kind of first fruits among his creatures	to be a kind of first fruits among the creatures	we should be a kind of first fruits of his creatures

vv. 19-27		vv. 19-21

| v. 19 you must understand this | v. 19a be sure of that | v. 19 know this |
| dear brothers | beloved brothers | beloved brothers |

vv. 19b-27

| everyone must be quick to hear speak be angry | let everyone be quick to listen talk be angry | let every man be quick to hear speak to anger |
| v. 20 men's anger does not produce the uprightness God wishes | v. 20 human anger does not promote divine righteousness | v. 20 anger of man does not work the righteousness of God |

v. 21
so strip yourselves of everything that soils you

in a humble spirit

let the message that has power to save your souls be planted in your hearts

v. 21
so clear away all the foul rank growth of malice

make a soil of modesty
for the word which roots itself inwardly with power to save your souls

v. 21
therefore put away all filthiness and rank growth of wickedness
receive with meekness
the implanted word which is able to save your souls

vv. 22-25

v. 22
obey the message

do not merely listen to it
deceive yourselves

v. 22
act on the word

instead of merely listening to it
deluding yourselves

v. 22
be doers of the word
not hearers only

deceiving yourselves

v. 23
anyone who merely listens to the message without obeying it
like a man who looks in a mirror at the face that nature gave him

v. 23
whoever listens and does nothing

like a man who glances at his natural face in a mirror

v. 23
if a man be a hearer of the word and not a doer

like a man who observes his natural face in a mirror

v. 24
then goes off

immediately forgets what he looked like

v. 24
he glances at himself, goes off
at once forgets what he was like

v. 24
he observes himself and goes away
at once forgets what he was like

GOODSPEED	MOFFATT	REVISED STANDARD VERSION
v. 25	v. 25	v. 25
but whoever looks at the faultless law that makes men free and keeps looking	whereas he who gazes into faultless law of freedom remains in that position	he who looks into the perfect law the law of liberty and perseveres
so that he does not just listen and forget	proving himself to be no forgetful listener	being no hearer that forgets
obeys and acts upon it	an active agent	a doer that acts
will be blessed in what he does	he will be blessed in his activity	he shall be blessed in his doing

vv. 26-27

GOODSPEED	MOFFATT	REVISED STANDARD VERSION
v. 26	v. 26	v. 26
if anyone thinks deceives himself	whoever considers deceives his own heart	if any one thinks deceives his heart
his religious observances are of no account	his religion is futile	this man's religion is vain
v. 27	v. 27	v. 27
a religious observance that is pure and stainless in the sight of God is this	pure unsoiled religion in the judgment of God means this	religion that is pure and undefiled before God and the Father is this
to look after orphans' trouble	to care for orphans' trouble	to visit orphans' affliction
keep one's self unstained by the world	keep oneself from the stain of the world	keep oneself unstained from the world

II. *Comparison and Contrast of Outlines*

The Epistle to the Colossians

The following three outlines occur in *Life Established,* by Roy L. Laurin, *The Analyzed Bible,* by G. C. Morgan, and *Outline Studies of the New Testament,* by William Moorehead. They are set forth in this fashion in order that the Bible student may note the method of outlining used by the respective authors and also that the paragraph limitations may be noted from the standpoint of agreement or disagreement between the outlines.

Life Established	*The Analyzed Bible*	*Outline Studies of the New Testament*
A. The Christian and His Christ 1:1-29	Introduction 1:1-8	A. Introduction 1:1-14
I. The Power of a True Life 1:1-12	I. The Salutation 1, 2	1. Address and greetings 1, 2
1. In Personality 1, 2, 7, 8	II. Thanksgiving 3-8	2. Thanksgiving 3-8
2. In Praise 3-6	1. Faith	a. For faith in Christ
3. In Prayer 9-12	2. Love	b. For love of saints
	3. Hope	c. For hope of glory
		3. His prayer for them 9-14
II. The Two Creations and One Creator 1:13-29	A. The Glorious Christ and His Church Provision 1:9—23:5	B. The Redeemer and His glory 1:15-23
1. Christ's relation to redemption 13, 14	Introductory Prayer 1:9-14	1. Titles as God
	1. The Need Indicated 9-12a	a. Image of Invisible God
2. Christ's relation to God 15	2. The Provision 12b-14	b. First-born of creation
	I. The Glorious Christ 15-23	c. Creator of all things
3. Christ's relation to the universe 16, 17	1. The Person 15-19	d. Eternally pre-existent
	2. The Purpose 20-23	e. Upholder of all things
4. Christ's rela-		2. His glory as Redeemer

Life Established   *The Analyzed Bible*   *Outline Studies of the New Testament*

Life Established

tion to the church 18-20
5. Christ's relation to the believer 21-29

Outline Studies of the New Testament

a. Head of the body
b. The beginning
c. First-born from dead
d. Preëminent
e. Possessor of all fullness
f. Reconcilor and Peace-maker, Sanctifier and Saviour

The Analyzed Bible

II. The Glorious Church 1:24—3
1. The Mystery of the Church 24-26
2. The Mystery of the Christian 27-29
3. The Mystery of the Christ 2:1-3

Outline Studies of the New Testament

C. Paul's Mission 1:24-29
1. Its Character 24
2. Its Glory 25, 26
3. Its Supreme Object 27
4. Its Aim 28
5. Its Support 29

Life Established

B. The Christian and His Creed 2:1-23
   I. The Preëminence of Christ 2:1-3

   II. The Perils of Christians 2:4-23
   1. Their state 5
   2. Their security 6, 7

   3. Warnings against four perils 8-23

The Analyzed Bible

Conclusion
   The reason for the statement 2:4, 5
B. The Church and Her Glorious Christ Possession 2:6—4:6
   Introductory 2:6-10
   1. The Central Injunction 6-7
   2. The Central Warning 8
   3. The Central Truth 9, 10

I. The Church Identi-

Outline Studies of the New Testament

D. Paul's Solicitude for the Church 2:1-7
1. For their unity of love 2
2. For their assured understanding 2
3. For their insight into the mystery of God 2, 3
4. For their security against delusions and snares 4
5. For their stability and order 6, 7
E. Believer's completeness in Christ 2:8-15
1. The threatening danger 8
2. Christ's infinite fullness 9
3. In Him believers are complete 10

Life Established	*The Analyzed Bible*	*Outline Studies of the New Testament*
	fied with Christ 2: 11—3:4	4. They have the true circumcision 11
	1. The Argument 2: 11-15 (Interpolated Application to Colossian Perils) 2:16-19	5. They have the true baptism 12
		6. They have the true life 13
		7. They have the perfect deliverance 14, 15
		F. Perilous Errors Named and Described 2:8, 16-23
		1. Philosophy 8
		2. Legalism 16, 17
		3. Angelolatry 18, 19
	2. The Appeal 2: 20—3:4	4. Asceticism 20-23
C. The Christian and His Character 3:1—4:1	II. Christ Identified with the Church 3:5—4:1	G. The True Christian Life 3:1-17
I. The New Wardrobe of Grace 3:1-14		1. Its source 1, 3
		2. Its characteristics 1-3
1. The Christian's Position 1-4	1. The general responsibility 3: 5-17	3. Its destiny 4
		4. Its twofold action
2. The Christian's Condition 5-14		a. Morification 5-8
		b. Vivification 10-17
II. Divine Revelation and Human revelations 3:15—4:1	2. The particular application 3:18—4: 1	H. Christian Behavior in Various Relations 3:18—4:6
1. The reciprocal relation of Christ and Church 15-17		
2. The reciprocal relation of husband and wife, 18, 19		1. In the family 3:18-21

Life Established	*The Analyzed Bible*	*Outline Studies of the New Testament*
3. The reciprocal relation of child and father 20, 21		
4. The reciprocal relation of employee and employer 3:22—4:1		2. Masters and servants 3:22—4-1
D. The Christian and His Career 4:2-18		
I. The Christian's Devotions 4:2-4		
1. For ourselves 2	Concluding Conditions 4:2-6	3. Prayer and social intercourse 4:2-6
2. For others 3, 4		
II. The Christian's Walk 4:5		
1. With discretion 5a		
2. With purpose 5b		
III. The Christian's Speech 4:6		
1. With grace		
2. With salt		
IV. The Christian's Companions 4:7-18	Conclusion 4:7-18	I. Personal Matters and and Messages 4:7-18
	I. Recommendations 7-9	
	II. Messages 10-14	
	III. Instructions 15-17	
	IV. The Last Words 18	

III. *Correlation of a Thematic, Chronological, and Geographical Outline*

The Acts of the Apostles

Thematic Outline	*Chronological Outline*	*Geographical Outline*
Introduction, 1:11	A.D. 30	Galilee, 1:3-11
1. Opening of the witness at Jerusalem, 1:12—8:3	A.D. 30	Jerusalem, 1:1—8:3
a. Preparation for Pentecost, 1:12-26		
b. Pentecost 2:1-41		
c. New fellowship, 2:42-47		
d. Lame man healed, 3:1-10		
e. Peter's second discourse, 3:11-26		
f. First persecution, 4:1-22		
g. A fresh baptism of the Spirit, 4:23-37		
h. Ananias and Sapphira, 5:1-11		
i. Spread of the gospel in Jerusalem, 5:12-16		
j. Second persecution, 5:17-42		
k. The Seven chosen, 6:1-7		
l. Preaching and seizing of Stephen, 6:8-15		
m. Third persecution 7:1-60		
n. General persecution, 8:1-3		

Thematic Outline	*Chronological Outline*	*Geographical Outline*
2. Extension of the witness to Judea and Samaria, 8:4 —9:43		
a. Samaritan ministry, 8:4-25	A.D. 34	Samaria, 8:4-40
b. Ministry of Philip in Judea, 8:26-40 (Ethiopian)		
c. Conversion of Saul, 9:1-22	A.D. 35	Damascus, 9:1-22
d. Plot to kill Paul, and his escape, 9:23-25		
e. Preaching of Paul in Jerusalem, 9:26-29		Jerusalem, 9:23-30
f. Paul sent to Tarsus, 9:30		Caesarea, Tarsus, 9:30
g. Progress of the church, 9:31		
h. Ministry of Peter, 9:32-35	A.D. 37	Lydda, Joppa, 9:31-43
3. Extension of the witness to the Gentiles, 10:1—28:31		
a. Conversion of Cornelius, 10:1-48		Caesarea, 10:1-48
b. Jerusalem council, 11:1-18		Jerusalem, 11:1-18
c. First Gentile church, 11:19-30	A.D. 41	Antioch, 11:19-26
d. Martyrdom of James, 12:1, 2	A.D. 43	Jerusalem, 11:27—12:23
e. Imprisonment and deliverance of Peter, 12:3-19		

Thematic Outline	*Chronological Outline*	*Geographical Outline*
f. Death of Herod, 12:20-23		
g. Growth of the Word of God, 12:24		
h. Return of Barnabas and Saul, 12:25		
i. Barnabas and Paul called 13:1-3		Antioch, 13:1
j. First missionary journey, 13:4–14:28	A.D. 45-48	Seleucia, 13:4 Cyprus, 13:4 Salamis, 13:5 Paphos, 13:6 Perga in Pamphylia, 13:13 Antioch of Pisidia, 13:14 Iconium, 14:1 Lystra, 14:6 Derbe, 14:20 Lystra, 14:21 Iconium, 14:21 Antioch of Pisidia, 14:21 Pamphylia, 14:24 Perga, 14:25 Attalia, 14:25 Antioch of Syria, 14:26
k. Council at Jerusalem, 15:1-35	A.D. 50	Jerusalem, 15:1-29 Antioch, 15:30-41
l. Second missionary journey, 15:36–18:22	A.D. 50-53	Derbe, Lystra, 16:1-5 Phrygia, 16:6 Galatia, 16:6 Mysia, 16:7 Troas, 16:8 Samothracia, 16:11 Neapolis, 16:11 Europe: Philippi, 16:13-40 Amphipolis, 17:1 Apollonia, 17:1 Thessalonica, 17:1-9 Berea, 17:10-14

Thematic Outline	*Chronological Outline*	*Geographical Outline*
	A.D. 51	Athens, 17:15-35
		Corinth, 18:1-17
	A.D. 53	Ephesus — Jerusalem
		— Antioch, 18:18-22
m. Third mission-ary journey, 18:23—21:16	A.D. 54-57	Galatia, Phrygia, 18:23
		Ephesus, 19:1-41
		Greece, 20:2
		Philippi, 20:6
		Troas, 20:6
		Assos, 20:13
		Mitylene, 20:14
		Samos, 20:15
		Miletus, 20:15
		Coos, 21:1
		Syria, 21:3
		Tyre, 21:3
		Ptolemais, 21:7
		Caesarea, 21:8
n. Paul at Jeru-salem, 21:17—23:30	A.D. 58	Jerusalem, 21:17—23:22
o. Paul at Cae-sarea, 23:31—26:32	Summer of A.D. 58 to fall of A.D. 60	Caesarea, 23:31—26:32
		Myra, 27:5
q. Paul's voyage and ship-wreck, 27:1-44	Fall of A.D. 60 to Spring of A.D. 61	Crete, 27:7
		Salmone, 27:7
q. Paul on the is-land of Melita, 28:1-10		Melita, 28:1-9
r. Voyage re-sumed, 28:11-15		Syracuse, 28:11
		Appi forum, 28:15
s. Arrival at Rome, 28:16		Rome, 28:15-31
t. Conference with the Jews, 28:17-29		
u. Paul a prisoner in his own hired house, 28:30, 31	A.D. 62-63	

COVENANT, DISPENSATION, AND BIBLE INTERPRETATION

There are two words found occasionally in the Bible and rather frequently in Christian theological works which the Bible student must know about, together with certain information about them, if he is to be a wise "scribe of the kingdom" bringing forth from his treasures "things old and new." These two words are *covenant* and *dispensation.*

Contrary to the apparent assumptions of some, neither of these words, nor the ideas they represent, is the property of any theological party. They were Biblical words before they became theological placards and belong to all Christians. One of the unhappy features of evangelical Christian thinking today is that controversy has seemed to cause one or the other of these ideas to receive improper emphasis in one or another quarter. Meanwhile the great body of Christians, happily, go on using both, seeking to keep both ideas in proper relation. Most Christians are neither "dispensational*ists*" nor "covenantal*ists*," as the terms go, though believing both in Scripture covenants and dispensations.

The first word, "covenant," in common speech is a bilateral contract (Greek, *sunthēkē*) between two parties, *both of whom have shared in framing its provisions.* We use contracts every day, especially in business and employment. In the Bible, both Old and New Testaments, however, this purely "bilateral" idea appears rarely, then only in contracts between men. In reference to covenants between God and men, this mutuality of responsibility in framing the provisions never appears. The Hebrew word (*berîth*) and the Greek word (*diathēkē*) are in such connections always used for a set of arrangements announced by almighty God and received by man. In this sense it may be said that a covenant of God with man (Hebrews, *berîth;* Greek, *diathēkē*) is scarcely to be distinguished from divine *law, enactment, arrangement,* etc. It is in a reduced sense a bilateral arrangement but the provisions are all stated by God, "the party of the first part." Man, the party of the second part may willingly agree or not agree; yet the arrangement prevails. He is bound to respect and obey it.

The second word, "dispensation," is hardly to be found in the English Bible. There is not one clear case of its occurrence at all in the special theological sense, unless it be Ephesians 1:10, where the total of God's management of history appears to be the meaning.

It is a good word in theology, however, and has a long history there. Dispensations were discussed at length 450 years ago by John Calvin in the *Institutes of the Christian Religion,*[1] and 150 years ago by Charles Hodge in his *Systematic Theology.* Both of these authors, so often of late supposed to be against belief in "dispensations," discuss them with approval and do not appear to sense that they might be, as such, a matter of difference among Christian believers. Though he does not define the word, Hodge, like most other theological writers of his time, thinks of a dispensation as a period of time during which God has administered something in a certain way, employing certain usages, regulations, etc.[2] This dispensation might then be replaced by another. With this understanding of things, that great man of God distinguished four dispensations: Adam to Abraham; Abraham to Moses; Moses to Christ; the "Gospel Dispensation."

Now there are certain fine present-day Christians who call themselves "dispensationalists" and agree with Mr. Hodge's idea of having the four dispensations. And, though tending to subdivide the period from Adam to Moses into three, and certainly to add a millennial dispensation, to make seven in all, they nevertheless disagree with the ideas of Mr. Hodge in another important way. Dr. Hodge introduces his four dispensations with the following definitive sentence: "Although the covenant of Grace has always been the same, the dispensations of *that covenant* have changed."

A respected contemporary advocate of "dispensationalism" asserts, "Dispensationalism views the world as a household run by God. In this household-world, God is administering its affairs according to His own will and in various stages of revelation in the process of time. These various stages mark off the distinguishably different economies in the outworking of His total purpose, and these economies are the dispensations. The understanding of God's differing economies is essential to a proper interpretation of His revelation within those various economies."[3]

Now at first look these two approaches appear to be the same. In fact, they are about the same except for one detail: the former views the dispensations as stages in God's administration of the so-called "covenant of Grace," while the latter views them as God's administration of "the world . . . [God's] total purpose." To the former the idea of "dispensation" is a "soteriological" (salvational) idea, while for the latter it is a "governmental" idea. This same difference prevails in their respective treatments of the kingdom of Christ.

Now how does this affect Bible interpretation? Well, happily, in the very most central areas of Christian truth, not at all. The doctrine of God, the person of Christ, etc., are not matters of important difference in this dispute. The doctrine of salvation is unaffected, for both parties are firm advocates of all the evangelical doctrines of the gospel. Wherein is there, then, great difference?

The areas of difference are chiefly these: The Old Testament prophecies of the kingdom of Messiah; the New Testament discourses on the kingdom of heaven (or "of God" or "of Christ"). Very briefly, the former (covenant of Grace emphasis) tends to apply Old Testament prophecies of Israel's national, visible, physical restoration and of the spread of a Jewish kingdom under Messiah over the whole world to the church of Christ and to its spread over the world.[4] In the New Testament the church is equated spiritually with Israel. The instrument used to support their indistinguishable unity is the "covenant of Grace," in which both receive one salvation and are members of one "household of faith."[5]

The "dispensationalist," on the other hand, holds that the promises regarding Israel in the Old Testament are to be fulfilled "literally" (i.e., spiritually, where spiritual promises are given, and physically where physical promises are given).[6] In the New Testament the idea of the "kingdom of heaven" (Matthew especially) and the "kingdom of God" are equated with the promised visible kingdom of the Old Testament promises to Israel. When Jesus came announcing a kingdom, it was this kingdom *in toto.* It was offered (not established) and when rejected by the Jews, the offer was withdrawn and the kingdom postponed[7] until the second coming of Christ and the Millennium.

The result is that in the Gospels the "dispensationalists" tend to restrict application of important teachings to the future kingdom to be manifested on earth after the return of Christ. The "covenantalist" will apply all the "kingdom" material in the New Testament to the church of today as likewise all Old Testament prophecies of the kingdom. The Messianic kingdom represented by the "stone" of Daniel (chap. 2), for example, will be interpreted as a prophecy of Christ and the church, certainly no visible kingdom of Christ on earth at His second advent.

In the treatment of those who use the dispensations mainly as a framework on which to group the facts of Biblical history and related revelation, there is nothing especially objectionable to covenant theologians, as Hodge's division of Bible history into dispensations indicates.

A famous dispensational work published nearly fifty years ago presents a fairly common scheme, as follows:

ETERNITY

CREATION

1. Edenic — Innocence
2. Antediluvian — Conscience
3. Postdiluvian — Human Government
4. Patriarchal — Family
5. Legal — Law
6. Church — Grace
7. Messianic — Millennium
8. Perfect Age — New Creation

ETERNITY

This scheme provides eight dispensations. This has been more commonly represented without the eighth, assuming the new earth to belong to "eternity" — hence the so-called "seven dispensations."

Important effects on Bible interpretation occur mainly when a certain refinement of the scheme is included. The "kingdom" proclamation of Jesus in His early ministry is held to relate to the seventh dispensation. This "millennial" dispensation, with restoration of the Jews to Palestine, the visible reign of Messiah, as spelled out in Old Testament prophecy, is held to be the heart of the proclamation of "the kingdom" in the Gospels. With, however, the rejection of Messiah, the message of Christ and His apostles shifted to the church of the sixth dispensation. Hence though, of course, all that is read in the Gospels is true, it must be discerned, according to this approach, that some of it — the "kingdom" truths — must wait until the coming of Christ in His kingdom to be fully applicable to men. Differences of opinion among dispensational interpreters arise as to the point in New Testament history when the shift of message occurs. Also some dispensational interpreters place more emphasis on the dispensational distinctions than do others. See the footnotes in the Scofield Bible on the Book of Matthew for what may be described as a moderate approach to interpretation from the dispensationalist viewpoint. The reader should know, however, that the majority of dispensational interpreters today seem to lay much less emphasis on interpretational distinctions based on dispensational divisions in Scripture than was the case in the recent past.

It must be emphasized that no Christian needs to feel himself in any wise obligated to join either of these "movements" or parties — though considerable pressure is sometimes exerted to do so. It is thoroughly in harmony with sound faith and sound interpretation to reject both *as systems* of interpretation while at the same time conserving certain valid insights of both. (Remember, both systems of thought exist *only* among evangelical believers.) This is what most Bible students have done. There are certain fine teachers who hold that Christ did not *offer* a kingdom when He first came, but *established* a spiritual realm (the church) only, planning from the first later to establish a visible realm with Israel, converted and restored at its heart, with the church, at His second coming. A well-known contemporary writer expounding this view is Erich Sauer.[8] He, like both Covenant and Dispensational theologians, believes in dispensations (seven of them) but rejects the "postponed kingdom" idea so precious to dispensationalists, and places no emphasis on a covenant of grace as the area of dispensational development through the ages. Another fine writer accepts the covenant idea; that is, the covenant of grace (and its correlate, the covenant of works in the law), but also believes in a coming kingdom of Christ on earth and starts "church truth" in the New Testament with the announcement of the kingdom of heaven in Matthew.[9] Evangelical interpreters of this sort are in the majority. Some who hesitantly accept labels such as "covenantal" or "dispensational" really stand far aside from what they obviously regard as one-sided emphases in the positions described above.

We suggest that in interpretation and application of both Testaments, the student follow the plain sense of the passage before him unless there are plain contextual reasons for seeking some other sense. Receive all the Old Testament as "profitable" for doctrine, reproof, and instruction (II Tim. 3:16) while keeping in mind that as a code of laws governing all of life, and especially as a ceremonial system, it has been superseded by a "new testament." In reading the New Testament, wherein the "dispensation" is that in which we live, either in process of establishment or fully established (see Hebrews 8 and 9 on old covenant and new), apply the ethical teaching to yourself. Take the commands to heart for yourself unless, as is occasionally true, the context or larger narrative setting shows it belongs to the apostles (e.g., Matt. 10:5 ff.), or to some other generation (e.g., Matt. 24:15 ff.), or was fulfilled long ago (Acts 1:4, 5), or awaits some future day (Rev. 18:4). Do the same for the promises. It is not true, as a bit of pietistical doggerel has it, that "Every promise in the Book is mine." But do not assign any promises (or commands) to the Old Testament saints, tribulation saints, millennial saints, or apostolic college unless there are demonstrably sound reasons for doing so!

Notes

1. Book II, Chap. IX treats "Christ, Although He Was Known to Jews Under the Law, Was at Length Clearly Revealed Only in the Gospel." Chapter XI, "The Difference Between the Two Testaments." Though much of this material would with our "hindsight" be called "Covenant Theology" after the name supplied to the theory of the Dutch theologian Cocceius (1602-1699), it is nevertheless true that much of it sounds distinctly "dispensational" (especially II, xi, 13, 14). Some of it is far more

"dispensational" even than, say, the *Scofield Bible* or the *Systematic Theology* of Lewis Sperry Chafter. J. O. Buswell makes some very interesting comments on the "dispensationalism" of Calvin and Charles Hodge in his *A Systematic Theology of the Christian Religion,* vol. I, pp. 316-319.

2. *Systematic Theology,* Vol. II, pp. 373-377.
3. Charles C. Ryrie, *Dispensationalism Today,* p. 31.
4. This will be seen most clearly in the Old Testament commentaries of such convinced amillenarian "covenant" writers as Edward J. Young (on Isaiah and Daniel), C. F. Keil (on Daniel and the Minor Prophets) and H. C. Leupold (on Daniel).
5. Geerhardus Vos. *The Teaching of Jesus Concerning the Kingdom and the Church* is one well-known example among many.
6. Ryrie, *op.cit.,* p. 47.
7. Given very extended exposition by A. J. McClain, *The Greatness of the Kingdom.* See his table of contents. Succinctly put in footnotes of *Scofield Bible* on the Gospel of Matthew. A few minutes' reading in Scofield's footnotes will acquaint one with the main features of the dispensational approach to the kingdom in the Gospels.
8. *From Eternity to Eternity,* especially pp. 171-178. Though claimed by certain dispensationalists as one of their protagonists, this author rejects a prime affirmation of dispensationalism, "The postponement of the kingdom" offered by Jesus in the early months of His ministry. Though he does discuss seven dispensations, he does not do so with the same intent that dispensationalists do — manifesting clearly that the name is misleading. His translator (from the German) is G. H. Lang, a thoroughly "non-dispensationalist" premillenarian British scholar.
9. J. O. Buswell, *ibid.* This approach seems clear in his Vol. ii, pp. 346-423.

QUESTIONS AND ANSWERS ON BIBLE CONTENT

The following material is presented as a device whereby individuals can quiz others, or each other, on their knowledge of Bible content. It may be used in connection with family Bible study, in Sunday school classes and in youth programs.

Which New Testament book or books deal extensively with the following subjects?

1. The church — *Ephesians*
2. Christian joy — *Philippians*
3. Law and Grace — *Galatians*
4. Faith and Works — *James*
5. The pre-eminence of Christ — *Colossians*
6. The most complete account of the birth of Christ — *Luke*
7. A Book which stresses the Son of God working among men — *Mark*
8. A Book of Christian ethics — *James*
9. The history of the church's foundation — *Acts*
10. The book that gives proof of the Deity of Christ — *John*
11. A book which shows Christianity superior to Judaism — *Hebrews*
12. Second coming in relation to the world — *II Thessalonians*
13. The liberty of the believer — *Galatians*
14. A book in which the Kingdom is mentioned most frequently — *Matthew*

The following lists of key words identify what three different books?

15.	straight-way (40)	Kingdom of God (14)	*Mark*
16.	High Priest (17)	blood (22)	
	faith (26)	covenant (14)	*Hebrews*
17.	fulfilled (14)	Heaven (74)	
	King-dom (50)	king (21)	*Matthew*

Locate the following by book:

18. Five periods of reformation   *II Chronicles*
19. Solomon   *I Kings*
20. Deborah, Gideon, Jephthah,
    Samson   *Judges*

Locate by book and chapter:

21. Definition of faith   *Hebrews 11*
22: Elijah and the ravens   *I Kings 17*
23. Parable of the talents   *Matthew 25*
24. Transfiguration   *Luke 9; Matthew 17;
                                     Mark 9*
25. Twelve spies   *Numbers 13*
26. Divorce and marriage   *Matthew 19; I Corin-
                                     thians 7*
27. "Lovest thou me?"   *John 21*
28. Story of the prodigal son   *Luke 15*
29. Wickedness of last days   *II Timothy 3*
30. Sending out the 70   *Luke 10*
21. Solomon's prayer of dedication *II Chronicles 6;
                                     I Kings 8*
32. Conversion of Lydia   *Acts 16*
33. A spiritual portrait of Christ *Revelation 1*
34. The shortest and middle chap-
    ter in Bible   *Psalm 117*
35. Matthias chosen   *Acts 1*
36. Brazen serpent   *Numbers 21*
37. The Vine and the Branches   *John 15*
38. Location of Ten Command-
    ments   *Exodus 20*
39. The disciples' prayer   *Matthew 6; Luke 11*
40. Sermon on the Mount   *Matthew 5-7*
41. Burning bush   *Exodus 3*
42. Parable of the virgins   *Matthew 25*

43. The seven churches of Asia Minor — *Revelation 2, 3*
44. Healing ten lepers — *Luke 17*
45. Institution of the Lord's Supper — *Matthew 26; Mark 14*
46. Elijah and the juniper tree — *I Kings 19*
47. Chapter on spiritual athletics — *Hebrews 12*
48. The Lord's Prayer — *John 17*
49. Resurrected life — *Colossians 3*
50. Nathan's parable — *II Samuel 12*
51. Conduct of the Lord's Supper — *I Corinthians 11*
52. Parable of the lost coin — *Luke 15*
53. Sending out twelve apostles — *Matthew 10*
54. Samson's death — *Judges 16*
55. Jesus raises Lazarus from the dead — *John 11*
56. Ethiopian baptized — *Acts 8*
57. Elijah and Mt. Carmel — *I Kings 18*
58. Songs of the Saviour's birth — *Luke 1, 2*
59. Paul's third missionary journey — *Acts 18-21*
60. Gideon — lamps and trumpets — *Judges 7*
61. Admonitions regarding the use of the tongue — *James 3*
62. Parable of the great supper — *Luke 14*
63. Feast of Belshazzar — *Daniel 5*
64. Samaritan woman — *John 4*
65. Visit of the Wise Men — *Matthew 2*
66. David and Goliath — *I Samuel 17*
67. Paul's first missionary journey — *Acts 13-14*
68. Longest chapter in the Bible — *Psalm 119*
69. Paul and Silas in prison — *Acts 16*
70. Lion's den — *Daniel 6*
71. Ananias and Sapphira — *Acts 5*
72. Parables of the Kingdom — *Matthew 13*
73. Good Samaritan — *Luke 10*

74. New Heaven and new earth   *Revelation 21*
75. Melchizedec   *Hebrews 7*
76. Five feasts   *Leviticus 23*
77. First and last resurrection   *Revelation 20*
78. Christ the chief cornerstone   *Ephesians 3; I Peter 2*

Identify the following chapters by content:

79. John 10   *New Testament Shepherd Psalm*
80. John 14   *Comfort chapter*
81. I Corinthians 15   *Gospel of resurrection*
82. Acts 9   *Conversion of Paul*
83. I Corinthians 13   *Love or charity*
84. I Corinthians 12   *Spiritual gifts*
85. I John 5   *Certainty*
86. Ephesians 6   *Armor of a Christian*
87. Isaiah 40   *Comfort*
88. Revelation 20   *Millennium*
89. Acts 3   *Healing of a lame man*
90. Isaiah 55   *Satisfaction guaranteed*
91. Matthew 4   *Temptations of Christ*
92. Acts 27   *Shipwreck*
93. Isaiah 6   *Call*
94. II Peter 3   *Life in the light of His return*
95. Acts 2   *Pentecost*
96. Isaiah 53   *Christ — Sacrifice*

Locate the point of division between creed and conduct in the following books:

97. Romans   *Chapters 11 and 12*
98. Ephesians   *Chapters 3 and 4*
99. II Corinthians   *Chapters 8 and 9*
100. Galatians   *Chapters 4 and 5*
101. Colossians   *Chapters 1 and 2*
102. I Thessalonians   *5:11 and 5:12*

Miscellaneous:

103. List the names of the six
     Jewish feasts.

     Passover
     Pentecost
     Trumpets
     Tabernacles
     Atonement
     Purim

104. The first prophecy of
     Christ's coming is found in
     what verse?

     Genesis 3:15

105. Name the 12 disciples

     Peter, Andrew, James,
     John, Philip, Bartholo-
     mew, Thomas, Matthew,
     James, Thaddaeus, Si-
     mon, Judas

106. List six great individuals in
     Genesis

     Adam, Noah, Abraham,
     Isaac, Jacob, Joseph

107. To the Christians of what
     famous Grecian commercial
     city did Paul write two let-
     ters?

     Corinth

108. What books parallel the two
     Books of Kings?

     I and II Chronicles

109. Who were the first to bring
     disciples to Jesus?

     Andrew and Philip

110. Locate the expression, "Van-
     ity of vanities."

     Ecclesiastes

111. Who said, "I am crucified
     with Christ"?

     Paul

112. In what book is the saying:
     "The people had a mind to
     work?"

     Nehemiah

113. Why is the book of Numbers so called? — *From its two censuses*

114. Who foretold the time when men should beat their swords into ploughshares and their spears into pruning hooks? — *Isaiah*

115. What is "the beginning of wisdom," according to the proverb? — *The fear of the Lord*

116. What book means "the second Law?" — *Deuteronomy*

117. Who said, "I am doing a great work, so that I cannot come down"? — *Nehemiah*

118. Where was John when he wrote the Revelation? — *Island of Patmos*

119. Of what church was Paul speaking when he said that he determined to know nothing among them but "Jesus Christ, and Him crucified"? — *Corinthian Church*

120. Which of the Judges won his victory using only an ox goad for a weapon? — *Shamgar*

121. Who succeeded Elijah? — *Elisha*

122. What is the significance of the phrase, "from Dan to Beersheba"? — *"Throughout Palestine"*

123. Who was Melchizedek? — *King of Salem, priest of the most high God*

124. What did Paul say is the wages of sin? — *Death*

125. What general won a great

victory through cutting his army down from 32,000 to 300? *Gideon*

126. What happened at the waters of Marah? *They were made sweet*

127. Locate the following "I AM's" in the Gospel of John by giving the chapter where each is found.

(1) I AM the bread of life *Chapter 6*
(2) I AM the good shepherd *Chapter 10*
(3) I AM the way, the truth, and the life *Chapter 14*
(4) I AM the light of the world *Chapter 8*
(5) I AM the true vine *Chapter 15*
(6) I AM the door of the sheep *Chapter 10*
(7) I AM the resurrection and the life *Chapter 11*

128. Identify the content of the following verses in John's Gospel:

John 3:3	*Except a man be born again*
John 4:1-42	*Samaritan woman*
John 5:39	*Search the scriptures*
John 9:25	*Whereas I was blind, now I see*
John 10:10	*I am come that they may have life*
John 11:35	*Jesus wept*
John 14:1	*Let not your heart be troubled*
John 14:6	*I am the way*
John 15:1	*I am the true vine*
John 15:7	*If ye abide in me*

129. Identify the content of the following verses in the Epistle to the Romans:

Romans 3:23	*All have sinned*
Romans 5:1	*Justification by faith*
Romans 5:8	*God commendeth his love*
Romans 6:23	*Wages of sin*
Romans 8:1	*No condemnation*
Romans 8:14	*For as many as are led by the Spirit*
Romans 8:28	*All things work together for good to them that love God*
Romans 8:35	*Who shall separate us*
Romans 10:9, 10	*Confess the Lord Jesus and believe*
Romans 10:13	*Whosoever shall call*
Romans 12:1	*Present bodies a living sacrifice*
Romans 13:14	*Put ye on the Lord Jesus Christ*

Questions on Prophetical Books

130. The Day of the Lord is especially characteristic of the book of   *Joel*

131. The minor prophet who had an unfaithful wife was   *Hosea*

132. The book especially noted for its visions is the book of   *Zechariah*

133. The minor prophet who was a herdsman was   *Amos*

134. The Prophet of love was   *Hosea*

135. The plumbline and basket of summer fruit were two word pictures found in the book of   *Amos*

136. "The just shall live by faith" is found in the book of   *Habakkuk*

137. The prophet who was a rebellious missionary was   *Jonah*

138. If one were to consider a series of five

	woes pronounced by God against a nation, he should read the book of	*Habakkuk*
139.	"saith Jehovah of hosts . . . Yet ye say" indicates the basic structure of the book of	*Malachi*
140.	The following key words characterize which book: Ephraim (36); backsliding (3); return (15); whoredom (16).	*Hosea*
141.	The prophet of Pentecost was	*Joel*
142.	The most quoted minor prophet by New Testament writers is	*Hosea*
143.	The eternal "why" is indicative of the book of	*Habakkuk*
144.	The clue given to the wise men as to the manger child is to be found in chapter 5 of	*Micah*
145.	"Consider your ways" was an admonition set forth by God through the prophet	*Haggai*
146.	The prophet of final things was	*Zechariah*

Indicate in which book each of the following quotations may be found:

147.	"Rejoice greatly, O daughter of Zion; shout, O daughter of Jerusalem: behold, thy King cometh unto thee: he is just, and having salvation; lowly and riding upon an ass, and upon a colt the foal of an ass."	*Zechariah*
148.	"Bring ye all the tithes into the storehouse . . . that there may be meat in my house. . . ."	*Malachi*
149.	"But the Lord is in his holy temple; let all the earth keep silence before Him."	*Habakkuk*
150.	"He hath showed thee, O man, what is	

good; and what doth the Lord require
of thee, but to do justly, and to love
mercy, and to walk humbly with thy
God."

Micah

THEMATIC DIAGRAMMING

INTRODUCTION

This type of study, which is similar to the procedure for diagramming sentences followed in English classes, is particularly helpful in determining the meaning of complicated Scripture passages, irrespective of their location in the Bible. It enables the student to visualize the relationships between words, phrases, and clauses within the structure of complex sentences.

For a further explanation of this procedure in Bible study the reader is referred to Merrill C. Tenney's, *Galatians, the Charter of Christian Liberty,* Chapter VIII.

I. EXPLANATION

1. The main statements, including declarations, questions, and commands, should be placed at the extreme left on the page.
2. Subordinate clauses and phrases should be placed below the main statements to which they refer.
3. Write the reference in brackets beneath each pronoun.
4. Note chapter and verse references in the margin.
5. The unit for thematic diagramming is the paragraph.
6. Lists of names, qualities, or actions should be tabulated in vertical columns.
7. Having completed the mechanical analysis, formulate a tabulated analysis of the material pertaining to certain selected items of importance.

II. EXEMPLIFICATION

A. *Mechanical Analysis of Romans 1:1-17*

v. 1 Paul
      a servant of Jesus Christ
      called an apostle
      separated unto the gospel of God
v. 2   which he had promised afore
              (God)
                by his prophets
                (God's)
                in the holy scriptures
v. 3   concerning his Son
              (God's)
                    Jesus Christ our Lord
                        (Christians)
                    which was made of the seed of
                    David, according to the flesh
v. 4 And declared to be the Son of God
      with power
      according to the spirit of holiness
      by the resurrection from the dead
v. 5   By whom we have received
        (Christ)
            grace
        (and) apostleship
              for obedience to the faith
              among all nations
              for his name
              (Christ's)
v. 6   Among whom are ye also
                    (all nations)
                  the called of Jesus Christ
v. 7 To all that be in Rome
      beloved of God

             called to be saints
             Grace to you
             (and) peace
                   from God our Father
                      (Christians)
             (and) the Lord Jesus Christ
v.   8 First, I thank my God
                      (Paul's)
                         through Jesus Christ
                         for you all
                         that your faith is spoken of
                            throughout the whole world
v.   9 For God is my witness
             whom I serve
             (God)
                with my spirit
                   (Paul's)
                in the gospel of his Son
                         (God's)
             that without ceasing I make mention of you always
             in my prayers
             (Paul's)
v.   10 Making request, if by any means
             I might have a prosperous journey by the will of
             God to còme unto you
v.   11 For I long to see you
             that I may impart unto you
                some spiritual gift
             to the end ye may be established
v.   12 That is, that I may be comforted together with you
             by the mutual faith
                both of you and me
v.   13 Now I would not have you ignorant, brethren
             that oftentimes I purposed to come unto you
             (but was let hitherto)

> that I might have some fruit among you also,
> even as among other Gentiles

v. 14 I am debtor
> (Paul) both to the Greeks   both to the wise
> and to the barbarians   and to the unwise

v. 15 So, as much as in me is, I am ready to preach the gos-
> (Paul) (Paul)   pel to you that are
> at Rome also

v. 16 For I am not ashamed of the gospel
> (Paul)   for it is the power of God
> (gospel)   unto salvation
> to everyone
> that believeth
> to the Jew first
> (and also) to the Greek

v. 17   for therein is the righteousness of God
> revealed from faith to faith

> as it is written:
> the just shall live by faith.

B. *Tabulated Analysis of Romans 1:1-17*

1. Paul

   a. Servant of Jesus Christ
   b. Called of God
   c. Separated unto gospel

2. Gospel of God

   a. Promised afore
      (1) by prophets
      (2) in Holy Scriptures
   b. Concerns Son
      (1) Our Lord
      (2) Incarnate God

3. Son of God

   a. Has power

    b. Holy
    c. Testimony of resurrection
    d. Gives
       (1) Grace
       (2) Apostleship

4. Christians at Rome
    a. Are beloved of God
    b. Are called saints
    c. Are recipients
       (1) of grace
       (2) of peace

5. Thanksgiving of Paul
    a. To God through Jesus Christ
    b. For Christians at Rome
    c. For their faith

6. Prayer of Paul
    a. Witnessed by God
    b. Persevering
    c. For safe journey to Rome
    d. For opportunity to impart spiritual gift
    e. For mutual comfort of faith

7. Further reasons for desire to come to Rome
    a. To have some fruit among them
    b. Because he was debtor
    c. Because he was ready to preach the gospel
    d. Because he was unashamed of the gospel
       (1) It is power of God unto salvation
       (2) Applicable to all who believe
       (3) Means of faith
       (4) Revelation of God's righteousness

Chapter VI

HOMILETICAL METHODS OF SEARCHING THE SCRIPTURES

A Biblical sermon must have Biblical subject-matter. This means that the foundation and superstructure of a Biblical sermon are based on searching the Scriptures.

The preacher must strive to develop a homiletical mind. Such a mind alerts him to sermon "starters" and sermonic material. The process of discovering such material is rhetorically called the process of invention. The other four rhetorical processes are arrangement, style, memory, and delivery.

.The specific methods of Bible study listed in the earlier sections of this book may be profitably employed by the preacher. His ability to discover preaching possibilities will increase as he develops this "homiletical mind." The sermon material discovered may be useful as illustrations within a sermon. The usefulness for purposes other than mere illustration will become evident as the homiletician has one of several possible preaching patterns in mind.[1] Having a preaching pattern in mind, he will then see how such material might fit into the framework of the sermon. Sensing the relevance of Bible material for sermonic purposes depends largely upon the preacher's knowledge of sermon construction methodology.

I. SURVEYING THE CONTEXT

A survey of the context of a preaching passage will provide illustrative material, descriptive material, and possibly ideas for a sermon title, subject, theme, or sermonic main points. It is wise to study a large portion and allow the Holy Spirit to narrow your homiletical vision later in the sermonizing process.

Dr. Charles Koller in his book *Expository Preaching without Notes* has listed seven items which he terms factual data:

1. Determine the speaker or writer of the large passage. The type of person presenting the passage as recorded in the Bible may give a valuable clue to the major thrust of the passage and its possible application.
2. Determine the addressee. The type of person or group who were the recipients of the original passage will give an indication of the type of individuals to whom the preacher can most easily direct the message.
3. Establish an approximate time for the incident or for the presentation of the original passage. The Westminster Atlas or a good study Bible will provide helpful information at this point. The homiletician will want to list other significant Biblical and extra-Biblical events which took place at about the same time.
4. Locate the place where the incident took place or where the passage was presented. The location of the incident in relation to other well-known spots and the listing of other incidents connected with this particular location will provide sermonic information.
5. Clarify the occasion which prompted the contents of the passage. There may be similar conditions at the present time to those which prompted the passage originally. If so, the pertinence of the passage will be more clearly seen.
6. Determine the aim of the passage so that it can be clarified as to whether or not the original aim was accomplished. The passage might be used as a

basis for a sermon to accomplish a similar purpose
to that of the original.

7. Formulate the theme of the larger passage. This will
help the preacher determine the subject and theme
of his sermon outline.

Whitesell and Perry, in their homiletical work *Variety in Your Preaching,* suggest that the preacher survey recent archaeological findings to locate information which might throw light upon the whole passage. They also suggest that a study of the distinctive doctrines, ideas, and stylistic traits of the Biblical writer may provide helpful suggestions for interpretation.

The information collected as factual data should be written in outline form and kept on file under the heading of the passage studied. The aim of the factual data is to give the homiletician an appreciation of the passage in relation to its Scriptural surroundings. The information will also be useful as Scriptural background for the text of the sermon.

II. SURVEYING THE CONTENT

Not only must the preacher survey the context of the preaching portion but he must also survey the content of the portion itself.

1. *Formulate an analytical outline of the passage.* The
paragraph divisions will serve to help determine the
major boundaries of segments of the outline. No
attempt should be made at this point to rearrange
the Biblical material so far as order is concerned.
Major and supporting ideas should be formulated in
wording as nearly Scriptural as possible and arranged
so that a logical relationship can be seen. The following writers provide help in formulating analytical out-

lines: Merrill Tenney, G. Campbell Morgan, W. H. Griffith Thomas, Roy Laurin, Guy King, and Lehman Strauss.

2. *Read the passage in several translations.* Each time you read it have a primary purpose in mind such as:
   (a) To determine the dominant impression from the passage.
   (b) To note major and minor personages.
   (c) To note repeated words and phrases.
   (d) To determine a distinctive name which might be given the passage as a means of identification.
   (e) To prepare to read the passage from the pulpit.

As each purpose is pursued, the findings should be recorded for possible sermon help. Some translations are listed in chapter 1 of this book. Others which might be used are:

1901. *American Standard Version,* by the American Revision Committee.

> This is the version set forth in A.D. 1611 but compared with the most ancient authorities and revised.

1907. *The Modern Reader's Bible,* by Richard Moulton.

> This places emphasis upon the types of literature within the Bible. It is based upon the English Revised Version.

1914. *The Douay Bible,* by John Murphy Company.

> This is the English translation of the Latin Vulgate with Dr. Challoner's notes.

1923. *The Riverside New Testament,* by William G. Ballantine.

> This is a very readable translation. It does not have verse numbers but does have an extensive index system.

1924. *The Centenary Translation of the New Testament,* by Helen Barrett Montgomery.

1925. *The Holy Bible in Modern English,* by Ferrar Fenton.

1950. *The Letters of St. Paul,* by Arthur S. Way.

1953. *A Literal Translation of the Holy Bible,* by Robert Young.

1958. *The Amplified New Testament,* by the Lockman Foundation.

1959. *Wuest's Expanded Translation of the Greek New Testament,* by Kenneth Wuest.

1960. *The New American Standard Bible New Testament,* by the Lockman Foundation.

1962. *Living Letters,* by Kenneth N. Taylor.

1965. *The New English Bible,* by Oxford University Press, Cambridge University Press.

3. *Produce a grammatical survey of the preaching portion.*

   (a) The diagramming of ideas after the manner used in diagramming sentences in school English courses will help to clarify the logical relationships between ideas. This process is called thematic diagramming and is illustrated on pages 256-260 of this book.

   (b) Special attention should be given to the punctuation marks. A series of declarations, exclamations, or questions might provide preaching points.

   (c) A study of the etymology of words will provide sermonic illustrative material. The meaning given in the dictionary can be made more relevant by checking the connotation of the word. The context often colors the meaning of the word.

   (d) Verb tenses have greater significance in the

Greek of the New Testament and the Hebrew of the Old Testament than in the English translations. Such translations as those by Montgomery and Williams will help the student who is handicapped at this point by not knowing the Greek language.

(e) A checking of the word order in the original language will clarify the emphasis within the sentence. In the Greek the emphatic words come first in the sentence.

(f) The Bible has an abundance of figures of speech. These figures should be identified and clarified as to their meaning and implications.

(g) Repeated, peculiar or distinctive terms will not only provide sermonic illustrative material but may also provide bases for sermon points.

4. *Analyze the theme of the passage.*

By this time in the process of sermonic invention, the theme of the passage should be clearly evident to the homiletician. The theme is the phrase which summarizes the major part of the subject matter of the preaching portion. The sermonizer should now ask himself whether this theme is *biographical, doctrinal,* or *ethical in nature.* A theme analysis should then be made according to the following list of questions:

Biographical

What is the meaning of the individual's name?
What is the ancestral background?
What significant religious and secular crises occurred in this life?
What advantages for personal development were enjoyed?

What traits of character were manifested?
What important friendships did this person have?
What important influences did this individual exert?
What failures and faults occurred in this life?
What important contributions were made?
What one main lesson is in this life for you?

Doctrinal

What is the definition of the terms of the theme?
  Etymological
  Bible usage
  Non-Biblical usage
What is the importance of this doctrine in the light of
  the whole pattern of Biblical truth?
What will be the results of the operation of this truth
  in personal experience?
How is personal faith related to this doctrine?

Ethical

What is the definition of the terms of the theme?
  Etymological
  Biblical and Non-Biblical
  Negation
  Quotations from great writers
  Synonyms and Antonyms
When this ethical principle prevails what relation-
  ship does it establish between the individual and
  God, and between the individual and his fellow-
  man?
How can this ethical principle be realized in the
  individual's experience?
What is the relationship to other ethical principles?

III.   SEARCHING FOR SERMON STARTERS

1. Seventy-five per cent of the main points of sermon
   outlines can be characterized by a key word. The

preacher should become so well acquainted with the words in this list that he will be able to spot them within his preaching passage. The key word may appear specifically or the wording may be such that it implies the presence of a key word. For example, the key word "reasons" may not actually appear in the passage, but there may be a clause worded "because. . . ." This is one way of stating a reason. All of the main points of a given sermon should be characterized by a single key word.

2. Relate the subject which appears to be predominant in the passage to the passage itself by determining whether the *when, where, why, who, wherefore, what,* or *how* of your subject is being discussed. If more than one of these is discussed in the passage, which appears to have the pre-eminence? Be sure that you can convince yourself and your audience that this is the predominant subject of the passage. The subject is often one word which is the core of the passage or the sermon.

3. Give special attention to the paragraph divisions. A good paragraph has one main idea. Find that main idea in each paragraph and relate it to the subject of the entire passage. The application of the interrogative words in the preceding paragraph will help. One of the paragraphs may provide the basis for a conclusion, or another may provide the basis for an introduction. In some passages, each paragraph provides the basis for a main point of the message. When the logical relationship has been determined between the major emphasis of each paragraph and the subject of the whole passage, a category of thought may emerge. A category of thought is a pattern of thinking such as the time pattern of past, present, and future.

4. If your preaching passage deals with an incident, determine the steps involved in the unfolding of that incident. These steps may give the basic idea for the points of a sermon.

5. From the standpoint of human reason, why should this passage be included within the scope of the Bible? Your answer to this question may help to show the relevance of this passage to present-day living. This will help the sermonizer apply the truths in the passage throughout his presentation.

6. Are there verses within the preaching portion which are regarded by many as familiar verses? These verses which already stand out in the minds of many of the listeners may serve as good verses for Scriptural bases for main points in the sermon. One of these familiar verses may also give you the key to the major thought emphasis of the passage.

7. Can you recall having read or heard sermons based upon this particular portion? Reflect upon these sermons which you have heard and read. If you have developed a method of sermon construction, you will not have to be afraid of plagiarism.

8. Is there a figure of speech which is at the core of this passage? If so, check the analogical preaching pattern. Be sure that you can give a clear explanation of the meaning of the figure of speech.

9. If the passage covers a period of time, determine the time order in the passage and the events which pertain to each period. If the passage deals with events which take place over a wide geographical area, determine the directional sequences within the preaching portion.

10. Are there cause and effect relationships within the passage? These may give helpful clues toward possible key words for the sermon.

Any time spent by the sermonizer in Bible study is time well spent. He cannot preach the Bible until he knows the Bible. Before worrying about the particular preaching pattern to be used in the sermon, he should make certain that he has an abundance of substance for the sermon. The Bible says that the world was created *Ex nihilo* (out of nothing). Sermons, however, are made out of substance. The preacher's head and heart should be full in order that he may be able to preach "out of the overflow."

1. Much of the material in this chapter is taken from *A Manual for Biblical Preaching*, by Lloyd M. Perry (Baker Book House, 1965).

CONCLUSION

A burning conviction has guided the authors and permeated the material within this work. There can be no hesitancy about the fact that "All scripture is given by inspiration of God, and is profitable for doctrine, for reproof, for correction, for instruction in righteousness: That the man of God may be perfect, thoroughly furnished unto all good works" (II Tim. 3:16, 17). It is only with such a conviction that real and lasting profit can be gained from searching the Scriptures.

This book has sought to develop in the reader an appreciation for the Bible, God's written Word. The comments on the Bible have upheld its uniqueness and wonder. The methods of Bible study practiced by certain men and women of our day have served to add a note of certainty to the truth that the Word of God is personal, practical, and powerful.

This book has sought to establish basic inductive methodology for personal study. This methodology has taken the form of eleven specific methods. These have included methods for studying Bible books, Bible chapters, Bible paragraphs, minute parts of Scripture, Bible doctrines, Bible biographies, Bible prayers, Bible miracles, Bible parables, Bible poetry, and Bible writers. In addition to these special methods, which grow out of the nature of the items being studied, there are also six general methods of study. These can be applied to units of Scripture, irrespective of their inherent nature. These include comparison and contrast of versions, comparison and contrast of outlines, correlation of thematic, chronological and geographical outlines, consideration of dispensational divisions, content questions and answers, and thematic diagramming.

The sixth section of the book will be of special interest to the preachers. It establishes a three-step process which should precede the actual formulation of the sermon outline.

Searching the Scriptures involves investigation and exploration. It should be carried out with thoroughness and regularity. The Bereans set a good example when they ". . . received the word with all readiness of mind, and searched the Scriptures daily . . ." (Acts 17:11).

Some read the Bible like the action of the hour glass, where all runs in and all runs out, leaving nothing behind. Some read the Bible after the manner in which a sponge gathers and gives forth without change. Some allow all the good material gained in Bible study to escape, holding only the husks. This is patterned after the old jelly bag process.

But blessed are those Bible students who study as though they were panning gold. They are careful to keep the pure metal. Such will prove to be of everlasting value. "How glad should be the man who has discovered his portion in the promises of Holy Writ" (Spurgeon).

BIBLIOGRAPHY FOR BIBLE STUDY METHODS

1. Adler, Mortimer J. *How to Read a Book*. New York: Simon and Schuster, 1940, 389 pp.
2. Allis, Oswald Thompson. *Bible Numerics*. Chicago: Moody Press, 1944, 24 pp.
3. Ashcraft, J. Robert. *Ways of Understanding God's Word*. Springfield, Missouri: Gospel Publishing House, 1960, 103 pp.
4. Avey, Albert Edwin. *Historical Method in Bible Study*. New York: Charles Scribners and Sons, 1924, 189 pp.
5. Baly, Denis. *The Geography of the Bible*. New York: Harper and Bros., 1957, 303 pp.
6. Baughman, Ray. *Bible History Visualized*. Chicago: Moody Colportage, 1963, 1281 pp.
7. Bjorklund, C. W. *According to Thy Word*. Chicago: Covenant Press, 1954, 444 pp.
8. Bratt, John H. *New Testament Guide*. Grand Rapids: William B. Eerdmans Publishing Company, 1961, 144 pp.
9. Briggs, Charles Augustus. *Biblical Study, Its Principles, Methods, and History*. New York: Charles Scribners and Sons, 1885, 488 pp.
10. Brown, Robert McAfee. *The Bible Speaks to You*. Philadelphia: Westminster Press, 1955, 320 pp.
11. Colson, Howard. *Preparing to Teach the Bible*. Convention Press.
12. Colwell, Ernest Cadman. *The Study of the Bible*. Chicago: University of Chicago Press, 1946, 172 pp.
13. Cooper, Clayton Sedgwick. *World Wide Bible Study*. Philadelphia: Sunday School Times, 1912, 234 pp.
14. Danker, Frederick W. *Multipurpose Tools for Bible*

Study. St. Louis: Concordia Publishing House, 1960, 289 pp.

15. Eade, Alfred Thompson. *The Expanded Panorama Bible Study Course.* Westwood, N.J.: Fleming H. Revell, 1961, 192 pp.

16. Eberhardt, Charles Richard. *The Bible in the Making of Ministers.* New York: The Association Press, 1949, 252 pp.

17. Eddins, J. Frank. *Finding and Filing Bible Facts and Features.* Boston: Chapman and Grimes, 1936, 115 pp.

18. Erdman, Charles R. *Your Bible and You.* Philadelphia: John C. Winston Co., 1950, 180 pp.

19. Evans, William. *The Book of Books.* Chicago: The Bible Institute Colportage Association, 1902, 222 pp.

20. Filson, Floyd V. *Opening the New Testament.* Philadelphia: Westminster Press, 1952, 224 pp.

21. Gaebelein, Frank E. *Exploring the Bible.* New York: "Our Hope" Publication Office, 1929, 204 pp.

22. Gettys, Joseph M. *How to Enjoy Studying the Bible.* Richmond: John Knox Press, 1959, 72 pp.

23. Goodspeed, Edgar J. *How to Read the Bible.* Philadelphia: John C. Winston Co., 1946, 238 pp.

24. Grant, F. W. *The Numerical Structure of Scripture.* New York: Loiseaux Brothers, 1956, 155 pp.

25. Gray, James M. *How to Master the English Bible.* Chicago: Moody Colportage Library.

26. Jensen, Irving. *Independent Bible Study.* Chicago: Moody Press, 1964, 188 pp.

27. Johnson, Douglas. *The Christian and His Bible.* Grand Rapids: William B. Eerdmans Publishing Company, 1953, 144 pp.

28. Jones, Kenneth E. *Let's Study the Bible.* Anderson, Ind.: Warner Press, 1962, 96. pp.

29. Kruist, Howard Tillman. *How to Enjoy the Bible.* Princeton, N.J.: Princeton Theological Seminary, 1939, 16 pp.

30. _____. *These Words Upon Thy Heart*. Richmond: John Knox Press, 1947, 181 pp.

31. Luck, G. Coleman. *The Bible Book by Book*. Chicago: Moody Press, 1955, 253 pp.

32. Manley, G. T. and Oldham, H. W. *Search the Scriptures*. Chicago: Intervarsity Press, 1962.

33. May, Herbert Gordon. *Our English Bible in the Making*. Philadelphia: Westminster, 1965.

34. Mears, Henrietta C. *What the Bible Is All About*. Glendale, Calif.: Gospel Light Publications.

35. Moody, D. L. *Pleasure and Profit in Bible Study*. Chicago: Moody Colportage Library.

36. Morgan, G. Campbell. *The Study and Teaching of the English Bible*. New York: Fleming H. Revell Co., 1910, 99 pp.

37. Moulton, Richard G. *The Literary Study of the Bible*. Boston: D. C. Heath and Company, 1895, 525 pp.

38. Needham, George, et ux. *Bible Briefs*. Vol. 1. New York: Fleming H. Revell Company, 1889, 224 pp.

39. Oakes, John P. *Exploring Your Bible*. Grand Rapids: Zondervan Publishing House, 1960, 155 pp.

40. Olson, Norman. *Short Course of Bible Study*. Grand Rapids: Zondervan Publishing House, 1959, 182 pp.

41. Patterson, Alexander. *Bird's Eye Bible Study*. Chicago: Moody Press, 1911, 131 pp.

42. Peirce, B. K. *The Bible-Scholar's Manual*. New York: Carlton and Porter, 1847, 291 pp.

43. Phillips, John. *Exploring the Scriptures*. Chicago: Moody Press, 1965, 288 pp.

44. Pierson, A. T. *Knowing the Scriptures*. New York: Gospel Publishing House, 1910, 459 pp.

45. Ramm, Bernard L. *Protestant Biblical Interpretation*. Boston: W. A. Wilde Company, 1950, 188 pp.

46. Rees, Howard. *A Handbook on Bible Study*. Nashville: Broadman Press.

47. Richardson, Alan. *A Preface to Bible Study*. Philadelphia: The Westminster Press, 1944, 128 pp.

48. ――――. *A Theological Word Book of the Bible*. MacMillan, 1950, 290 pp.

49. Ridout, Samuel. *How to Study the Bible*. New York: Loiseaux Brothers, 1947, 269 pp.

50. Sell, Henry T. *Bible Studies in Vital Questions*. New York: Fleming H. Revell Company, 1916, 160 pp.

51. Simow, Martin P. *How to Know and Use Your Bible*. Zondervan Publishing House, 1963, 285 pp.

52. Smith, Wilbur M. *Profitable Bible Study*. Boston: W. A. Wilde Company, 1939, 205 pp.

53. Spotts, Charles D. *You Can Read the Bible*. Philadelphia: The Christian Education Press, 1949.

54. Stibbs, Alan M. *Understanding God's Word*. London: The Inter-Varsity Fellowship, 1950, 64 pp.

55. Swaim, J. Carter. *Right and Wrong Ways to Use the Bible*. Philadelphia: The Westminster Press, 176 pp.

56. Tenney, Merrill C. *Galatians: The Charter of Christian Liberty*. Grand Rapids: William B. Eerdmans Publishing Company, 1950, 193 pp.

57. Terry, Milton S. *Biblical Hermeneutics*. New York: Eaton and Mains, 1911, 782 pp.

58. Thomas, W. H. Griffith. *Methods of Bible Study*. New York: Harper and Brothers, 1926.

59. Tidwell, Josiah Blake. *Bible Study Period by Period*. Nashville: Broadman Press, 1937, 360 pp.

60. ――――. *Thinking Straight about the Bible*. Nashville: Broadman Press, 1935, 152 pp.

61. Torrey, R. A. *How to Study the Bible for Greatest Profit*. London: James Nisbet & Company, 1898, 121 pp.

62. Traina, Robert A. *Methodical Bible Study*. New York: Ganis & Harris, 1952, 265 pp.

63. Trumbull, H. Clay, and Others. *Hints on Bible Study*. Philadelphia: John D. Wattles & Company, 1898, 257 pp.

64. Vos, Howard F. *Effective Bible Study.* Grand Rapids: Zondervan Publishing House, 1956, 224 pp.

65. Waffle, A. E. *The Interpreter with His Bible.* New York: Anson D. F. Randolph & Company, 1891, 106 pp.

66. Weatherspoon, J. B. *The Book We Teach.* Nashville: Sunday School Board of the Southern Baptist Convention, 1934, 131 pp.

67. Weddell, J. W. *Your Study Bible.* Philadelphia: Sunday School Times, 1918.

68. White, Wilbert Webster. *The Divine Library — Its Abuse and Use.* New York: International Committee of the Y.M.C.A., 15 pp.

69. White, William Parker. *Thinking Through the Scriptures.* Doubleday, Doran & Co., 1928, 176 pp.

70. Whitesell, Faris D., and LeFever, Ruth H. *Let's Study.* Chicago: Moody Press, 1954, 128 pp.

71. Wirt, Sherwood E. *Open Your Bible.* Fleming H. Revell, 1962, 128 pp.

DATE DUE

F			
F			
OC 5 '81			
GAYLORD			PRINTED IN U.S.A